TABE

SECRETS

Study Guide
Your Key to Exam Success

TABE Exam Review for the
Test of Adult Basic Education

Published by
Mometrix Test Preparation
TABE Exam Secrets Test Prep Team

Written and edited by the TABE Exam Secrets Test Prep Staff

Printed in the United States of America

This paper meets the requirements of ANSI/NISO Z39.48-1992 (Permanence of Paper).

Mometrix offers volume discount pricing to institutions. For more information or a price quote, please contact our sales department at sales@mometrix.com or 888-248-1219.

* TABE® is a registered trademark of CTB/McGraw-Hill ®, which was not involved in the production of, and does not endorse, this product.

ISBN 13: 978-1-5167-0530-6

Dear Future Exam Success Story:

Congratulations on your purchase of our study guide. Our goal in writing our study guide was to cover the content on the test, as well as provide insight into typical test taking mistakes and how to overcome them.

Standardized tests are a key component of being successful, which only increases the importance of doing well in the high-pressure high-stakes environment of test day. How well you do on this test will have a significant impact on your future- and we have the research and practical advice to help you execute on test day.

The product you're reading now is designed to exploit weaknesses in the test itself, and help you avoid the most common errors test takers frequently make.

How to use this study guide

We don't want to waste your time. Our study guide is fast-paced and fluff-free. We suggest going through it a number of times, as repetition is an important part of learning new information and concepts.

First, read through the study guide completely to get a feel for the content and organization. Read the general success strategies first, and then proceed to the content sections. Each tip has been carefully selected for its effectiveness.

Second, read through the study guide again, and take notes in the margins and highlight those sections where you may have a particular weakness.

Finally, bring the manual with you on test day and study it before the exam begins.

Your success is our success

We would be delighted to hear about your success. Send us an email and tell us your story. Thanks for your business and we wish you continued success-

Sincerely,

Mometrix Test Preparation Team

Need more help? Check out our flashcards at: http://MometrixFlashcards.com/TABE

TABLE OF CONTENTS

Top 20 Test Taking Tips

1. Carefully follow all the test registration procedures
2. Know the test directions, duration, topics, question types, how many questions
3. Setup a flexible study schedule at least 3-4 weeks before test day
4. Study during the time of day you are most alert, relaxed, and stress free
5. Maximize your learning style; visual learner use visual study aids, auditory learner use auditory study aids
6. Focus on your weakest knowledge base
7. Find a study partner to review with and help clarify questions
8. Practice, practice, practice
9. Get a good night's sleep; don't try to cram the night before the test
10. Eat a well balanced meal
11. Know the exact physical location of the testing site; drive the route to the site prior to test day
12. Bring a set of ear plugs; the testing center could be noisy
13. Wear comfortable, loose fitting, layered clothing to the testing center; prepare for it to be either cold or hot during the test
14. Bring at least 2 current forms of ID to the testing center
15. Arrive to the test early; be prepared to wait and be patient
16. Eliminate the obviously wrong answer choices, then guess the first remaining choice
17. Pace yourself; don't rush, but keep working and move on if you get stuck
18. Maintain a positive attitude even if the test is going poorly
19. Keep your first answer unless you are positive it is wrong
20. Check your work, don't make a careless mistake

Mathematics Section

Number Sense

Numbers and Their Classifications

There are several different kinds of numbers. When you learn to count as a child, you start with *Natural Numbers*. You may know them as counting numbers. These numbers begin with 1, 2, 3, and so on. *Whole Numbers* are all natural numbers and zero. *Integers* are all whole numbers and their related negative values (...-2, -1, 0, 1, 2...). Fractions with an integer in the numerator and a non-zero integer in the denominator are called

Rational Numbers. Numbers such as pi (π) that do not end or repeat and cannot be given as a fraction are known as *Irrational Numbers*. Any number that has the imaginary number i, where $i^2 = -1$ and $i = \sqrt{-1}$ is known as a *Complex Number*. All natural numbers, whole numbers, integers, rational numbers, and irrational numbers are *Real Numbers*. Complex numbers are not real numbers.

Aside from the number 1, all natural numbers are known as prime or composite. *Prime Numbers* are natural numbers that are greater than 1 and have factors that are 1 and itself (e.g., 3). On the other hand, *Composite Numbers* are natural numbers that are greater than 1 and are not prime numbers. The number 1 is a special case because it is not a prime number or composite number.

Numbers are the basic building blocks of mathematics. These terms show some elements of numbers:

Integers – The set of positive and negative numbers. This set includes zero. Integers do not include fractions $\left(\frac{1}{3}\right)$, decimals (0.56), or mixed numbers $\left(7\frac{3}{4}\right)$.

Even number – Any integer that can be divided by 2 and does not leave a remainder. Example: 2, 4, 6, 8, etc.

Odd number – Any integer that cannot be divided evenly by 2. For example: 3, 5, 7, 9, and so on.

Decimal number – a number that uses a decimal point to show the part of the number that is less than one. Example: 1.234.

Decimal point – a symbol used to separate the ones place from the tenths place in decimals. This symbol is used to separate dollars from cents in currency.

Decimal place – the position of a number to the right of the decimal point. In the decimal 0.123, the 1 is in the first place to the right of the decimal point. This is the place for tenths. The 2 is in the second place. This is the place for hundredths. The 3 is in the third place. This is the place for thousandths.

The decimal, or base 10, system is a number system that uses ten different digits (0, 1, 2, 3, 4, 5, 6, 7, 8, 9). Another system is the binary, or base 2, number system. This system is used by computers and uses the numbers 0 and 1. Some think that the base 10 system started because people had only their 10 fingers for counting.

> ➢ **Review Video: Numbers and Their Classification**
> *Visit **mometrix.com/academy** and enter **Code: 461071***

Place Value and the Number Line

Write the place value of each digit in the following number: 14,059
    1: ten thousands
    4: thousands
    0: hundreds
    5: tens
    9: ones

A number line is a graph to see the distance between numbers. Basically, this graph shows the relationship between numbers. So, a number line may have a point for zero and may show negative numbers on the left side of the line. Also, any positive numbers are placed on the right side of the line. Before you work with negative numbers, you need to understand absolute values. Basically, a number's *Absolute Value* is the distance away from zero that a number is on the number line. The absolute value of a number is always positive and is written as $|x|$. If a number like -4 is added with a +2, then the sum is -2. So, the absolute value of $|-2|$ is +2.

Example
Name each point on the number line below:

Answer

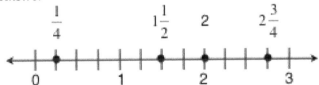

Ordering Numbers from Least to Greatest

<u>Example 1</u>
Write each list of numbers from least to greatest
a) 4,002; 280; 108,511; 9
b) 5,075,000,600; 190,800,330; 7,000,300,001

Answer
a) 9; 280; 4,002; and 108,511
b) 190,800,330; 5,075,000,600; 7,000,300,001

<u>Example 2</u>
Write each list of numbers from least to greatest
a) 0.06; 6.0; 0.6
b) 0.11; 0.09; 0.43

Answer
a) 0.06; 0.6; 6.0
b) 0.09; 0.11; 0.43

Mathematics Computation

Operations

There are four basic operations in math: addition, subtraction, multiplication, and division.

Addition increases the value of one number by the value of another number.
Example: 2 + 4 = 6; 8 + 9 = 17. The result is called the sum. With addition, the order does not matter. 4 + 2 or 2 + 4 equals 6. This is the commutative property for addition.

Subtraction decreases the value of one number by the value of another number. The result is called the difference. Example: 6 – 4 = 2 and 17 – 8 = 9. Note for subtraction that the order does matter. For example, 6 – 4 and 4 – 6 do not have the same difference.

Multiplication is like repeated addition. This operation tells how many times one number needs to be added to the other number. Example: 3 × 2 (three times two) = 2 + 2 + 2 = 6. With multiplication, the order does not matter. 2 × 3 (or 3 + 3) = 3 × 2 (or 2 + 2 + 2). This is the commutative property for multiplication.

Division is the opposite operation to multiplication. This operation shows how much of a number is in another number. The first number is known as the dividend. The second number is known as the divisor. The answer to the division problem is known as the quotient.
Example: 20 ÷ 4 = 5. If 20 is split into 4 equal parts, then each part is 5. With division, the order of the numbers does matter. 20 ÷ 4 and 4 ÷ 20 do not give the same result. Note that you cannot divide a number by zero. If you try to divide a number by zero, then the answer is known as undefined.

Decimals

Decimal Illustration
Use a model to represent the decimal: 0.24. Write 0.24 as a fraction.

The decimal 0.24 is twenty four hundredths. One possible model to represent this fraction is to draw 100 pennies, since each penny is worth 1 one hundredth of a dollar. Draw one hundred circles to represent one hundred pennies. Shade 24 of the pennies to represent the decimal twenty four hundredths.

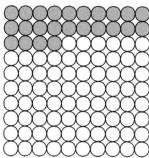

To write the decimal as a fraction, write a fraction: $\frac{\#\ shaded\ spaces}{\#\ total\ spaces}$. The number of shaded spaces is 24, and the total number of spaces is 100, so as a fraction 0.24 equals $\frac{24}{100}$. $\frac{24}{100}$ can then be reduced to $\frac{6}{25}$.

- 4 -

Adding and Subtracting Decimals

When adding and subtracting decimals, the decimal points must always be aligned. Adding decimals is just like adding regular whole numbers.
Example: 4.5 + 2 = 6.5.

If the problem-solver does not properly align the decimal points, an incorrect answer of 4.7 may result. An easy way to add decimals is to align all of the decimal points in a vertical column visually. This will allow one to see exactly where the decimal should be placed in the final answer. Begin adding from right to left. Add each column in turn, making sure to carry the number to the left if a column adds up to more than 9. The same rules apply to the subtraction of decimals.

> **Review Video: Adding and Subtracting Decimals**
> *Visit mometrix.com/academy* and enter *Code:* **381101**

Multiplying Decimals

A simple multiplication problem has two components: a multiplicand and a multiplier. When multiplying decimals, work as though the numbers were whole rather than decimals. Once the final product is calculated, count the number of places to the right of the decimal in both the multiplicand and the multiplier. Then, count that number of places from the right of the product and place the decimal in that position. For example, 12.3 x 2.56 has three places to the right of the respective decimals. Multiply 123 x 256 to get 31488. Now, beginning on the right, count three places to the left and insert the decimal. The final product will be 31.488.

> **Review Video: Multiplying Decimals**
> *Visit mometrix.com/academy* and enter *Code:* **731574**

Dividing Decimals

Every division problem has a divisor and a dividend. The dividend is the number that is being divided. In the problem 14 ÷ 7, 14 is the dividend and 7 is the divisor. In a division problem with decimals, the divisor must be converted into a whole number. Begin by moving the decimal in the divisor to the right until a whole number is created. Next, move the decimal in the dividend the same number of spaces to the right. For example, 4.9 into 24.5 would become 49 into 245. The decimal was moved one space to the right to create a whole number in the divisor, and then the same was done for the dividend. Once the whole numbers are created, the problem is carried out normally: 245 ÷ 49 = 5.

> **Review Video: Dividing Decimals**
> *Visit mometrix.com/academy* and enter *Code:* **560690**

Fractions

A fraction has one integer that is written above another integer with a dividing line between them $(\frac{x}{y})$. It represents the quotient of the two numbers "x divided by y." Also, this can be thought of as x out of y equal parts. The x and y in this fraction are known as variables. When the value for a symbol can change, a variable is given to that value. So, a number like 3 is a constant. A value that does not change is a constant.

The top number of a fraction is called the numerator. This number stands for the number of parts. The 1 in $\frac{1}{4}$ means that this is one part out of the whole. The bottom number of a fraction is called the denominator. This stands for the total number of equal parts. The 4 in $\frac{1}{4}$ means that the whole has four equal parts. A fraction cannot have a denominator of zero. This fraction is known as "undefined." The reverse of a fraction is known as the reciprocal. For example, the reciprocal of 1/2 is 2, and the reciprocal of 3 is 1/3.

Fractions can be changed by multiplying or dividing the numerator and denominator by the same number. This will not change the value of the fraction. You cannot do this with addition or subtraction. If you divide both numbers by a common factor, you will reduce or simplify the fraction. Two fractions that have the same value but are given in different ways are known as equivalent fractions. For example, $\frac{2}{10}, \frac{3}{15}, \frac{4}{20}$, and $\frac{5}{25}$ are equivalent fractions. Also, they can be reduced or simplified to $\frac{1}{5}$.

Two fractions can be changed to have the same denominator. This is known as finding a common denominator. The number for the common denominator should be the least common multiple of the original denominators. Example: $\frac{3}{4}$ and $\frac{5}{6}$; the least common multiple of 4 and 6 is 12. So, you can change these fractions to have a common denominator: $\frac{3}{4} = \frac{9}{12}$ and $\frac{5}{6} = \frac{10}{12}$.

If two fractions have a common denominator, you can add or subtract the fractions with the two numerators. Example: $\frac{1}{2} + \frac{1}{4} = \frac{2}{4} + \frac{1}{4} = \frac{3}{4}$. If the two fractions do not have the same denominator, one or both of them must be changed to have a common denominator. This needs to be done before they can be added or subtracted.

Two fractions can be multiplied. The two numerators need to be multiplied to find the new numerator. Also, the two denominators need to be multiplied to find the new denominator. Example: $\frac{1}{3} \times \frac{2}{3} = \frac{1 \times 2}{3 \times 3} = \frac{2}{9}$. Two fractions can be divided. First, flip the numerator and denominator of the second fraction. Then multiply the numerators and denominators. Example: $\frac{2}{3} \div \frac{3}{4}$ becomes $\frac{2}{3} \times \frac{4}{3}$. Now, $\frac{8}{9}$ is your answer.

A fraction with a denominator that is greater than the numerator is known as a proper fraction. A fraction with a numerator that is greater than the denominator is known as an improper fraction. Proper fractions have values less than one. Improper fractions have values greater than one.

A mixed number is a number that has an integer and a fraction. Any improper fraction can be rewritten as a mixed number. Example: $\frac{8}{3} = \frac{6}{3} + \frac{2}{3} = 2 + \frac{2}{3} = 2\frac{2}{3}$.

Also, any mixed number can be rewritten as an improper fraction. Example: $1\frac{3}{5} = 1 + \frac{3}{5} = \frac{5}{5} + \frac{3}{5} = \frac{8}{5}$.

A fraction that has a fraction in the numerator, denominator, or both is called a *Complex Fraction*. These can be solved in many ways. The easiest way to solve the equation is to use order of operations.

For example, $\left.\left(\frac{4}{7}\right)\middle/\left(\frac{5}{8}\right)\right. = 0.571/0.625 = 0.914$. Another way to solve this problem is to multiply the

fraction in the numerator by the reciprocal of the fraction in the denominator. For example,
$\left.\left(\frac{4}{7}\right)\middle/\left(\frac{5}{8}\right)\right. = \frac{4}{7} \times \frac{8}{5} = \frac{32}{35} = 0.914$.

> ➤ **Review Video: <u>Fractions</u>**
> *Visit **mometrix.com/academy** and enter **Code: 262335***

Fraction Illustrations

Alex's mom brings $6\frac{3}{4}$ oranges to a soccer game. Draw the number of oranges she brought to the game. The whole number is the number of whole oranges brought to the game. Each of these can be represented by a circle. Shade the entire circle to show the whole orange was used.

The fraction of an orange is only a portion of a circle. Divide a circle into three equal spaces, and shade two of them to represent the $\frac{3}{4}$ of an orange.

Percentages, Ratios, and Proportions

Percentages

You can think of percentages as fractions that are based on a whole of 100. In other words, one whole is equal to 100%. The word percent means "per hundred." Fractions can be given as percents by using equivalent fractions with an amount of 100. Example: $\frac{7}{10} = \frac{70}{100} = 70\%$; Another example is $\frac{1}{4} = \frac{25}{100} = 25\%$. To give a percentage as a fraction, divide the percentage by 100. Then, reduce the fraction to its simplest possible terms. Example: $60\% = \frac{60}{100} = \frac{3}{5}$; $96\% = \frac{96}{100} = \frac{24}{25}$.

Converting decimals to percentages and percentages to decimals is as simple as moving the decimal point. To convert from a decimal to a percent, move the decimal point two places to the right. To convert from a percent to a decimal, move the decimal two places to the left.
Example: $0.23 = 23\%$; $5.34 = 534\%$; $0.007 = 0.7\%$; $700\% = 7.00$; $86\% = 0.86$; $0.15\% = 0.0015$.

A percentage problem can come in three main ways.
- Type 1: What percentage of 40 is 8?
- Type 2: What number is 20% of 40?
- Type 3: What number is 8 20% of?

- 7 -

The three parts in these examples are the same: a whole (W), a part (P), and a percentage (%).
To solve type (1), use the equation % = P/W.
To solve type (2), use the equation: P = W × %.
To solve type (3), use the equation W = P/%.

Percentage Problems

Percentage problems can be difficult because many are word problems. So, a main part of solving them is to know which quantities to use.

Example 1

In a school cafeteria, 7 students choose pizza, 9 choose hamburgers, and 4 choose tacos. Find the percentage that chose tacos. To find the whole, you must add all of the parts: 7 + 9 + 4 = 20. Then, the percentage can be found by dividing the part by the whole (% = P/W): $\frac{4}{20} = \frac{20}{100} = 20\%$.

Example 2

At a hospital, 40% of the nurses work in labor and delivery. If 20 nurses work in labor and delivery, how many nurses work at the hospital?
To answer this problem, first think about the number of nurses that work at the hospital. Will it be more or less than the number of nurses who work in a specific department such as labor and delivery? More nurses work at the hospital, so the number you find to answer this question will be greater than 20.
40% of the nurses are labor and delivery nurses. "Of" indicates multiplication, and words like "is" and "are" indicate equivalence. Translating the problem into a mathematical sentence gives
$40\% \cdot n = 20$, where n represents the total number of nurses. Solving for n gives
$n = \frac{20}{40\%} = \frac{20}{0.40} = 50$.
Fifty nurses work at the hospital.

Example 3

A patient was given 40 mg of a certain medicine. Later, the patient's dosage was increased to 45 mg. What was the percent increase in his medication? To find the percent increase, first compare the original and increased amounts. The original amount was 40 mg, and the increased amount is 45 mg, so the dosage of medication was increased by 5 mg (45 − 40 = 5). Note, however, that the question asks not by how much the dosage increased but by what percentage it increased. Percent
increase $= \frac{\text{new amount} - \text{original amount}}{\text{original amount}} \cdot 100\%$.
So, $\frac{45 \text{ mg} - 40 \text{ mg}}{40 \text{ mg}} \cdot 100\% = \frac{5}{40} \cdot 100\% = 0.125 \cdot 100\% \approx 12.5\%$
The percent increase is approximately 12.5%.

> ➤ **Review Video: Percentages**
> *Visit **mometrix.com/academy** and enter **Code: 141911***

Ratios

A ratio is a comparison of two numbers in a certain order. Example: There are 14 computers in a lab, and the class has 20 students. So, there is a student to computer ratio of 20 to 14. Normally, this is written as 20:14. Ratios can be listed as *a to b*, *a:b*, or *a/b*. Examples of ratios are miles per hour (miles/hour), meters per second (meters/second), and miles per gallon (miles/gallon).

> ➤ **Review Video: Ratios**
> *Visit **mometrix.com/academy** and enter **Code: 996914***

Proportions and Cross Products
A proportion is a relationship between two numbers. This relationship shows how one changes when the other changes. A direct proportion is a relationship where a number increases by a set amount with every increase in the other number. Another way is for the number to decrease by that same amount for every decrease in the other quantity. Example: For every 1 sheet cake, 18 people can have cake. The number of sheet cakes and the number of people that can be served from them is a direct proportion.

Inverse proportion is a relationship where an increase in one number has a decrease in the other. This can work the other way where a decrease in a number has an increase in the other. Example: The time needed for a car trip decreases as the speed increases. Also, the time for the trip increases as the speed decreases. So, the time needed for the trip is inversely proportional to the speed of the car.

Two equal ratios have cross products that are equal. This can be written as $\frac{m}{b} = \frac{w}{z}$. For example, Fred travels 2 miles in 1 hour, and Jane travels 4 miles in 2 hours. So, their speeds are proportional because $\frac{2}{1} = \frac{4}{2}$. In a proportion, the product of the numerator of the first ratio and the denominator of the second ratio is equal to the product of the denominator of the first ratio and the numerator of the second ratio. In other words, you can see that $m \times z = b \times w$. So, $2 \times 2 = 1 \times 4$.

Example
A room has dimensions of 12' wide by 15' long. Using a scale of $\frac{1}{4}$ in. :1 foot, draw a blueprint of the room. First, determine the dimensions of the room on the blueprint. Let w represent the width in inches and l represent the length in inches of the room on the scale drawing.

$$\frac{\frac{1}{4} \text{ in}}{1 \text{ ft}} = \frac{w}{12 \text{ ft}}$$

Using cross-multiplication, $1 \cdot w = \left(\frac{1}{4}\right)(12) = 3$. The width of the room on the blueprint is 3 in.

$$\frac{\frac{1}{4} \text{ in}}{1 \text{ ft}} = \frac{l}{15 \text{ ft}}$$

Again using cross-multiplication, $1 \cdot l = \left(\frac{1}{4}\right)(15) = \frac{15}{4} = 3\frac{3}{4}$. The length of the room on the blueprint is $3\frac{3}{4}$ in.

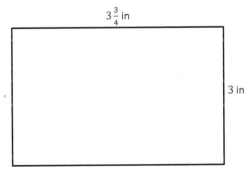

➤ **Review Video: Proportions**
*Visit **mometrix.com/academy** and enter **Code: 505355***

Copyright © Mometrix Media. You have been licensed one copy of this document for personal use only. Any other reproduction or redistribution is strictly prohibited. All rights reserved.

Decimal and Fraction Equivalents

Fraction	Decimal	Percentage
1/4	0.25	25%
1/2	0.50	50%
3/4	0.75	75%
1/3	$0.\overline{3}$ *	$33.\overline{3}$%
2/3	$0.\overline{6}$ *	$66.\overline{6}$%
1/5	0.20	20%
3/5	0.60	60%
4/5	0.80	80%
1/6	$0.1\overline{6}$ *	$16.\overline{6}$%
5/6	$0.8\overline{3}$ *	$83.\overline{3}$%
1/8	0.125	12.5%
3/8	0.375	37.5%
5/8	0.625	62.5%
7/8	0.875	87.5%

* the symbol ¯ above a number indicates that the number to the right is repeated infinitely.

Converting Decimals to Fractions

A fraction can be turned into a decimal and vice versa. In order to convert a fraction into a decimal, simply divide the numerator by the denominator. For example, the fraction $\frac{5}{4}$ becomes 1.25. This is done by dividing 5 by 4. The fraction $\frac{4}{8}$ becomes 0.5 when 4 is divided by 8. This remains true even if the fraction $\frac{4}{8}$ is first reduced to $\frac{1}{2}$. The decimal conversion will still be 0.5. In order to convert a decimal into a fraction, count the number of places to the right of the decimal. This will be the number of zeros in the denominator. The numbers to the right of the decimal will become the whole number in the numerator.

> ➤ **Review Video: <u>Converting Decimals to Fractions and Percentages</u>**
> Visit *mometrix.com/academy* and enter **Code: 986765**

Example 1: $0.45 = \frac{45}{100}$ and $\frac{45}{100}$ reduces to $\frac{9}{20}$

Example 2: $0.237 = \frac{237}{1000}$

Example 3: $0.2121 = \frac{2121}{10000}$

Working with Positive and Negative Numbers

Addition: If the signs are the same, then add the absolute values of the addends and use the original sign with the sum. The addends are the numbers that will be added to have the sum. For example, $(+4) + (+8) = +12$ and $(-4) + (-8) = -12$. When the signs are different, take the absolute values of the addends and subtract the smaller value from the larger value. Then, put the original sign of the larger value on the difference. For example, $(+4) + (-8) = -4$ and $(-4) + (+8) = +4$.

Subtraction: For signed numbers, change the sign of the number after the minus symbol. Then, follow the same rules for addition. For example, $(+4) - (+8)$ becomes $(+4) + (-8) = -4$.

Multiplication: If the signs are the same, then the product is positive. For example, $(+4) \times (+8) = +32$ and $(-4) \times (-8) = +32$. If the signs are different, then the product is negative. For example, $(+4) \times (-8) = -32$ and $(-4) \times (+8) = -32$. When more than two factors are multiplied together, the sign of the product is decided by how many negative factors are in the equation. If there are an odd number of negative factors, then the product is negative. An even number of negative factors gives a positive product. For example, $(+4) \times (-8) \times (-2) = +64$ and $(-4) \times (-8) \times (-2) = -64$.

Division: The rules for dividing signed numbers are similar to multiplying signed numbers. If the dividend and divisor have the same sign, the quotient is positive. If the dividend and divisor have opposite signs, the quotient is negative. For example, $(-4) \div (+8) = -0.5$.

Translating

Words to Mathematical Expression
Write "four less than twice x" as a mathematical expression.

Remember that an expression does not have an equals sign. "Less" indicates subtraction, and "twice" indicates multiplication by two. Four less than $2x$ is $2x - 4$. Notice how this is different than $4 - 2x$. You can plug in values for x to see how these expressions would yield different values.

Words to Mathematical Equation
Translate "three hundred twenty-five increased by six times $3x$ equals three hundred forty-three" into a mathematical equation.

The key words and phrases are "increased by," "times," and "equals."
Three hundred twenty-five increased by six times $3x$ equals three hundred forty-three:
$$325 + 6(3x) = 343$$
The mathematical sentence is $325 + 6(3x) = 343$.

Mathematical Expression to a Phrase
Write a phrase which represents this mathematical expression: $75 - 3t + 14^2$.

Because there are many words which indicate various operations, there are several ways to write this expression, including "seventy-five minus three times t plus fourteen squared."

Order of Operations

Order of Operations is a list of rules that gives the order of doing each operation in an expression. If you have an expression that with many different operations, Order of Operations tells you which operations to do first. An easy way to remember Order of Operations is PEMDAS.

This is written out as "Please Excuse My Dear Aunt Sally." PEMDAS stands for Parentheses, Exponents, Multiplication, Division, Addition, Subtraction. You need to understand that multiplication and division are equal as steps. Also, addition and subtraction are equal as steps. So, those pairs of operations are worked from left to right.

Example: Use order of operations for the expression $5 + 20 \div 4 \times (2 + 3)^2 - 6$.
P: Work on the operations inside the parentheses, $(2 + 3) = 5$.
E: Simplify the exponents, $(5)^2 = 25$.
The equation now looks like this: $5 + 20 \div 4 \times 25 - 6$.
MD: Work on multiplication and division from left to right, $20 \div 4 = 5$; then $5 \times 25 = 125$.
The equation now looks like this: $5 + 125 - 6$.
AS: Work on addition and subtraction from left to right, $5 + 125 = 130$; then $130 - 6 = 124$.

> ➤ **Review Video: Order of Operations**
> *Visit **mometrix.com/academy** and enter **Code: 259675***

Exponents and Parentheses

A number like 7, 23, or 97 is a base number. A number that is connected to the base number like 7^3, 23^4, or 97^2 is a superscript number. An exponent is a superscript number placed at the top right of a base number. Exponents are a short form of a longer math operation. This superscript number shows how many times the base number is to be multiplied by itself.

Example: $a^2 = a \times a$ or $2^4 = 2 \times 2 \times 2 \times 2$. A number with an exponent of 2 is said to be *squared*. A number with an exponent of 3 is said to be *cubed*. The value of a number raised to an exponent is called its power. So, 8^4 is read as *8 to the 4th power* or *8 raised to the power of 4*. A negative exponent can be written as a fraction to have a positive exponent. Example: $a^{-2} = 1/a^2$.

Laws of Exponents
The laws of exponents are as follows:
1) Any number to the power of 1 is equal to itself: $a^1 = a$.
   - Examples: $2^1 = 2$ | $-3^1 = -3$
2) The number 1 raised to any power is equal to 1: $1^n = 1$.
   - Examples: $1^3 = 1$ | $1^{30} = 1$
3) Any number raised to the power of 0 is equal to 1: $a^0 = 1$.
   - Examples: $8^0 = 1$ | $(-10)^0 = 1$ | $(1/2)^0 = 1$
4) Add exponents to multiply powers of the same base number: $a^n \times a^m = a^{n+m}$.
   - Example: $2^3 \times 2^4 = 2^{3+4} = 2^7 = 128$
5) Subtract exponents to divide powers of the same base number: $a^n \div a^m = a^{n-m}$.
   - Example: $\dfrac{2^5}{2^3} = 2^{5-3} = 2^2 = 4$

6) When a power is raised to a power, the exponents are multiplied: $(a^n)^m = a^{n \times m}$.
   - Example: $(3^2)^3 = 3^2 \times 3^2 \times 3^2 = 3^6 = 729$
7) Multiplication and division operations that are inside parentheses can be raised to a power. This is the same as each term being raised to that power: $(a \times b)^n = a^n \times b^n; (a \div b)^n = a^n \div b^n$.
   - Multiplication: $(2 \times 3)^2 = 2^2 \times 3^2 = 4 \times 9 = 36$
   - Division: $(4 \div 3)^3 = 4^3 \div 3^3 = 64 \div 27 = 2.37$

Note: Exponents do not have to be integers. Fractional or decimal exponents follow all the rules above as well. Example: $5^{\frac{1}{4}} \times 5^{\frac{3}{4}} = 5^{\frac{1}{4} + \frac{3}{4}} = 5^1 = 5$.

> ➤ **Review Video:** <u>Law of Exponents</u>
> *Visit **mometrix.com/academy** and enter **Code: 532558***

Parentheses are used to show which operation should be done first when there is more than one operation. Example: 4 – (2 + 1) = 1. So, the first step for this problem is to add 2 and 1. Then, subtract the sum from 4.

Coefficients and the Distributive Property

Coefficients
A coefficient is a number or symbol that is multiplied by a variable. For example, in the expression 2(ab), the number 2 is the coefficient of (ab). The expression can be written in other ways to have a different coefficient. For example, the expression can be 2a(b). This means that 2a is the coefficient of (b).

Distributive Property
The distributive property can be used to multiply each addend in parentheses. Then, the products are added to reach the result. The formula for the distributive property looks like this:
$$a(b + c) = ab + ac$$
Example: 6(2+4)
First, multiply 6 and 2. The answer is 12.
Then, multiply 6 and 4. The answer is 24.
Last, we add 12 and 24. So, the final answer is 48.

Inequalities

In algebra and higher areas of math, you will work with problems that do not equal each other. The statement comparing such expressions with symbols such as < (less than) or > (greater than) is called an *Inequality*. An example of an inequality is $7x > 5$. To solve for x, divide both sides by 7. So, the solution is $x > \frac{5}{7}$.

One way to remember these symbols is to see that the sign for "less than" looks like an *L* for *L*ess. Also, the sign for "greater than" looks like half of an *R* in g*R*eater. The terms *less than or equal to, at most*, or *no more than* are for the symbol ≤. Also, the terms *greater than or equal to, at least*, and *no less than* are for the symbol ≥.

Applied Mathematics

Rounding and Estimation

Rounding

Rounding is lowering the digits in a number and keeping the value similar. The result will be less accurate. However, this will be in a simpler form and will be easier to use. Whole numbers can be rounded to the nearest ten, hundred or thousand. Also, fractions and decimals can be rounded to the nearest whole number.

Example 1

Round each number to the nearest ten: 11 | 47 | 118

When rounding to the nearest ten, anything ending in 5 or greater rounds up.
So, 11 rounds to 10 | 47 rounds to 50 | 118 rounds to 120.

Example 2

Round each number to the nearest hundred: 78 | 980 | 248

When rounding to the nearest hundred, anything ending in 50 or greater rounds up.
So, 78 rounds to 100 | 980 rounds to 1000 | 248 rounds down to 200.

Example 3

Round each number to the nearest thousand: 302 | 1274 | 3756

When rounding to the nearest thousand, anything ending in 500 or greater rounds up.
So, 302 rounds to 0 | 1274 rounds to 100 | 3756 rounds to 4000.

Example 4

Round each number to the nearest whole number: $\frac{5}{8}$ | 2.12 | $\frac{14}{3}$

When rounding fractions and decimals, anything half or higher rounds up.
So, $\frac{5}{8}$ rounds to 1 | 2.12 rounds to 2 | $\frac{14}{3}$ rounds to 5.

Estimation

Estimation is the process of finding an approximate answer to a problem. Estimation may involve rounding to the nearest whole number to make addition or subtraction easier.

Example 1

There are 24 people in an English class. Miss Foster decides to order three exam books for each student, plus 6 extras. She estimates that she should order 90 exam books. Identify if her solution is reasonable.

Write an expression to determine the total number of exam books to order. Since three books are ordered for each student, first multiply the number of books per student by the number of students: 3 books per student · 24 students = 72 books. Next, add the six extra exam books that Miss Foster would like to order. The total number of books to order is: 72 + 6 = 78 books. Her original estimate of 90 exam books is too large.

Example 2
The following food items are available in a school cafeteria for lunch:
Sandwich: $3.15; Soup: $1.84
Salad: $2.62; Pretzels: $0.95
Milk: $0.40

Daniel has $4.00 and wants to purchase a milk, sandwich, and soup. Emily has $4.00 and wants to purchase a salad, pretzels, and milk. Estimate the cost of each student's lunch and determine if they have enough money to purchase the food they would like for lunch.

Daniel wants to purchase a milk, sandwich, and soup. Rounded to the nearest fifty cents, the cost of his items is $0.50, $3.00, and $2.00. The total for his three items would be approximately:
$$0.50 + 3.00 + 2.00 = 5.50$$
It will cost Daniel approximately $5.50 for his lunch. He does not have enough money to purchase the items he has selected.

Emily wants to purchase a salad, pretzels, and milk. Rounded to the nearest fifty cents, the cost of her items is $2.50, $1.00, and $0.50. The total for her three items would be approximately:
$$2.50 + 1.00 + 0.50 = 4.00$$
It will cost Emily approximately $4.00 for her lunch. She has approximately enough money to purchase the items she has selected.

Sequencing

Example 1
Use the sequence to find each of the following.
6, 13, 20, 27, 34, 41, …
a) Find the position of 34.
b) Find the value of the term in position 7.

a) The position of a term is its place in the sequence. The sequence begins with 6, in position 1, 13 is position 2, etc. The term 34 has a position of 5.
b) The terms in positions 1 through 6 are given. To find the term in position 7, identify the difference between each term.
13 – 6 = 7
20 – 13 = 7
27 – 20 = 7
34 – 27 = 7
41 – 34 = 7
The terms are increasing by 7. To find the 7th term, add 7 to the sixth term, 41:
41 + 7 = 48
The term in position 7 is 48.

Example 2
The *n*th term of a sequence is: $4n - 6$. Find the terms in position: 1, 4, and 10.

To find the terms in each given position, evaluate the expression for the *n*th term at the given position values.
1st term: $4(1) - 6 = 4 - 6 = -2$
4th term: $4(4) - 6 = 16 - 6 = 10$
10th term: $4(10) - 6 = 40 - 6 = 34$

Example 3
Write an algebraic expression to determine the *n*th term of the arithmetic sequence:
31, 25, 19, 13, ...

To find the *n*th term, find the common difference between each pair of given terms.
2nd term – 1st term: $25 - 31 = -6$
3rd term – 2nd term: $19 - 25 = -6$
4th term – 3rd term: $13 - 19 = -6$
The first term is 31, so when $n = 1$, the term is 31.
1st term: $31 + -6(n - 1)$

Simplify this expression and check it for terms 2, 3, and 4 by evaluating the expression at $n = 2, 3,$ and 4.
$31 + -6(n - 1) = 31 - 6n + 6 = -6n + 37$
2nd term: $-6(2) + 37 = -12 + 37 = 25$
3rd term: $-6(3) + 37 = -18 + 37 = 19$
4th term: $-6(4) + 37 = -24 + 37 = 13$
The *n*th term of the arithmetic sequence is $-6n + 37$.

Factors and Multiples

Factors are numbers that are multiplied for a product. An example is the equation $2 \times 3 = 6$. The numbers 2 and 3 are factors. A prime number has only two factors: 1 and itself. Other numbers can have many factors.

> **Review Video: Factors**
> *Visit **mometrix.com/academy** and enter **Code: 920086***

A common factor is a number that divides exactly into two or more numbers. For example, the factors of 12 are 1, 2, 3, 4, 6, and 12. The factors of 15 are 1, 3, 5, and 15. So, the common factors of 12 and 15 are 1 and 3. A prime factor is a factor that is a prime number. Thus, the prime factors of 12 are 2 and 3. For 15, the prime factors are 3 and 5.

The greatest common factor (GCF) is the largest number that is a factor of two or more numbers. For example, the factors of 15 are 1, 3, 5, and 15. The factors of 35 are 1, 5, 7, and 35. So, the greatest common factor of 15 and 35 is 5.

A multiple of a number is the product of the number and some other integer. Common multiples are multiples that are shared by two numbers. The least common multiple (LCM) is the smallest number that is a multiple of two or more numbers. For example, the multiples of 3 are 3, 6, 9, 12, 15, etc. The multiples of 5 are 5, 10, 15, 20, etc. Therefore, the least common multiple of 3 and 5 is 15.

➤ **Review Video: Multiples**
Visit mometrix.com/academy and enter Code: 626738

Roots and Square Roots

A root, or *Square Root*, is a number that when multiplied by itself gives a real number. For example, $\sqrt{4} = +2$ and -2 because $(-2) \times (-2) = 4$ and $(2) \times (2) = 4$. Now, $\sqrt{9} = +3$ and -3 because $(-3) \times (-3) = 9$ and $(3) \times (3) = 9$. So, +2 and -2 are square roots of 4. Also, +3 and -3 are square roots of 9.

Instead of using a superscript (e.g., a^x), roots use the radical symbol (e.g., $\sqrt{}$) for the operation. A radical will have a number underneath the bar (i.e., radical symbol). Also, a number can be placed in the index. This is the upper left where n is placed: $\sqrt[n]{a}$. So, this is read as *the nth root of a*. There are two special cases for the use of n. When n = 2, this is a square root. When n = 3, this is a cube root.

If there is no number to the upper left, it is understood to be a square root (n = 2). Almost all of the roots that you will face will be square roots. A square root is the same as a number raised to the $\frac{1}{2}$ power. When we say that a is the square root of b ($a = \sqrt{b}$), we mean that the variable multiplied by itself equals b: ($a \times a = b$). A perfect square is a number that has an integer for its square root. There are 10 perfect squares from 1 to 100: 1, 4, 9, 16, 25, 36, 49, 64, 81, 100. These are the squares for integers: 1, 2, 3, 4, 5, 6, 7, 8, 9, and 10.

Scientific Notation

Scientific notation is a way of writing long numbers in a shorter form. The form $a \times 10^n$ is used in scientific notation. This form means that *a* is greater than or equal to 1 but less than 10. Also, *n* is the number of places the decimal must move to get from the original number to *a*.

Example: The number 230,400,000 is long to write. To see this value in scientific notation, place a decimal point between the first and second numbers. This includes all digits through the last non-zero digit (a = 2.304).

To find the correct power of 10, count the number of places the decimal point had to move (n = 8). The number is positive if the decimal moved to the left. Thus, the number is negative if it moved to the right. So, 230,400,000 can be written as 2.304×10^8.

Now, let's look at the number 0.00002304. We have the same value for *a*. However, this time the decimal moved 5 places to the right (n = -5). So, 0.00002304 can be written as 2.304×10^{-5}. This notation makes it easy to compare very large or very small numbers. By comparing exponents, you can see that 3.28×10^4 is smaller than 1.51×10^5 because 4 is less than 5.

Addition and Subtraction

To add and subtract numbers in scientific notation, you need the numbers to have the same power of 10. Next, you can add the constants. Then, you can use the power of 10 with the result.

If the constant is greater than 10 or less than 1, you need to move the decimal place. For constants less than 1, the decimal is moved to the right. For constants greater than 10, the decimal is moved to the left. Also, the power of 10 needs to change as you move the decimal place.

Example 1

In the problem $(4.8 \times 10^4) + (2.2 \times 10^4)$, the numbers have the same power of 10. So, add 4.8 and 2.2. So, you have 7 as the result. Now, the number can be written as (7×10^4).

Example 2

In the problem $(3.1 \times 10^8) - (2.4 \times 10^8)$, the numbers have the same power of 10. So, subtract 3.4 and 1.1. So, you have 0.7 as the result. Remember that you cannot have a constant that is less than 1. So, you need to move the decimal place one time to the right: (7×10^8). Also, the power of 10 has to change. Now, the number can be written as (7×10^{-1}).

The power of 10 is -1 because we moved the decimal place one time to the right. Now you have $(7 \times 10^{-1}) \times 10^8$. The reason is that we still have the power of 10 as 8. Now, you can add the -1 to the +8 for an answer of (7×10^7).

Example 3

In the problem $(5.3 \times 10^6) + (2.7 \times 10^7)$, the numbers do not have the same power of 10. So, you need one of the terms to have the same power. So, take (5.3×10^6) and change it to (0.53×10^7). Now, you can add 0.53 and 2.7. So, the number can be written as (3.23×10^7).

Multiplication

In the problem $(2.4 \times 10^3) \times (5.7 \times 10^5)$, you need to multiply 2.4 and 5.7. Then, you need to add the powers of 10 which are 3 and 5 for this example. So, you have (13.68×10^8). Remember that this cannot be an answer for scientific notation. The 13.68 for a constant is higher than 10. So, move the decimal to the left one time and change the exponent. Now, you have (1.368×10^9) as the answer.

Division

In the problem $(5.6 \times 10^6) \div (2.3 \times 10^2)$, you need to divide 5.6 and 2.3. Then, you need to subtract the powers of 10 which are 6 and 2 for this example. So, you have (2.43×10^4).

Substitute an Integer

Polynomial Expressions

Solve the expression $(x^2+4)+(3x^2+4x+2)$, when x=5.

First, put in 3 for every x: $(5^2 + 4) + (3(5)^2 + 4(5) + 2) =$

Second, solve the parentheses: $(29) + (81) =$

Third, add 29 and 81: $(29) + (81) = 110$

<u>Linear Expressions</u>
Solve the expression $(x - 4) + (4x + 10)$, when x=6.

First, put in 6 for every x: $(6 - 4) + (4(6) + 10)$
Second, solve the parentheses: $(2) + (34) =$
Third, add 2 and 34: $(2) + (34) = 36$

<u>Rational Expressions</u>
Solve the expression: $\frac{x+7}{10-x}$, when x=9

First, put in 9 for every x: $\frac{9+7}{10-9}$

Second, solve the numerator and the denominator: $\frac{16}{1}$

Third, divide 16 and 1: $\frac{16}{1}=16$.

Solving for a Variable

Similar to order of operation rules, algebraic rules must be obeyed to ensure a correct answer. Begin by locating all parentheses and brackets, and then solving the equations within them. Then, perform the operations necessary to remove all parentheses and brackets. Next, convert all fractions into whole numbers and combine common terms on each side of the equation.

Beginning on the left side of the expression, solve operations involving multiplication and division. Then, work left to right solving operations involving addition and subtraction. Finally, cross-multiply if necessary to reach the final solution.

Example 1:
    4a-10=10

Constants are the numbers in equations that do not change. The variable in this equation is *a*. Variables are most commonly presented as either *x* or *y*, but they can be any letter. Every variable is equal to a number; one must solve the equation to determine what that number is. In an algebraic expression, the answer will usually be the number represented by the variable. In order to solve this equation, keep in mind that what is done to one side must be done to the other side as well. The first step will be to remove 10 from the left side by adding 10 to both sides. This will be expressed as 4a-10+10=10+10, which simplifies to 4a=20. Next, remove the 4 by dividing both sides by 4. This step will be expressed as 4a÷4=20÷4. The expression now becomes *a*=5.

Since variables are the letters that represent an unknown number, you must solve for that unknown number in single variable problems. The main thing to remember is that you can do anything to one side of an equation as long as you do it to the other.

Example 2:
    Solve for x in the equation 2x + 3 = 5.

Answer: First you want to get the "2x" isolated by itself on one side. To do that, first get rid of the 3. Subtract 3 from both sides of the equation 2x + 3 – 3 = 5 – 3 or 2x = 2. Now since the x is being multiplied by the 2 in "2x", you must divide by 2 to get rid of it. So, divide both sides by 2, which gives 2x / 2 = 2 / 2 or x = 1.

Manipulating Equations

Sometimes you will have variables missing in equations. So, you need to find the missing variable. To do this, you need to remember one important thing: whatever you do to one side of an equation, you need to do to the other side. If you subtract 100 from one side of an equation, you need to subtract 100 from the other side of the equation. This will allow you to change the form of the equation to find missing values.

Example
Ray earns $10 an hour. This can be given with the expression $10x$, where x is equal to the number of hours that Ray works. This is the independent variable. The independent variable is the amount that can change. The money that Ray earns is in y hours. So, you would write the equation: $10x = y$. The variable y is the dependent variable. This depends on x and cannot be changed. Now, let's say that Ray makes $360. How many hours did he work to make $360?

$$10x = 360$$

Now, you want to know how many hours that Ray worked. So, you want to get x by itself. To do that, you can divide both sides of the equation by 10.

$$\frac{10x}{10} = \frac{360}{10}$$

So, you have: $x = 36$. Now, you know that Ray worked 36 hours to make $360.

Word Problems

Inequalities
To write out an inequality, you may need to translate a sentence into an inequality. This translation is putting the words into symbols. When translating, choose a variable to stand for the unknown value. Then, change the words or phrases into symbols. For example, the sum of 2 and a number is at most 12. So, you would write: $2 + b \leq 12$.

Example
Write an inequality that represents "64 plus 25f is less than or equal to 23 plus the quantity x minus 44."

The key words and phrases are "plus," "less than or equal to," "the quantity," and "minus." The first part of the number sentence is 64 plus 25f. "Plus" indicates addition. So this can be written as 64 + 25f which will go on the left hand side of the inequality sign.

"Less than or equal to" is represented with the inequality symbol ≤.
The second part of the number sentence is 23 plus the quantity x minus 44. "Plus" indicates addition. "The quantity x minus 44" means that 44 must be subtracted from x before it is added to the 23; in other words, the "x minus 44" needs to be grouped together inside parentheses. All together, this can be written as 23 + (x – 44), which goes on the right hand side of the inequality sign. The final answer is 64 + 25f ≤ 23 + (x – 44).

Rational Expressions
John and Luke play basketball every week. John can make 5 free throws per minute faster than Luke can make three-point shots. On one day, John made 30 free throws in the same time that it took Luke to make 10 three-point shots. So, how fast are Luke and John scoring points?

First, set up what you know. You know that John made 30 free throws, and he had a rate of 5 free throws per minute faster than Luke's three point shots: $\frac{30}{x+5}$. The x is for Luke's speed. Also, you know that Luke made 20 three point shots in the same amount of time that John scored his free throws: $\frac{20}{x}$. So, we can set up proportions because their times are equal.

$$\frac{30}{x+5} = \frac{20}{x}$$

Cross factor the proportion: $30x = 20(x+5)$

Then, distribute the 20 across the parentheses: $30x = 20x + 100$
Now, you can subtract 20x from both sides of the equation, and you are left with: $10x = 100$

So, you can divide both sides by 10: $\frac{10x}{10} = \frac{100}{10}$
Now, you are left with: $x = 10$. So, Luke's speed was 10 three-point shots per minute. Then, John's speed was 15 free throws per minute.

Polynomial Expressions
Fred buys some CDs for $12 each. He also buys two DVDs. The total that Fred spent is $60. So, write an equation that shows the connection between the number of CDs and the average cost of a DVD.

Let c stand for the number of CDs that Fred buys. Also, let d stand for the average cost of one of the DVDs that Fred buys. The expression $12c$ gives the cost of the CDs. Also, the expression $2d$ gives the cost of the DVDs. So, the equation $12c + 2d = 60$ states the number of CDs and the average cost of a DVD.

Unit Prices
A supermarket promotes a special price of $3.00 for 5 oranges. The regular price is $2.50 for 4 oranges. Compare the unit prices of sale-price and regular-priced oranges.

First, find the price of one orange (i.e., the price per orange). The price of one orange can be found by dividing the total price by the total number of oranges.
Sale price: $\frac{\$3.00}{5 \; oranges} = \frac{\$0.60}{1 \; orange}$

Regular price: $\frac{\$2.50}{4 \; oranges} = \frac{\$0.625}{1 \; orange}$

The sale price can be found by subtracting $0.625 and $0.60. So, the sale price is $0.025 less than the regular price of one orange.

Simple Interest
Simple Interest: Interest that is paid once per year for the principal amount. The principal amount is the original amount that someone borrows from another person or a bank. The formula is $I = Prt$, where I is the amount of interest, P is the principal, r is the annual interest rate, and t is the amount of time in years.

Real World Problems with Percents

Example 1
A car dealer has two promotions. The first promotion is a discount of 4% off the price of the car. The second promotion is $500 cash back. The car that Mark wants to buy is $15,000. Which promotion should Mark choose?

First: Find the discount to the purchase price for each promotion. For the first promotion, the purchase price is discounted by 4%. To find 4% of the purchase price, multiply the price by 4% as a decimal: 0.04: $15,000 $\times$ 0.04 $=$ $600

The discount of the purchase price with the second promotion is $500. This is the amount of cash given to the customer. Mark wants to have a greater discount off the purchase price. So, he should go with the first promotion of 4% off.

Example 2
A pair of jeans has a retail price of $54.00. The jeans are on sale for 15% off the retail price. A sales tax of 6% is charged on the discounted price of the jeans. Find the total cost of the jeans by including the discount and the tax.

First, find the discounted price of the jeans. Subtract the 15% off the retail price of the jeans from the original retail price.
$$54 - (0.15 \cdot 54) =$$
$$54 - 8.1 = 45.9$$
So, the discounted price is $45.90.
Next, calculate the tax on the jeans. The tax will be 6% of the discounted price.
$$45.9 \cdot 0.06 = 2.754$$

Rounded to the nearest cent, the tax on the jeans will be $2.75.
The total price of the jeans is the discounted price plus the tax:
$$45.90 + 2.75 = 48.65$$
So, the jeans will cost $48.65.

Example 3
The bill for dinner is $62.00. The group decides to leave their server a 20% tip. Find the total cost of eating at the restaurant and include the tip.

First, change 20% to a decimal: $20\% = \frac{20}{100} = 0.20$.
Next, multiply the bill by 0.20 to find the amount of the tip: $62.00(0.20) = $12.40
The total cost of dining will be the sum of the bill for dinner and the tip: $62.00 + $12.40 = $74.40
So, the total cost is $74.40.

- 22 -

Measurement

Temperature

Find the temperature, in degrees Fahrenheit, on the thermometer below. Use the thermometer to find the temperature if the temperature increased by 5° Fahrenheit.

The temperature, on the thermometer, is 75° F. If the temperature increases by 5° F, change the thermometer to show the increase in 5°:

If the temperature increases by 5° F, the new temperature is 80° F.

Time

Lindsay leaves for school at 7:00am. It takes her 20 minutes to get to school. Use a clock to determine the time Lindsay arrives at school. 7:00 am means the large clock hand is on 12, and the small hand is on 7.

In 20 minutes, the big hand will move 20 minutes clockwise, to the 4. The big hand will also move closer to the 8. 20 minutes is: $\frac{20}{60} = \frac{1}{3}$ of an hour, so the big hand will move one third of the way from the 7 to the 8.

The ending time is 7:20am, which is when Lindsay arrives at school.

Measurement Conversion

When going from a larger unit to a smaller unit, multiply the number of the known amount by the equivalent amount. When going from a smaller unit to a larger unit, divide the number of the known amount by the equivalent amount. Also, you can set up conversion fractions. In these fractions, one fraction is the conversion factor. The other fraction has the unknown amount in the numerator. So, the known value is placed in the denominator. Sometimes the second fraction has the known value from the problem in the numerator, and the unknown in the denominator. Multiply the two fractions to get the converted measurement.

<u>Measurement Equivalents</u>
12 inches = 1 foot
1 yard = 3 feet
1 yard = 36 inches

1 mile = 5280 feet
1 mile = 1760 yards
1 acre = 43,560 square feet

1 quart = 2 pints
1 quart = 4 cups

1 gallon = 4 quarts
1 gallon = 8 pints
1 gallon = 16 cups

1 pound = 16 ounces

Don't think that because something weighs one pound that its volume is one pint. Ounces of weight are not equal to fluid ounces which measure volume.

1 ton = 2000 pounds

<u>Metric Measurements</u>
1 liter = 1000 milliliters
1 liter = 1000 cubic centimeters

Do not confuse *cubic centimeters* with *centiliters*.
1 liter = 1000 cubic centi*meters*, but 1 liter = 100 centi*liters*.

1 meter = 1000 millimeters
1 meter = 100 centimeters

1 gram = 1000 milligrams
1 kilogram = 1000 grams

Kilo, centi, and milli
Kilo-: one thousand
Centi-: one hundredth
Milli-: one thousandth

Example 1
There are 100 centimeters in 1 meter. Convert the measurements below.
a. Convert 1.4 m to cm
b. Convert 218 cm to m

Write a ratio with the conversion factor: $\frac{100 \text{ cm}}{1 \text{ m}}$. Use proportions to convert the given units.

a. $\frac{100 \text{ cm}}{1 \text{ m}} = \frac{x \text{ cm}}{1.4 \text{ m}}$. Cross multiply to get $x = 140$. So, there are 1.4 m in 140 cm.

b. $\frac{100 \text{ cm}}{1 \text{ m}} = \frac{218 \text{ cm}}{x \text{ m}}$. Cross multiply to get $100x = 218$, or $x = 2.18$. So, there are 218 cm in 2.18 m.

Example 2
There are 12 inches in 1 foot. Also, there are 3 feet in 1 yard. Convert the following measurements.
a. 42 inches to feet
b. 15 feet to yards

Write ratios with the conversion factors: $\frac{12 \text{ in}}{1 \text{ ft}}$ and: $\frac{3 \text{ ft}}{1 \text{ yd}}$. Use proportions to convert the given units.

a. $\frac{12 \text{ in}}{1 \text{ ft}} = \frac{42 \text{ in}}{x \text{ ft}}$. Cross multiply to get $12x = 42$, or $x = 3.5$. So, there are 42 inches in 3.5 feet.

b. $\frac{3 \text{ ft}}{1 \text{ yd}} = \frac{15 \text{ ft}}{x \text{ yd}}$. Cross multiply to get $3x = 15$, or $x = 5$. So, there are 15 feet in 5 yards.

Geometry and Spatial Sense

Lines and Planes
A point is a fixed location in space. This point has no size or dimensions. Commonly, this fixed location is a dot. A collinear point is a point which is on the line. A non-collinear point is a point that is not on a line.

A line is a set of points that go forever in two opposite directions. The line has length but no width or depth. A line can be named by any two points that are on the line. A line segment is a part of a line that has definite endpoints. A ray is a part of a line that goes from a single point and goes in one direction along the line. A ray has a definite beginning but no ending.

A plane is a two-dimensional flat surface that has three non-collinear points. A plane goes an unending distance in all directions in those two dimensions. This plane has an unending number of points, parallel lines and segments, intersecting lines and segments. Also, a plane can have an unending number of parallel or intersecting rays. A plane will never have a three-dimensional figure or skew lines. Two given planes will be parallel, or they will intersect to form a line. A plane may intersect a circular conic surface (e.g., a cone) to make conic sections (e.g., the parabola, hyperbola, circle, or ellipse).

Perpendicular lines are lines that intersect at right angles. The symbol ⊥ stands for perpendicular lines. The shortest distance from a line to a point that is not on the line is a perpendicular segment from the point to the line. Parallel lines are lines in the same plane that have no points in common and never meet. The lines can be in different planes, have no points in common, and never meet. However, the lines will not be parallel because they are in different planes.

A bisector is a line or line segment that divides another line segment into two equal lengths. A perpendicular bisector of a line segment has points that are equidistant (i.e., equal distances) from the endpoints of the segment. Intersecting lines are lines that have exactly one point in common. Concurrent lines are several lines that intersect at a single point. A transversal is a line that intersects at least two other lines. The lines may or may not be parallel to one another. A transversal that intersects parallel lines is common in geometry.

Angles
An angle is made when two lines or line segments meet at a point. The angle may be a starting point for a pair of segments or rays. Also, angles come from the intersection of lines. The symbol ∠ stands for angles.

Angles that are opposite to one another are called vertical angles, and their measures are equal. The vertex is the point where two segments or rays meet to make an angle. Angles that are made from intersecting rays, lines, and/or line segments have four angles at the vertex.

An acute angle is an angle with a degree measure less than 90°. A right angle is an angle with a degree measure of exactly 90°. An obtuse angle is an angle with a degree measure greater than 90° but less than 180°. A straight angle is an angle with a degree measure of exactly 180°. A reflex angle is an angle with a degree measure greater than 180° but less than 360°. A full angle is an angle with a degree measure of exactly 360°.

> **Review Video: Angles**
*Visit **mometrix.com/academy** and enter **Code: 264624***

Two angles with a sum of exactly 90° are known as complementary. The two angles may or may not be adjacent (i.e., *next to* or *beside*). In a right triangle, the two acute angles are complementary.

Two angles with a sum that is exactly 180° are known as supplementary. The two angles may or may not be adjacent. Two intersecting lines always make two pairs of supplementary angles. Adjacent supplementary angles will always make a straight line. Two angles that have the same vertex and share a side are known as adjacent. Vertical angles are not adjacent because they share a vertex, but they have no common side.

Adjacent
Share vertex and side

Not adjacent
Share part of side, but not vertex

When two parallel lines are cut by a transversal, the angles that are between the two parallel lines are interior angles. In the diagram below, angles 3, 4, 5, and 6 are interior angles.

When two parallel lines are cut by a transversal, the angles that are outside the parallel lines are exterior angles. In the diagram below, angles 1, 2, 7, and 8 are exterior angles.

When two parallel lines are cut by a transversal, the angles that match the position of other angles are corresponding angles. The diagram below has four pairs of corresponding angles: angles 1 and 5; angles 2 and 6; angles 3 and 7; and angles 4 and 8. Corresponding angles made by parallel lines are congruent. For congruent angles, we mean that they have the same angle measures.

When two parallel lines are cut by a transversal, the two interior angles that are on opposite sides of the transversal are alternate interior angles. In the diagram below, there are two pairs of alternate interior angles: angles 3 and 6 and angles 4 and 5. Alternate interior angles made by parallel lines are congruent.

When two parallel lines are cut by a transversal, the two exterior angles that are on opposite sides of the transversal are alternate exterior angles. In the diagram below, there are two pairs of alternate exterior angles: angles 1 and 8 and angles 2 and 7. Alternate exterior angles made by parallel lines are congruent.

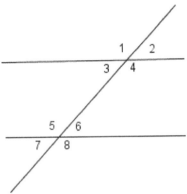

When two lines intersect, four angles are formed. The non-adjacent angles at this vertex are vertical angles. Vertical angles are congruent. The symbol for congruence is ($\cong$) In the diagram, $\angle ABD \cong \angle CBE$ and $\angle ABC \cong \angle DBE$.

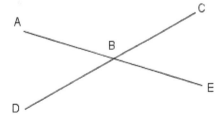

Triangles

An equilateral triangle is a triangle with three congruent sides. Also, an equilateral triangle will have three congruent angles and each angle will be 60°. All equilateral triangles are acute triangles.

An isosceles triangle is a triangle with two congruent sides. An isosceles triangle will have two congruent angles as well.

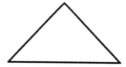

A scalene triangle is a triangle with no congruent sides. Also, a scalene triangle will have three angles of different measures. The angle with the largest measure is opposite from the longest side. The angle with the smallest measure is opposite from the shortest side.

An acute triangle is a triangle whose three angles are all less than 90°. If two of the angles are equal, the acute triangle is also an isosceles triangle. If the three angles are all equal, the acute triangle is also an equilateral triangle.

A right triangle is a triangle with exactly one angle equal to 90°. All right triangles follow the Pythagorean Theorem. A right triangle can never be acute or obtuse.

An obtuse triangle is a triangle with one angle greater than 90°. The other two angles may or may not be equal. If the two remaining angles are equal, the obtuse triangle is also an isosceles triangle.

Important Vocabulary for Triangles

Altitude of a Triangle: A line segment that is drawn from one vertex and is perpendicular to the opposite side. In the diagram below, $\overline{BE}$, $\overline{AD}$, and $\overline{CF}$ are altitudes. The three altitudes in a triangle are always concurrent (i.e., three or more lines that meet at one point). This concurrent point is also known as the point of concurrency.

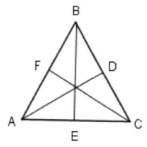

Height of a Triangle: The length of the altitude. Often, the two terms are used in place of the other.

Orthocenter of a Triangle: The point of concurrency of the altitudes of a triangle. In an obtuse triangle, the orthocenter will be outside the triangle. In a right triangle, the orthocenter is the vertex of the right angle.

Median of a Triangle: A line segment drawn from one vertex to the midpoint of the opposite side. This is not the same as the altitude, but sometimes the same line can be used for both. This is true for the altitude to the base of an isosceles triangle and all three altitudes of an equilateral triangle.

Centroid of a Triangle: The point of concurrency of the medians of a triangle. This is the same point as the orthocenter. However, this point is for equilateral triangles. Unlike the orthocenter, the centroid is always inside the triangle.

The centroid can be thought of as the exact center of the triangle. Any shape triangle can be perfectly balanced on a tip placed at the centroid. The centroid is the point that is two-thirds the distance from the vertex to the opposite side.

> **Review Video: <u>Orthocenter and Centroid of a Triangle</u>**
> *Visit **mometrix.com/academy** and enter **Code: 598260***

Pythagorean Theorem
The side of a triangle opposite to the right angle is called the hypotenuse. The other two sides are called the legs. The Pythagorean Theorem explains the relationship among the legs and the hypotenuse of a right triangle. This explanation is in the formula: $a^2 + b^2 = c^2$, where a and b are the lengths of the legs of a right triangle, and c is the length of the hypotenuse. This formula will only work with right triangles.

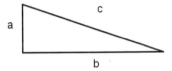

> **Review Video: <u>Pythagorean Theorem</u>**
> *Visit **mometrix.com/academy** and enter **Code: 906576***

General Rules of Triangles
The Triangle Inequality Theorem says that the sum of the measures of any two sides of a triangle is always greater than the measure of the third side. For example, one side of a triangle is 5, and the other side is 10. So, the third side must be less than or greater than 15. The third side cannot be 15.

If the sum of the measures of two sides were equal to the third side, a triangle would be impossible. The reason is that the two sides would lie flat across the third side, and there would be no vertex. If the sum of the measures of two of the sides was less than the third side, a closed shape would be impossible. The reason is that the two shortest sides would never meet.

The triangle sum theorem says that the sum of the measures of the interior angles of a triangle is always 180°. So, a triangle can never have more than one angle that is greater than or equal to 90°.

In any triangle, the angles that are opposite to congruent sides are congruent. The sides that are opposite to congruent angles are congruent. The largest angle is always opposite the longest side. The smallest angle is always opposite to the shortest side.

The line segment that joins the midpoints of any two sides of a triangle is always parallel to the third side. Also, this line segment is exactly half the length of the third side.

Polygons

Each straight line segment of a polygon is called a side. The point at which two sides of a polygon intersect is called the vertex. In a polygon, the number of sides is always equal to the number of vertices. A polygon with all sides congruent and all angles equal is called a regular polygon.

A line segment from the center of a polygon that is perpendicular to a side of the polygon is called the apothem. A line segment from the center of a polygon to a vertex of the polygon is called a radius. In a regular polygon, the apothem can be used to find the area of the polygon using the formula $A = \frac{1}{2}ap$, where a is the apothem, and p is the perimeter.

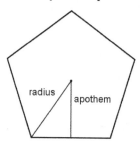

Triangle – 3 sides
Quadrilateral – 4 sides
Pentagon – 5 sides
Hexagon – 6 sides
Heptagon – 7 sides
Octagon – 8 sides
Nonagon – 9 sides
Decagon – 10 sides
Dodecagon – 12 sides

Generally, an n-gon is a polygon that has more than 12 angles and sides. The space of n is for the number of sides. Also, an 11-sided polygon is known as an 11-gon.

The sum of the interior angles of an n-sided polygon is $(n - 2)180°$. For example, in a triangle n = 3. So, the sum of the interior angles is $(3 - 2)180° = 180°$. In a quadrilateral, n = 4, and the sum of the angles is $(4 - 2)180° = 360°$.

A diagonal is a line segment that joins two non-adjacent vertices of a polygon. A convex polygon is a polygon whose diagonals all lie within the interior of the polygon. A concave polygon is a polygon with a least one diagonal that is outside the polygon. In the diagram below, quadrilateral *ABCD* is concave because diagonal $\overline{AC}$ lies outside the polygon.

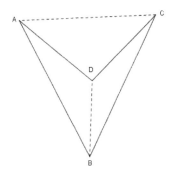

The number of diagonals that a polygon has can be found by using the formula:
$\frac{n(n-3)}{2}$ = number of diagonals; where n is the number of sides in the polygon. This formula works for all polygons.

Congruent figures are geometric figures that have the same size and shape. All corresponding angles are equal, and all corresponding sides are equal. Congruence is shown by the symbol $\cong$.

Congruent polygons

Similar figures are geometric figures that have the same shape, but may not have the same size. All corresponding angles are equal, and all corresponding sides are proportional. However, they do not have to be equal. Similarity is shown by the symbol $\sim$.

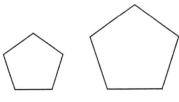

Similar polygons

Note that all congruent figures are also similar. However, not all similar figures are congruent.

Line of Symmetry: The line that divides a figure or object into equal parts. Each part is congruent to the other. An object may have no lines of symmetry, one line of symmetry, or multiple (i.e., more than one) lines of symmetry.
Lines of symmetry:

None

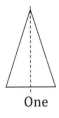

One

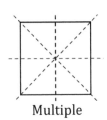

Multiple

Quadrilateral: A closed two-dimensional geometric figure that has four straight sides. The sum of the interior angles of any quadrilateral is 360°. A quadrilateral whose diagonals divide each other is a parallelogram.

A quadrilateral whose opposite sides are parallel (i.e., 2 pairs of parallel sides) is a parallelogram. A quadrilateral whose diagonals are perpendicular bisectors of each other is a rhombus. A quadrilateral whose opposite sides (i.e., both pairs) are parallel and congruent is a rhombus.

Parallelogram: A quadrilateral that has two pairs of opposite parallel sides. The sides that are parallel are also congruent. The opposite interior angles are always congruent, and the consecutive interior angles are supplementary. The diagonals of a parallelogram divide each other. Each diagonal divides the parallelogram into two congruent triangles.

A parallelogram that has a right angle is a rectangle. In the diagram below, the top left corner and the bottom left corner are consecutive angles. Consecutive angles of a parallelogram are supplementary. If there is one right angle in a parallelogram, there are four right angles in that parallelogram.

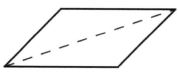

Trapezoid: Normally, a quadrilateral has one pair of parallel sides. Some define a trapezoid as a quadrilateral that has at least one pair of parallel sides. There are no rules for the second pair of sides. So, there are no rules for the diagonals of a trapezoid.

Rectangles, rhombuses, and squares are all special forms of parallelograms.

Rectangle: A parallelogram with four right angles. All rectangles are parallelograms, but not all parallelograms are rectangles. The diagonals of a rectangle are congruent.

Rhombus: A parallelogram with four congruent sides. All rhombuses are parallelograms, but not all parallelograms are rhombuses. The diagonals of a rhombus are perpendicular to each other. A rhombus with one right angle is a square. The rhombus is a special form of a parallelogram. So, the rules about the angles of a parallelogram are true for the rhombus.

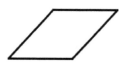

Square: A parallelogram with four right angles and four congruent sides. All squares are also parallelograms, rhombuses, and rectangles. The diagonals of a square are congruent and perpendicular to each other.

Area and Perimeter Formulas
The **perimeter of any triangle** is found by adding the three side lengths $P = a + b + c$. For an equilateral triangle, this is the same as $P = 3s$, where s is any side length. The reason is that the three sides are the same length.

Find the side of a triangle
You may have problems that give you the perimeter of a triangle. So, you are asked to find one of the sides.
Example: The perimeter of a triangle is 35 cm. One side length is 10 cm. Another side length is 20cm. Find the length of the missing side.
    First: Set up the equation to set apart a side length.
        Now, the equation is $35 = 10 + 20 + c$. So, you are left with $35 = 30 + c$.

    Second: Subtract 30 from both sides: $35 - 30 = 30 - 30 + c$
        Then, you are left with $5 = c$

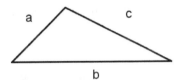

The **area of any triangle** can be found by taking half of the base (i.e., b). Then, multiply that result by the height (i.e., h) of the triangle. So, the standard formula for the area of a triangle is $A = \frac{1}{2}bh$. For many triangles, it may be difficult to calculate h. So, other formulas are given here that may be easier.

Find the height or the area of the base
You may have problems that give you the area of a triangle. So, you are asked to find the height or the base.
Example: The area of a triangle is 70 cm², and the height is 10. Find the base.
    First: Set up the equation to set apart the base.
        The equation is $70 = \frac{1}{2}10b$. Now, multiply both sides by 2: $70 \times 2 = \frac{1}{2}10b \times 2$.
        So, you are left with: $140 = 10b$.

    Second: Divide both sides by 10 to get the base: $\frac{140}{10} = \frac{10b}{10}$
        Then, you have $14 = b$.

Note: When you need to find the height, you can follow the steps above to find it.

Another formula that works for any triangle is $A = \sqrt{s(s-a)(s-b)(s-c)}$, where A is the area, s is the semi-perimeter $s = \frac{a+b+c}{2}$, and a, b, and c are the lengths of the three sides.

The area of an equilateral triangle can found by the formula $A = \frac{\sqrt{3}}{4}s^2$, where A is the area and s is the length of a side. You could use the $30° - 60° - 90°$ ratios to find the height of the triangle. Then, use the standard triangle area formula.

The area of an isosceles triangle can found by the formula, $A = \frac{1}{2}b\sqrt{a^2 - \frac{b^2}{4}}$, where A is the area, b is the base, and a is the length of one of the two congruent sides. If you do not remember this formula, you can use the Pythagorean Theorem to find the height. Then, you can use the standard formula for the area of a triangle.

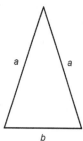

> ➤ **Review Video:** <u>Area and Perimeter of a Triangle</u>
> *Visit **mometrix.com/academy** and enter **Code: 817385**

The **area of a square** is found by using the formula $A = s^2$, where A is the area and s is the length of one side.

Find the side of a square
You may have problems that give you the area of a square. So, you are asked to find the side.
Example: The area of a square is 9 cm². Find the side.
    First: Set up the equation to set apart s.
            The equation is $9 = s^2$.

    Second: Now, you can take the square root of both sides: $\sqrt{9} = \sqrt{s^2}$.
            So, you are left with: $3 = s$

The **perimeter of a square** is found by using the formula $P = 4s$, where P is the perimeter, and s is the length of one side. All four sides are equal in a square. So, you can multiply the length of one side by 4. This is faster than adding the same number four times.

Find the side of a square
You may have problems that give you the perimeter of a square. So, you are asked to find the side.
Example: The perimeter of a square is 60 cm. Find the side.

First: Set up the equation to set apart s.
         The equation is $60 = 4s$.

Second: Now, you can divide both sides by 4: $\frac{60}{4} = \frac{4s}{4}$. You are left with $15 = s$

> **Review Video: <u>Area and Perimeter of a Square</u>**
> *Visit **mometrix.com/academy** and enter **Code: 620902***

The **area of a rectangle** is found by the formula $A = lw$, where A is the area of the rectangle, l is the length and w is the width. Usually, the longer side is the length, and the shorter side is the width. However, the numbers for l and w can used be for one or the other.

Find the width or length of a rectangle
You may have problems that give you the area of a rectangle. So, you are asked to find the width.
Example: The area of a rectangle is 150cm², and the length is 10cm. Find the width.

First: Set up the equation to set apart width.
       The equation is $150 = 10w$.

Second: Divide both sides by 10: $\frac{150}{10} = \frac{10w}{10}$. You are left with $15 = w$

The **perimeter of a rectangle** can be found with two formulas $P = 2l + 2w$ or $P = 2(l + w)$, where l is the length, and w is the width.

Find the width or length of a rectangle
You may have problems that give you the perimeter of a rectangle. So, you are asked to find the width.
Example: The perimeter of a rectangle is 100cm, and the length is 20cm. Find the width.

First: Set up the equation to set apart the width.
         The equation is $100 = 2(20 + w)$

Second: Distribute the 2 across $(20 + w)$: $100 = 40 + 2w$
        Then, subtract 40 from both sides: $100 - 40 = 40 + 2w - 40$
        So, you are left with: $60 = 2w$. Then, divide both sides by 2: $\frac{60}{2} = \frac{2w}{2}$.
        Now, you have $30 = w$.

Note: When you need to find the length, you can follow the steps above to find it.

> **Review Video: <u>Area and Perimeter of a Rectangle</u>**
> *Visit **mometrix.com/academy** and enter **Code: 933707***

The **area of a parallelogram** is found by the formula $A = bh$, where b is the length of the base, and h is the height. Note that the base and height match with the length and width in a rectangle. So, this formula can be used for rectangles as well. Do not confuse the height of a parallelogram with the length of the second side. They have the same measure only with rectangles.

Find the length of the base or the height of a parallelogram
You may have problems that give you the area of a parallelogram. So, you are asked to find the area of the base or the height.
Example: The area of the parallelogram is 84 cm². The base is 7cm. Find the height.

Set up the equation to set apart the height.

So, you have $84 = 7h$. Now, divide both sides by 7: $\frac{84}{7} = \frac{7h}{7}$.

Then, you are left with $12 = h$

The **perimeter of a parallelogram** is found by the formula $P = 2a + 2b$ or $P = 2(a + b)$, where a and b are the lengths of the two sides.

Find the missing side of a parallelogram
You may have problems that give you the perimeter of a parallelogram. So, you are asked to find one of the sides. Example: The perimeter of a parallelogram is 100cm, and one side is 20cm. Find the other side.

First: Set up the equation to set apart one of the side lengths.
The equation is $100 = 2(20 + b)$

Second: Distribute the 2 across $(20 + b)$: $100 = 40 + 2b$
Then, subtract 40 from both sides: $100 - 40 = 40 + 2b - 40$
So, you are left with: $60 = 2b$. Then, divide both sides by 2: $\frac{60}{2} = \frac{2b}{2}$
Now, you have $30 = b$.

> ➢ **Review Video:** <u>Area and Perimeter of a Parallelogram</u>
> *Visit **mometrix.com/academy** and enter **Code: 718313***

The **area of a trapezoid** is found by the formula $A = \frac{1}{2}h(b_1 + b_2)$, where h is the height, and b_1 and b_2 are the two parallel sides (i.e., bases). The height is the segment that joins the parallel bases.

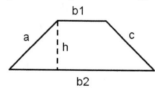

Find the height of a trapezoid
You may have problems that give you the area of a trapezoid. So, you are asked to find the height.
Example: The area of a trapezoid is 30cm². B_1 is 3cm, and B_2 is 9cm. Find the height.

First: Set up the equation to set apart the height.
The equation is $30 = \frac{1}{2}h(3 + 9)$.

Second: Now, multiply both sides by 2: $30 \times 2 = \frac{1}{2}(12)h \times 2$.
So, you are left with: $60 = (12)h$.

Third: Divide both sides by 12: $\frac{60}{12} = \frac{(12)h}{12}$. Now, you have $5 = h$

- 36 -

Find a base of a trapezoid
You may have problems that give you the area of a trapezoid and the height. So, you are asked to find one of the bases.
Example: The area of a trapezoid is 90cm². b_1 is 5cm, and the height is 12cm. Find b_2.
> First: Set up the equation to set apart b_2.
> > The equation is $90 = \frac{1}{2}12(5 + b_2)$.
> Second: Now, multiply the height by $\frac{1}{2}$: $90 = 6(5 + b_2)$.
> > So, you can distribute the 6 across $(5 + b_2)$: $90 = 30 + 6b_2$
> Third: Subtract 30 from both sides $90 - 30 = 30 + 6b_2 - 30$.
> > Now, you have $60 = 6b_2$.
> > Then, divide both sides by 6: $\frac{60}{6} = \frac{6b_2}{6}$. So, $b_2 = 10$.

The **perimeter of a trapezoid** is found by the formula $P = a + b_1 + c + b_2$, where a, b_1, c, and b_2 are the four sides of the trapezoid.

Find the missing side of a trapezoid
Example: The perimeter of a trapezoid is 50cm. B_1 is 20cm, B_2 is 10cm, and a is 5cm. Find the length of side c.
> First: Set up the equation to set apart the missing side.
> > The equation is $50 = 5 + 20 + c + 10$. So, you have $50 = 35 + c$
> Second: Subtract 35 from both sides: $50 - 35 = 35 + c - 35$.
> > So, you are left with $15 = c$

> ➤ **Review Video: <u>Area and Perimeter of a Trapezoid</u>**
> *Visit mometrix.com/academy and enter Code: 587523*

<u>Circles</u>
The center is the single point inside the circle that is equidistant from every point on the circle. The point O is in the diagram below. The radius is a line segment that joins the center of the circle and any one point on the circle. All radii of a circle are equal. The segments OX, OY, and OZ are in the diagram below.

The diameter is a line segment that passes through the center of the circle and has both endpoints inside the circle. The length of the diameter is twice the length of the radius. The segment XZ is in the diagram below. Concentric circles are circles that have the same center but not the same length of radii. A bulls-eye target is an example of concentric circles.

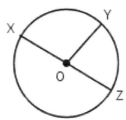

The **area of a circle** is found with the formula $A = \pi r^2$, where r is the length of the radius. If the diameter of the circle is given, divide it in half to get the radius before using the formula. (Note: In the following formulas, 3.14 is used for π.)

Find the radius of a circle
You may have problems that give you the area of a circle. So, you are asked to find the radius.
Example: The area of a circle is 30cm². Find the radius.

First: Set up the equation to set apart the radius.

The equation is $30 = \pi r^2$. Now, divide both sides by π: $\dfrac{30}{\pi} = \dfrac{\pi r^2}{\pi}$

Second: Take the square root of both sides: $\sqrt{9.55} = \sqrt{r^2}$.
So, you are left with: $3.09 = r$.

Note: You may have the area, and you are asked to find the diameter of the circle. So, follow the steps above to find the radius. Then, multiply the radius by 2 for the diameter.

The **circumference of a circle** is found by the formula $C = 2\pi r$, where r is the radius.

Find the radius of a circle
You may have problems that give you the circumference of a circle. So, you are asked to find the radius. Example: The circumference is 20cm. Find the radius.

First: Set up the equation to set apart the radius.

The equation is $20 = 2\pi r$. Now divide both sides by 2: $\dfrac{20}{2} = \dfrac{2\pi r}{2}$.

Second: Divide both sides by π: $\dfrac{10}{\pi} = \dfrac{\pi r}{\pi}$. So, you are left with $3.18 = r$

Note: You may have the circumference, and you are asked to find the diameter of the circle. So, follow the steps above to find the radius. Then, multiply the radius by 2 for the diameter.

➢ **Review Video:** <u>Area and Circumference of a Circle</u>
*Visit **mometrix.com/academy** and enter **Code: 243015***

Surface Area and Volume Formulas

The surface area of a solid object is the area of all sides or exterior surfaces. For objects like prisms and pyramids, there is a difference between base surface area (B) and lateral surface area (LA). For a prism, the total surface area (SA) is $SA = LA + 2B$. For a pyramid or cone, the total surface area is $SA = LA + B$.

<u>Sphere</u>

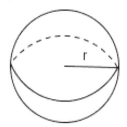

The **surface area of a sphere** can be found with the formula $SA = 4\pi r^2$, where r is the radius.

Find the radius of a sphere
You may have problems that give you the surface area of a sphere. So, you are asked to find the radius.
Example: The surface area of a sphere is 100 cm². Find the radius.

First: Set up the equation to set apart the radius.

You begin with: $SA = 4\pi r^2$. Then, you move 4π to the other side of the equal sign and cancel out the 4π on the right side of the formula: $\frac{SA}{4\pi} = r^2$.

Next, you square both sides to set apart the radius:

$\sqrt{\frac{SA}{4\pi}} = \sqrt{r^2}$. So, you are left with $r = \sqrt{\frac{SA}{4\pi}}$.

Second: Solve the equation.

$\sqrt{\frac{100}{4\pi}} = \sqrt{\frac{100}{12.57}} = 2.82$. So, the radius equals 2.82 cm.

The **volume of a sphere** can be found with the formula $V = \frac{4}{3}\pi r^3$, where r is the radius. Sometimes, you may be asked to give the volume of a sphere in terms of π. For example, the volume of the sphere is 30π.

Find the radius of a sphere
You may have problems that give you the volume of a sphere. So, you are asked to find the radius.
Example: The volume of a sphere is 100 cm³. Find the radius.

First: Set up the equation and cancel out the fraction.

$\frac{3}{4} \times \frac{4}{3}\pi r^3 = 100 \times \frac{3}{4}$. So, you are left with: $\pi r^3 = 75$

Second: Cancel out π.

$\frac{\pi r^3}{\pi} = \frac{75}{\pi}$. So, you are left with: $r^3 = \frac{75}{\pi} = 23.87$

Third: Take the cubed root of r³ and 23.87 to solve for the radius.

$\sqrt[3]{r^3} = \sqrt[3]{23.87}$. So, you have the result of r= 2.88

> ➤ **Review Video:** <u>Volume and Surface Area of a Sphere</u>
> *Visit **mometrix.com/academy** and enter **Code: 786928***

Prism

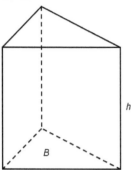

The **volume of any prism** is found with the formula $V = Bh$, where B is the area of the base, and h is the height. The perpendicular distance between the bases is the height.

Find the area of the base or the height of a prism
You may have problems that give you the volume of a prism. So, you are asked to find the area of the base or the height.
Example: The volume of the prism is 200 cm³. The area of the base is 10cm. Find the height.
    First: Set up the equation to set apart the height.
              So, you have $200 = 10h$.

    Second: Now, divide both sides by 10: $\frac{200}{10} = \frac{10h}{10}$.
              Then, you are left with $20 = h$

Note: When you need to find the area of the base, you can follow the steps above to solve for it.

The **surface area of any prism** is the sum of the areas of both bases and all sides. So, the formula for a sphere is $SA = 2B + Ph$, where B is the area of the base, P is the perimeter of the base, and h is the height of the prism.

Find the area of the base
You may have problems that give you the surface area of a prism. So, you are asked to find the area of the base.
Example: The surface area of the prism is 100 cm². The perimeter of the base is 10cm, and the height is 2cm. Find the area of the base.
    First: Set up the equation to set apart the area of the base.
              So, you have $100 = 2B + 20$.

    Second: Subtract 20 from both sides: $100 - 20 = 2B + 20 - 20$.
              Now, you are left with $80 = 2B$. So, divide both sides by 2.
              Then, you have $40 = B$.

Find the perimeter of the base or the height of a prism
You may have problems that give you the surface area of a prism and the area of the base. So, you are asked to find the perimeter of the base or the height.
Example: The surface area of the prism is 280 cm². The area of the base is 15cm², and the perimeter of the base is 10cm. Find the height.

First: Set up the equation to set apart the height.
         The equation is $280 = 2(15) + (10)h$. So, you have $250 = 30 + (10)h$

Second: Subtract 30 from both sides: $280 - 30 = 30 + (10)h - 30$.
         Now, you are left with: $250 = (10)h$.
         Then, divide both sides by 10.
         $\frac{250}{10} = \frac{(10)h}{10} = 25$. So, the height of the prism is 25cm.

Note: When you need to find the perimeter of the base, you can follow the steps above to find it.

Rectangular Prism

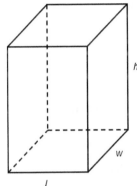

The **volume of a rectangular prism** can be found with the formula $V = lwh$, where V is the volume, l is the length, w is the width, and h is the height.

Find the length, width, or height of a rectangular prism
You may have problems that give you the volume of a rectangular prism. So, you are asked to find the length, width, or height.
Example: The volume of the rectangular prism is 200 cm³. The width is 10cm, and the height is 10cm. Find the length.

First: Set up the equation to set apart the length.
         So, you have $200 = l(10)(10)$ that becomes $200 = (100)l$.

Second: Divide both sides by 100.
         Now, you have $\frac{200}{100} = \frac{(100)l}{100}$. So, you are left with $2 = l$.

Note: When you need to find the width or height, you can follow the steps above to solve for either.

The **surface area of a rectangular prism** can be calculated as $SA = 2lw + 2hl + 2wh$ or $SA = 2(lw + hl + wh)$.

Find the length, width, or height of a rectangular prism
You may have problems that give you the surface area of a rectangular prism. So, you are asked to find the length, width, or height.
Example: The surface area of the rectangular prism is 200 cm². The width is 15cm, and the height is 5cm. Find the length.

First: Set up the equation to set apart the length.
So, you have $200 = 2(15)l + 2(5)l + 2(15)(5)$ that becomes $200 = (40)l + 150$.

Second: Subtract 150 from both sides.
So, $200 - 150 = (40)l + 150 - 150$ becomes $50 = (40)l$.
Then, divide both sides by 40 to set apart l: $\frac{50}{40} = \frac{(40)l}{40}$.
You are left with $1.25 = l$.

Note: When you need to find the width or height, you can follow the steps above to solve for either.

> **Review Video:** <u>Volume and Surface Area of a Rectangular Solid</u>
> *Visit **mometrix.com/academy** and enter **Code: 386780***

<u>Cube</u>
The **volume of a cube** can be found with the formula $V = s^3$, where s is the length of a side.

Find the side of a cube
You may have problems that give you the volume of a cube. So, you are asked to find the side.
Example: The volume of a cube is 20 cm³. Find the side.

First: Set up the equation to set apart the side length. Then, take the cube root of both sides. So, $20 = s^3$ becomes $\sqrt[3]{20} = \sqrt[3]{s^3}$ Then, you are left with $\sqrt[3]{20} = s$

Second: Solve for the side length.
$\sqrt[3]{20} = 2.71$. So, s equals 2.71.

The **surface area of a cube** is calculated as $SA = 6s^2$, where SA is the total surface area and s is the length of a side. These formulas are the same as the ones used for the volume and surface area of a rectangular prism. However, these are simple formulas because the three numbers (i.e., length, width, and height) are the same.

Find the side of a cube
You may have problems that give you the surface area of a cube. So, you are asked to find the side.
Example: The surface area of a cube is 60 cm². Find the side.

First: Set up the equation to set apart the side length.
So, $60 = 6s^2$ becomes $\frac{60}{6} = \frac{6s^2}{6}$. Then, you are left with $10 = s^2$

Second: Take the square root of both sides to set apart the s.
So, $10 = s^2$ becomes $\sqrt{10} = \sqrt{s^2}$.
Then, you are left with $3.16 = s$

Cylinder

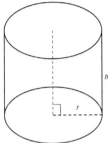

The **volume of a cylinder** can be found with the formula $V = \pi r^2 h$, where r is the radius, and h is the height.

Find the height of a cylinder
You may have problems that give you the volume of a cylinder. So, you are asked to find the height.
Example: The volume of a cylinder is 300 cm³ and the radius is 10 cm. Find the height.

     First: Set up the equation and put in the known numbers.
            You begin with $300 = \pi 5^2 h$. Now, $\pi 5^2 h = 78.5h$.
            So, you have $300 = 78.5h$

     Second: Set apart h to solve for the height.
            $\frac{300}{78.5} = \frac{78.5h}{78.5}$. So, you are left with: $\frac{300}{78.5} = h$

            Solve: $\frac{300}{78.5} = 3.82$cm is the height.

Find the radius of a cylinder
You may have problems that give you the volume of a cylinder. So, you are asked to find the radius.
Example: The volume of a cylinder is 200 cm³ and the radius is 15cm. Find the radius.

     First: Set up the equation to set apart the radius.
            You begin with $200 = \pi(15)r^2$. Now, you move π and (15) to both sides of the
            equation: $\frac{200}{\pi(15)} = \frac{\pi(15)r^2}{\pi(15)}$. Then, you are left with: $\frac{200}{\pi(15)} = r^2$.

     Second: Take the square root of both sides to solve for the radius: $\sqrt{\frac{200}{\pi(15)}} = \sqrt{r^2}$.

     Then, you have $\sqrt{4.25} = r$. So, the radius is equal to 2.06.

The **surface area of a cylinder** can be found with the formula $SA = 2\pi r^2 + 2\pi r h$.
The first term (i.e., $2\pi r^2$) is the base area multiplied by two. The second term (i.e., $2\pi r h$) is the perimeter of the base multiplied by the height.

Find the height of a cylinder
You may have problems that give you the surface area of a cylinder. So, you are asked to find the height. Example: The surface area of a cylinder is 150 cm² and the radius is 2 cm. Find the height.

     First: Set up the equation and put in the known numbers.
            You begin with $150 = 2\pi 2^2 + 2\pi(2)h$.
            So, you have $150 = 25.12 + 12.56h$.

Second: Subtract 25.12 from both sides of the equation.

So, $150 - 25.12 = 25.12 + 12.56h - 25.12$ becomes $124.85 = 12.56h$.

Then, divide both sides by 12.56.

Now, you are left with $9.94 = h$.

Find the radius of a cylinder

You may have problems that give you the surface area of a cylinder. So, you are asked to find the radius. Example: The surface area of a cylinder is 327 cm², and the height is 12cm. Find the radius.

First: Set up the equation and put in the known numbers.

You begin with $327 = 2\pi r^2 + 2\pi 12(r)$. So, you have $327 = 2\pi r^2 + 75.36r$.

Second: Set up the quadratic formula.

So, you now have $6.28r^2 + 75.36r - 327 = 0$

Third: Solve the equation using the quadratic formula steps.

Now, radius $= \frac{-75.36 \pm \sqrt{(75.36)^2 - 4(6.28)(-327)}}{2(6.28)}$

So, the radius equals a positive 3.39.

➤ **Review Video:** <u>Volume and Surface Area of a Right Circular Cylinder</u>
*Visit **mometrix.com/academy** and enter **Code: 226463***

<u>Pyramid</u>

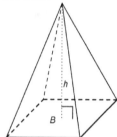

The **volume of a pyramid** is found with the formula $V = \frac{1}{3}Bh$, where B is the area of the base, and h is the height. The perpendicular distance from the vertex to the base is the height. This formula is the same as $\frac{1}{3}$ times the volume of a prism. Like a prism, the base of a pyramid can be any shape.

Find the area of the base or the height of a pyramid

You may have problems that give you the volume of a pyramid. So, you are asked to find the area of the base or the height.

Example: The volume of the pyramid is 100 cm³. The area of the base is 5cm². Find the height.

First: Set up the equation to set apart the height.

The equation is $100 = \frac{1}{3}5h$.

Now, you start by multiplying both sides by 3: $100 \times 3 = \frac{1}{3}5h \times 3$.

Second: You have $300 = 5h$. Now, divide both sides by 5: $\frac{300}{5} = \frac{5h}{5}$.

So, you have found that the height is 60.

Note: When you need to find the area of the base, you can follow the steps above to find it.

- 44 -

A right pyramid means that the base is a regular polygon. Also, the vertex is directly over the center of that polygon. If the pyramid is a right pyramid, the **surface area** can be calculated as $SA = B + \frac{1}{2}Ph_s$, where P is the perimeter of the base, and h_s is the slant height. The distance from the vertex to the midpoint of one side of the base is the slant height.

If the pyramid is irregular, the area of each triangle side must be calculated one at a time. Then, take the sum of the areas and the base to have the surface area.

Find the area of the base, the perimeter of the base, or the height
You may have problems that give you the surface area of a pyramid. So, you are asked to find the area of the base, the perimeter of the base, or the height.
Example: The surface area of the pyramid is 100 cm². The area of the base is 40cm², and the height is 12cm.

First: Set up the equation to set apart the perimeter of the base.

The equation is $100 = 40 + \frac{1}{2}12P$

Now, you can multiply the height by $\frac{1}{2}$. So, you have: $100 = 40 + 6P$

Second: Subtract both sides of the equation by 40: $100 - 40 = 40 + 6P - 40$.
So, you have: $60 = 6P$
Now, divide both sides by 6: $\frac{60}{6} = \frac{6P}{6}$. So, you are left with: P=10cm.

Note: When you need to find the area of the base or the height, you can follow the steps above.

> ➤ **Review Video: <u>Volume and Surface Area of a Pyramid</u>**
> *Visit **mometrix.com/academy** and enter **Code: 621932***

Cone

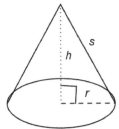

The **volume of a cone** is found with the formula $V = \frac{1}{3}\pi r^2 h$, where r is the radius, and h is the height. This formula is the same as $\frac{1}{3}$ times the volume of a cylinder.

Find the radius or height of a cone
You may have problems that give you the volume of a cone. So, you are asked to find the radius or the height.
Example: The volume of the cone is 47.12 cm³. The height is 5cm. Find the radius.

First: Set up the equation to set apart the radius.

The equation is $47.12 = \frac{1}{3}\pi 5r^2$

Now, you can multiply both sides by 3: $47.12 \times 3 = \frac{1}{3}\pi 5r^2 \times 3$

So, you have $141.36 = \pi 5r^2$.

Second: Divide both sides by 5: $\frac{141.36}{5} = \frac{\pi 5 r^2}{5}$.

Now, you have: $28.27 = \pi r^2$.

You can divide both sides by π: $\frac{28.27}{\pi} = \frac{\pi r^2}{\pi}$.

So, you have $9 = \pi r^2$.

Third: Take the square root of both sides: $\sqrt{9} = \sqrt{r^2}$.

Now, you have $3 = r$

Note: When you need to find the height, you can follow the steps above to find it.

The **surface area of a cone** can be found with the formula $SA = \pi r^2 + \pi r s$, where s is the slant height. The slant height can be found with the Pythagorean Theorem to be $\sqrt{r^2 + h^2}$. So, the surface area formula for a cone can also be written as $SA = \pi r^2 + \pi r \sqrt{r^2 + h^2}$.

Find the radius of a cone
You may have problems that give you the surface area of a cone. So, you are asked to find the radius.
Example: The surface area of the cone is 43.96 cm². The slant height is 5cm. Find the radius.

First: Set up the equation to set apart the radius.

The equation is $43.96 = \pi r^2 + 5\pi r$

Then, you can factor out the π: $43.96 = \pi(r^2 + 5r)$

Second: Now, you can divide both sides by π: $\frac{43.96}{\pi} = \frac{\pi(r^2 + 5r)}{\pi}$

So, you have: $14 = r^2 + 5r$.

Then, subtract 14 from both sides, and you have: $x = r^2 + 5r - 14$

Third: Use the quadratic formula

$$x = \frac{-5 \pm \sqrt{5^2 - 4(1)(-14)}}{2(1)}$$

So, the radius equals a positive 2.

Find the slant height of a cone
You may have problems that give you the surface area of a cone. So, you are asked to find the slant height.
Example: The surface area of the cone is 37.68 cm². The radius is 2cm. Find the slant height.

First: Set up the equation to set apart the slant height.

The equation is $37.68 = \pi 2^2 + \pi 2 s$

Now, calculate both sides: $37.68 = 12.56 + 6.28s$

Second: Divide 6.28 across all three terms: $\frac{37.68}{6.28} = \frac{12.56}{6.28} + \frac{6.28s}{6.28}$

Then, you have $6 = 2 + s$. Now, subtract 2 from both sides: $6 - 2 = 2 + s - 2$

So, you are left with $4 = s$

➤ **Review Video: <u>Volume and Surface Area of a Right Circular Cone</u>**
*Visit **mometrix.com/academy** and enter **Code: 573574***

- 46 -

Statistics

Statistics is the branch of mathematics that deals with collecting, recording, interpreting, illustrating, and reviewing large amounts of data. The following terms are used when talking about data and statistics:

Data – the collective name for pieces of information. The singular form is datum.

Quantitative data – measurements (e.g., length, mass, and speed) that give information about something in numbers

Qualitative data – information (e.g., colors, scents, tastes, and shapes) that cannot be measured by using numbers

Discrete data – information that can be given only by a specific value (e.g., whole or half numbers). For example, people can be counted only in whole numbers. So, a population count would be discrete data.

Continuous data – information (e.g., time and temperature) that can be given by any value within a specific range

Primary data – information that has been collected directly from a survey, investigation, or experiment. Examples are questionnaires or the recording of daily temperatures. Primary data that has not yet been organized or reviewed is called raw data.

Secondary data – information that has been collected, sorted, and processed by the researcher

Ordinal data – information that can be placed in numerical order (e.g., age or weight)

Nominal data – information that cannot be placed in numerical order (e.g., names or places)

Measures of Central Tendency

The quantities of mean, median, and mode are known as measures of central tendency. Each can give a picture of what a whole set of data looks like with a single number. Knowing what each value stands for is important to understanding the information from these measures.

Mean
The mean, or the arithmetic mean or average, of a data set is found by adding all of the values in the set. Then you divide the sum by how many values that you had in a set. For example, a data set has 6 numbers, and the sum of those 6 numbers is 30. So, the mean is 30/6 = 5.

When you know the average, you may be asked to find a missing value. Look over the following steps for how this is done.
Example: You are given the values of 5, 10, 12, and 13. Also, you are told that the average is 9.6. So, what is the one missing value?

> First: Add the known values together: $5 + 10 + 12 + 13 = 40$.
> Now, set up an equation with the sum of the known values in the divisor. Then, put the number of values in the dividend.

> For this example, you have 5 values. So, you have $\frac{40+?}{5} = 9.6$. Now, multiply both sides by 5:
> $5 \times \frac{40+?}{5} = 9.6 \times 5$

> Second: You are left with $40+? = 48$. Now, subtract 40 from both sides: $40 - 40+? = 48 - 40$. So, you know that the missing value is 8.

Median

The median is the middle value of a data set. The median can be found by putting the data set in numerical order (e.g., 3, 7, 26, 28, 39). Then, you pick the value that is in the middle of the set. In the data set (1, 2, 3, 4, 5), there is an odd number of values. So, the median is 3. Sometimes, there is an even number of values in the set. So, the median can be found by taking the average of the two middle values. In the data set (1, 2, 3, 4, 5, 6), the median would be (3 + 4)/2 = 3.5.

Mode

The mode is the value that appears the most in a data set. In the data set (1, 2, 3, 4, 5, 5, 5), the number 5 appears more than the other numbers. So, the value 5 is the mode. If more than one value appears the same number of times, then there are multiple values for the mode. For example, a data set is (1, 2, 2, 3, 4, 4, 5, 5). So, the modes would be 2, 4, and 5. Now, if no value appears more than any other value in the data set, then there is no mode.

Probability

Probability is a branch of statistics that deals with the likelihood of something taking place. One classic example is a coin toss. There are only two possible results: heads or tails. The likelihood, or probability, that the coin will land as heads is 1 out of 2 (i.e., 1/2, 0.5, 50%). Tails has the same probability. Another common example is a 6-sided die roll. There are six possible results from rolling a single die. So, each side has an equal chance of happening. So, the probability of any number coming up is 1 out of 6.

> ➤ **Review Video: Simple Probability**
> *Visit mometrix.com/academy and enter Code:* **212374**

Terms often used in probability:

Simple event – a situation that produces results of some sort (e.g., a coin toss)

Compound event – event that involves two or more items (e.g., rolling a pair of dice and taking the sum)

Outcome – a possible result in an experiment or event (e.g., heads and tails)

Desired outcome (or success) – an outcome that meets a particular set of requirements (e.g., a roll of 1 or 2 when we want a number that is less than 3)

Independent events – two or more events whose outcomes do not affect one another (e.g., two coins tossed at the same time)

Dependent events – two or more events whose outcomes affect one another (e.g., drawing two specific cards right after the other from the same deck)

Certain outcome – probability of outcome is 100% or 1

Impossible outcome – probability of outcome is 0% or 0

Mutually exclusive outcomes – two or more outcomes whose requirements cannot all be done in a single outcome. An example is a coin coming up heads and tails on the same toss.

Theoretical probability is the likelihood of a certain outcome happening for a given event. It can be known without actually doing the event. Theoretical probability can be calculated as:

$$P(\text{probability of success}) = \frac{(\text{Desired Outcomes})}{(\text{Total Outcomes})}$$

Example:
There are 20 marbles in a bag and 5 are red. The theoretical probability of randomly selecting a red marble is 5 out of 20, (i.e., 5/20 = 1/4, 0.25, or 25%).

When we talk about probability, we mean theoretical probability most of the time. Experimental probability, or relative frequency, is the number of times an outcome happens in an experiment or a certain number of observed events.

Theoretical probability is based on what *should* happen. Experimental probability is based on what *has* happened. Experimental probability is calculated in the same way as theoretical. However, actual desired outcomes are used instead of possible desired outcomes.

Theoretical and experimental probability do not always line up with one another. Theoretical probability says that out of 20 coin tosses 10 should be heads. However, if we were actually to toss 20 coins, we might record just 5 heads. This doesn't mean that our theoretical probability is incorrect; it just means that this particular experiment had results that were different from what was predicted.

> **Review Video: <u>Theoretical and Experimental Probability</u>**
> *Visit **mometrix.com/academy** and enter **Code:** 444349*

When trying to calculate the probability of an event using the (desired outcomes)/(total outcomes) formula, you may find that there are too many outcomes to count each one. Permutation and combination formulas offer a shortcut to counting outcomes.

The main distinction between permutations and combinations is that permutations take into account order and combinations do not. To calculate the number of possible groupings, there are two necessary limits. The limits are the number of items available for selection and the number to be selected.

When you have a set of n items, the number of permutations of r items can be calculated as $_nP_r = \frac{n!}{(n-r)!}$. The number of combinations of r items given a set of n items can be calculated as $_nC_r = \frac{n!}{r!(n-r)!}$ or $_nC_r = \frac{_nP_r}{r!}$.

Example:
You want to know how many different 5-card hands can be drawn from a deck of 52 cards. This is a combination because the order of the cards in a hand does not matter. There are 52 cards available and 5 to be selected. So, the number of different hands is $_{52}C_5 = \frac{52!}{5! \times 47!} = 2,598,960$.

Common Charts and Graphs

Charts and *Tables* are ways of organizing information into separate rows and columns. These rows and columns are labeled to find and to explain the information in them. Some charts and tables are organized horizontally with rows giving the details about the labeled information. Other charts and tables are organized vertically with columns giving the details about the labeled information.

A *Bar Graph* is one of the few graphs that can be drawn correctly in two ways: horizontally and vertically. A bar graph is similar to a line plot because of how the data is organized on the graph. Both axes must have their categories defined for the graph to be useful. A thick line is drawn from zero to the exact value of the data. This line can be used for a number, a percentage, or other numerical value. Longer bar lengths point to greater data values. To understand a bar graph, read the labels for the axes to know the units being reported. Then look where the bars end and match this to the scale on the other axis. This will show you the connection between the axes. This bar graph shows the responses from a survey about the favorite colors of a group.

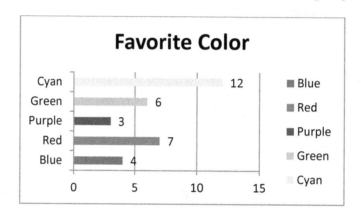

Line Graphs have one or more lines of different styles (e.g., solid or broken). These lines show the different values for a data set. Each point on the graph is shown as an ordered pair. This is similar to a Cartesian plane. In this case, the *x*- and *y*- axes are given certain units (e.g., dollars or time). Each point that is for one measurement is joined by line segments. Then, these lines show what the values are doing.

The lines may be increasing (i.e., line sloping upward), decreasing (i.e., line sloping downward), or staying the same (i.e., horizontal line). More than one set of data can be put on the same line graph. This is done to compare more than one piece of data. An example of this would be graphing test scores for different groups of students over the same stretch of time. This allows you to see which group had the greatest increase or decrease in performance over a certain amount of years. This example is shown in the graph below.

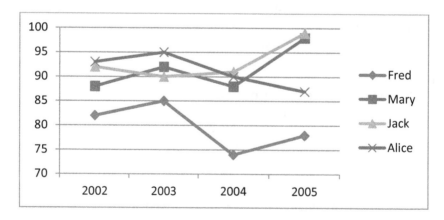

A *Pictograph* is a graph that is given in the horizontal format. This graph uses pictures or symbols to show the data. Each pictograph must have a key that defines the picture or symbol. Also, this key should give the number that stands for each picture or symbol. The pictures or symbols on a pictograph are not always shown as whole elements.

In this case, the fraction of the picture or symbol stands for the same fraction of the quantity that a whole picture or symbol represents. For example, there is a row in the pictograph with $3\frac{1}{2}$ ears of corn. Each ear of corn represents 100 stalks of corn in a field. So, this would equal $3\frac{1}{2} \times 100 = 350$ stalks of corn in the field.

Circle Graphs, or *Pie Charts*, show the relationship of each type of data compared to the whole set of data. The circle graph is divided into sections by drawing radii (i.e., plural for radius) to make central angles. These angles stand for a percentage of the circle. Each 1% of data is equal to 3.6° in the graph. So, data that stands for a 90° section of the circle graph makes up 25% of the whole. The pie chart below shows the data from the frequency table where people were asked about their favorite color.

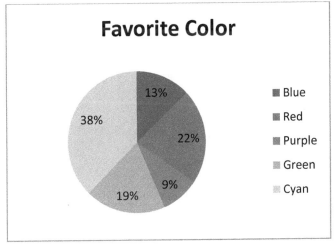

A *Stem and Leaf Plot* can outline groups of data that fall into a range of values. Each piece of data is split into two parts: the first, or left, part is called the stem. The second, or right, part is called the leaf. Each stem is listed in a column from smallest to largest. Each leaf that has the common stem is listed in that stem's row from smallest to largest.

For example, in a set of two-digit numbers, the digit in the tens place is the stem. So, the digit in the ones place is the leaf. With a stem and leaf plot, you can see which subset of numbers (10s, 20s, 30s, etc.) is the largest. This information can be found by looking at a histogram. However, a stem and leaf plot also lets you look closer and see which values fall in that range. Using all of the test scores from the line graph, we can put together a stem and leaf plot:

Test Scores								
7	4	8						
8	2	5	7	8	8			
9	0	0	1	2	2	3	5	8	9

Again, a stem-and-leaf plot is similar to histograms and frequency plots. However, a stem-and-leaf plot keeps all of the original data. In this example, you can see that almost half of the students scored in the 80s. Also, all of the data has been maintained. These plots can be used for larger numbers as well. However, they work better for small sets of data.

Functions

Example 1
The table shows some data points for a linear function. What is the missing value in the table?

x	y
0	?
3	50
5	80

The data in the table represent a linear function. For a linear function, the rate of change is equal to the slope. To find the slope, calculate the change in y divided by the change in x for the two given points from the table: $m = \frac{80-50}{5-3} = \frac{30}{2} = 15$

The rate of change of the linear function is 15. This means for each increase of 1 in the value of x, the value of y increases by 15. Similarly, each decrease of 1 in the value of x decreases the value of y by 15. The x-value 0 is 3 less than 3, so subtract $3 \cdot 15 = 45$ from 50 to get $y = 5$. This is the missing value in the table.

Example 2
Which linear function represents the values in the table?

x	0	1	2	3
y	3	1	−1	−3

Based on the table, the rate of change is -2 and the y-intercept is $(0, 3)$. Plugging this information into the slope-intercept form $y = mx + b$, the equation is $y = -2x + 3$.

Problem Solving and Reasoning

<u>Example 1</u>
Jamie had $6.50 in his wallet when he left home. He spent $4.25 on drinks and $2.00 on a magazine. Later, his friend repaid him $2.50 that he had borrowed the previous day. How much money does Jamie have in his wallet now?

Jamie had $2.75 in his wallet. To solve this problem, you subtract $4.25 and $2.00 from the first sum of $6.50. So, you are left with $0.25. Then, you add $2.50. So, you come to the final answer of $2.75.

<u>Example 2</u>
Lauren had $80 in her savings account. When she received her paycheck, she put some money in her savings account. This brought the balance up to $120. By what percentage did the total amount in her account increase by putting this amount in her savings account?

The rate of increase equals the change in the account balance divided by the original amount: $80. Multiply that decimal by 100 to know the percentage of increase. So, to find the change in the balance, subtract the original amount from the new balance: Change = $120 - $80 = $40 Now, you can find the percentage of increase: $Percent = \frac{\$40}{\$80} \times 100 = 50\%$

Example 3
In a game of chance, 3 dice are thrown at the same time. What is the probability that all three will land with a 6?

For each die there is 1 in 6 chance that a 6 will be on top. The reason is that the die has 6 sides. The probability that a 6 will show for each die is not affected by the results from another roll of the die. In other words, these probabilities are independent. So, the overall probability of throwing 3 sixes is the product of the individual probabilities: $P = \frac{1}{6} \times \frac{1}{6} \times \frac{1}{6} = \frac{1}{6^3} = \frac{1}{216}$

The chart below is needed for Examples 4 and 5.

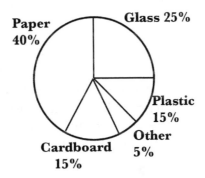

Example 4
The Charleston Recycling Company collects 50,000 tons of recyclable material every month. The chart shows the kinds of materials that are collected by the company's five trucks. What is the second most common material that is recycled?

This pie chart shows the relative amounts of each variable as a slice of the whole circle. The larger variables have larger slices. Also, the percentage of each variable (e.g., recycled material) is shown next to each slice. In this chart, paper is the most common recycled material (i.e., the largest variable). This is 40% of the total. The next largest is glass at 25% of the total. All of the other materials stand for smaller portions of the total.

Example 5
About how much paper is recycled every month?

The chart indicates that 40% of the total recycled material is paper. Since 50,000 tons of material are recycled every month, the total amount of paper will be 40% of 50,000 tons, or $\frac{40}{100} \times 50,000 = 20,000$ tons.

- 53 -

<u>Example 6</u>
An 11'×13' room contains a 3' wide, 7' tall doorway and two 5'x3' windows. The ceiling height is 9'. Determine :

- The price to install baseboards which cost $1.25 per linear foot.
- The price to install flooring which costs $5 per square foot.
- If one gallon of paint which covers 400 square feet of surface is sufficient to paint the walls of the room.

Baseboards run along the edge of the room, but not across doorways. To determine the price for the baseboards, first determine how many feet are needed for the perimeter of the room, excluding the doorway. Use the formula for the perimeter of a rectangle to find the perimeter of the room: $2l + 2w = 2(11 \text{ ft}) + 2(13 \text{ ft}) = 48 \text{ ft}$. After adjusting for the width of the doorway, 45ft of baseboard is needed for the room. The price of baseboards is 45×1.25=$56.25.

To determine the price for flooring, first determine the area of the room. Use the formula for the area of a rectangle to find the area of the room: $lw = (11 \text{ ft})(13 \text{ ft}) = 143 \text{ ft}^2$. The price for the flooring is 143×5=$715.

To determine the amount of paint needed for the walls, first determine the total surface area to be covered. Two walls are 11'×9' and the other two walls are 13'×9'. Disregarding doors and windows, the total area of the walls is $2(11 \text{ ft})(9 \text{ ft}) + 2(13 \text{ ft})(9 \text{ ft}) = 198 \text{ ft}^2 + 234 \text{ ft}^2 = 432 \text{ ft}^2$. Take away the area of the door, which is $(3 \text{ ft})(7 \text{ ft}) = 21 \text{ ft}^2$, and the area of the windows, which is $2(5 \text{ ft})(3 \text{ ft}) = 30 \text{ ft}^2$: $432 \text{ ft}^2 - 21 \text{ ft}^2 - 30 \text{ ft}^2 = 381 \text{ ft}^2$. The amount of surface which needs paint is 381 ft^2. Purchasing one gallon of paint should be sufficient to cover the walls if only one coat of paint is needed.

Reading Section

Organizing and Understanding Graphic Information

Tables show information that has been seen in a field of study and put into a viewable layout. This layout is for easy reading and understanding. At the top of the table, you will see a title. The title says what information is in the table. An example of a title: *Average Income for Different Levels of Education.* Another example: *Price of Milk Compared to Demand.* A table gives information in vertical (i.e., up and down) columns and horizontal (i.e., left to right) rows. Normally, each column will have a label. For example, *Average Income for Different Levels of Education* is the title. Then, the two columns could be labeled *Education Level* and *Average Income.* Each location on the table is called a cell. Cells are named by their column and row (e.g., second column, fifth row). The information for a table is placed in those cells.

Like a table, a **graph** will show information that has been collected. The purpose of the graph is to give information in a layout that keeps track of changes. The graph will have a title that may simply give the names of the two axes (e.g., Income vs. Education). Or, the title may have more description: *A Comparison of Average Income with Level of Education.*

The bar and line graphs are given on two perpendicular lines (i.e., axes). The vertical axis (Note: axes is plural and axis is only one) is called the y-axis, and the horizontal axis is called the x-axis. The x-axis is the independent variable, and the y-axis is the dependent variable. A variable is an unknown or changing value or quantity. The independent variable is the one being changed or controlled by the person who created the graph. Let's continue with the *Income and Education* example. The independent variable would be *level of education.* The maker of the graph will decide the levels of education (e.g., high school, college, master's degree, etc.). The dependent value is not controlled by the maker of the graph. Instead, the value is a result of the independent variable.

Think about the purpose and the type of graph layout. For example, a bar graph is good for showing specific numbers or amounts and the change among those numbers or amounts. For example, you want to show the amount of money spent on groceries during the months of a year. In that case, a bar graph would be best. The vertical axis would be for values of money. The horizontal axis would give the bar showing each month. On the other hand, let's say that the cost of groceries is put on a line graph, not a bar graph. Then, you would want to know if your amount of spending rose or fell during the year.

A bar graph is good for showing the relationships between the different values placed on a graph. The line graph is good for showing if the values will grow, shrink, or stay the same. Often, the bar graph is chosen over the line graph. There has to be some built-in relationship between the data points because the graph hints at a relationship. The amount of different apples at a store is one example. There is a relationship between the store and the number of apples that the store has for sell. The speed of popular rollercoasters at an amusement park is another example. There is a relationship between the amusement park and the different speeds of roller coasters at the amusement park.

In some examples, the line graph is better (e.g., periods of time or growth). A line graph shows the speed of change between periods of time in a visual layout. Watching a stock on the Dow Jones rise and fall over the course of a month is a good example. Or, keeping track of the height of a child over a period of years is another good use of a line graph.

A **line graph** is used for measuring changes over time. The graph is set up on a vertical and a horizontal axis. The measured variables are listed along the left side and the bottom side of the axes. Points are then placed along the graph. For example, a line graph measures a person's income for each month of the year. If the person earned $1500 in January, there should be a point directly above January and directly to the right of $1500. When all of the amounts are placed on the graph, they are connected with a line from left to right. This line gives a nice picture of the general changes. If the line sloped up, you would see that the person's income had increased over the course of the year.

The **bar graph** is one of the most common pictures of information. The bar graph has two parts: the vertical axis and the horizontal axis. The vertical axis uses numbers or amounts. The horizontal axis uses categories or names. A bar graph that gives the heights of famous basketball players is a good example. The vertical axis would have numbers going from five to eight feet. The horizontal axis would have the names of the players. The length of the bar above the player's name would show his height. In this graph, you would see that Yao Ming is taller than Michael Jordan because Yao's bar would be higher.

A **pie chart** is good for showing how a single thing or group is divided. The standard pie chart is a circle with labeled wedges. Each wedge is proportional in size to a part of the whole. For example, think about a pie chart that shows a student's budget. The whole circle represents all of the money that the student has to spend. Let's say that the student spends half of his or her money on food. So, the pie chart will be divided in half with one half labeled food. The other half is what remains in the student's budget. Now, let's say that he or she spends a quarter of his or her money on movies. Now, the unlabeled half will be divided to show that a quarter of his or her budget is left over. This picture would make it easy to see that the student spends twice the amount of money on food as on movies. So, the wedge of the graph labeled food is proportional to the actual amount of money spent on food. The wedge takes up half of circle, and the amount spent on food is half of the budget.

As you review the information in the graph, ask questions. Has the author chosen the correct format for the information? Did the author remove variables or other information that might upset his or her argument? Be aware of how one variable reacts to a change in another variable. Let's say that someone's education level increases. Does the graph show that there is a rise for income as well? The same can be done with a table.

Be sure that your conclusions come from the information in the graph. In other words, don't infer unknown values from a graph to draw conclusions that have no evidence. Think about a graph that compares the price of eggs to the demand. If the price and demand rise and fall together, you would be right to say that the demand for eggs and the price are connected. However, this simple graph does not say which variable causes the other. So, you cannot say that the price of eggs raises or lowers the demand. With more information, you may find that the demand for eggs could be connected to other things.

Vocabulary, Spelling, and Figurative Language

Denotative and Connotative Meaning

There is more to a word than the dictionary definition. The denotative meaning of a word is the actual meaning found in a dictionary. For example, a house and a home are places where people live. The connotative meaning is what comes to mind when you think of a word. For example, a house may be a simple, solid building. Yet, a home may be a comfortable, welcoming place where a family stays. Most non-fiction is fact-based with no use of figurative language. So, you can assume that the writer will use denotative meanings. In fiction, drama, and poetry, the author may use the connotative meaning. Use context clues to know if the author is using the denotative or connotative meaning of a word.

> ➤ **Review Video: <u>Denotative and Connotative Meanings</u>**
> *Visit **mometrix.com/academy** and enter **Code: 736707***

Readers of all levels will find new words in passages. The best way to define a word in context is to think about the words that are around the unknown word. For example, nouns that you don't know may be followed by examples that give a definition. Think about this example: *Dave arrived at the party in hilarious garb: a leopard-print shirt, buckskin pants, and tennis shoes.* If you didn't know the meaning of garb, you could read the examples (i.e., a leopard-print shirt, buckskin pants, and tennis shoes) and know that *garb* means *clothing.* Examples will not always be this clear. Try another example: *Parsley, lemon, and flowers were just a few of items he used as garnishes.* The word *garnishes* is explained by parsley, lemon, and flowers. From this one sentence, you may know that the items are used for decoration. Are they decorating a food plate or an ice table with meat? You would need the other sentences in the paragraph to know for sure.

> ➤ **Review Video: <u>Context</u>**
> *Visit **mometrix.com/academy** and enter **Code: 613660***

Also, you can use contrasts to define an unfamiliar word in context. In many sentences, authors will not describe the unfamiliar word directly. Instead, they will describe the opposite of the unfamiliar word. So, you are given some information that will bring you closer to defining the word. For example: *Despite his intelligence, Hector's bad posture made him look obtuse. Despite* means that Hector's posture is at odds with his intelligence. The author explains that Hector's posture does not prove his intelligence. So, *obtuse* must mean *unintelligent.* Another example: *Even with the horrible weather, we were beatific about our trip to Alaska.* The weather is described as *horrible.* So, *beatific* must mean something positive.

Substitution

Sometimes, there will be very few context clues to help you define an unknown word. When this happens, substitution is a helpful tool. First, try to think of some synonyms for the words. Then, use those synonyms in place of the unknown words. If the passage makes sense, then the substitution has given some information about the unknown word. For example: *Frank's admonition rang in her ears as she climbed the mountain.* Don't know the definition of *admonition*? Then, try some substitutions: *vow, promise, advice, complaint,* or *compliment.* These words hint that an *admonition* is some sort of message. Once in a while substitution can get you a precise definition.

Description

Usually, you can define an unfamiliar word by looking at the descriptive words in the context. For example: *Fred dragged the recalcitrant boy kicking and screaming up the stairs.* The words *dragged*, *kicking*, and *screaming* all hint that the boy hates going up the stairs. So, you may think that *recalcitrant* means something like unwilling or protesting. In this example, an unfamiliar adjective was identified.

Description is used more to define an unfamiliar noun than unfamiliar adjectives. For example: *Don's wrinkled frown and constantly shaking fist labeled him as a curmudgeon.* Don is described as having a *wrinkled frown* and *constantly shaking fist.* This hints that a *curmudgeon* must be a grumpy, old man. Contrasts do not always give detailed information about the unknown word. However, they do give you some clues to understand the word.

Many words have more than one definition. So, you may not know how the word is being used in a sentence. For example, the verb *cleave* can mean *join* or *separate.* When you see this word, you need to pick the definition that makes the most sense. For example: *The birds cleaved together as they flew from the oak tree.* The use of the word *together* hints that *cleave* is being used to mean *join.* Another example: *Hermione's knife cleaved the bread cleanly.* A knife cannot join bread together. So, the word must hint at separation. Learning the purpose of a word with many meanings needs the same tricks as defining an unknown word. Look for context clues and think about the substituted words.

Synonyms and Antonyms

To learn more from a passage, you need to understand how words connect to each other. This is done with understanding synonyms (e.g., words that mean the same thing) and antonyms (e.g., the opposite meaning of a word). For example, *dry* and *arid* are synonyms. However, *dry* and *wet* are antonyms. There are pairs of words in English that can be called synonyms. Yet, they have somewhat different definitions.

For example, *friendly* and *collegial* can be used to describe a warm, close relationship. So, you would be correct to call them synonyms. However, *collegial* (linked to *colleague*) is used for professional or academic relationships. *Friendly* is not linked to professional or academic relationships.

Words should not be called synonyms when their differences are too great. For example, *hot* and *warm* are not synonyms because their meanings are too different. How do you know when two words are synonyms? First, try to replace one word for the other word. Then, be sure that the meaning of the sentence has not changed. Replacing *warm* for *hot* in a sentence gives a different meaning. *Warm* and *hot* may seem close in meaning. Yet, *warm* means that the temperature is normal. And, *hot* means that the temperature is very high.

Antonyms are words with opposite meanings. *Light* and *dark*, *up* and *down*, *right* and *left*, *good* and *bad* are sets of antonyms. However, there is a difference between antonyms and pairs of words that are different. *Black* and *gray* are not antonyms. *Black* is not the opposite of *gray*. On the other hand, *black* and *white* are antonyms. Not every word has an antonym. For example, many nouns do not have an antonym. What would be the antonym of chair?

During your exam, the questions about antonyms are likely to be about adjectives. Remember that adjectives are words that describe a noun. Some common adjectives include *red*, *fast*, *skinny*, and *sweet*. From those four adjectives, *red* is the one that does not have an antonym.

> ➢ **Review Video:** <u>Synonyms and Antonyms</u>
> *Visit **mometrix.com/academy** and enter **Code: 105612***

Consonants and Vowels

The English vowels are *a, e, i, o,* and *u*. The letter *y* is considered a vowel in words like *fly* and *rhythm*. Also, the letter *w* can be considered a vowel in words like *now* and *brown*. All of the other letters in the English language are consonants.

Spelling

<u>Words ending with a consonant</u>
Usually the final consonant is doubled on a word before adding a suffix. This is the rule for single syllable words, words ending with one consonant, and multi-syllable words with the last syllable accented. The following are examples:
- *beg* becomes *begging* (single syllable)
- *shop* becomes *shopped* (single syllable)
- *add* becomes *adding* (already ends in double consonant, do not add another *d*)
- *deter* becomes *deterring* (multi-syllable, accent on last syllable)
- *regret* becomes *regrettable* (multi-syllable, accent on last syllable)
- *compost* becomes *composting* (do not add another *t* because the accent is on the first syllable)

<u>Words ending with *y* or *c*</u>
The general rule for words ending in *y* is to keep the *y* when adding a suffix if the *y* is preceded by a vowel. If the word ends in a consonant and *y* the *y* is changed to an *i* before the suffix is added (unless the suffix itself begins with *i*). The following are examples:
- *pay* becomes *paying* (keep the *y*)
- *bully* becomes *bullied* (change to *i*)
- *bully* becomes *bullying* (keep the *y* because the suffix is *–ing*)

If a word ends with *c* and the suffix begins with an *e, i,* or *y*, the letter *k* is usually added to the end of the word. The following are examples:
- *panic* becomes *panicky*
- *mimic* becomes *mimicking*

<u>Words containing *ie* or *ei*, and/or ending with *e*</u>
Most words are spelled with an *i* before *e*, except when they follow the letter *c*, **or** sound like *a*. For example, the following words are spelled correctly according to these rules:
- piece, friend, believe (*i* before *e*)
- receive, ceiling, conceited (except after *c*)
- weight, neighborhood, veil (sounds like *a*)

To add a suffix to words ending with the letter *e*, first determine if the *e* is silent. If it is, the *e* will be kept if the added suffix begins with a consonant. If the suffix begins with a vowel, the *e* is dropped. The following are examples:
- *age* becomes *ageless* (keep the *e*)
- *age* becomes *aging* (drop the *e*)

An exception to this rule occurs when the word ends in *ce* or *ge* and the suffix *able* or *ous* is added; these words will retain the letter *e*. The following are examples:
- *courage* becomes *courageous*
- *notice* becomes *noticeable*

Words ending with *ise* or *ize*
A small number of words end with *ise*. Most of the words in the English language with the same sound end in *ize*. The following are examples:
- advertise, advise, arise, chastise, circumcise, and comprise
- compromise, demise, despise, devise, disguise, enterprise, excise, and exercise
- franchise, improvise, incise, merchandise, premise, reprise, and revise
- supervise, surmise, surprise, and televise

Words that end with *ize* include the following:
- accessorize, agonize, authorize, and brutalize
- capitalize, caramelize, categorize, civilize, and demonize
- downsize, empathize, euthanize, idolize, and immunize
- legalize, metabolize, mobilize, organize, and ostracize
- plagiarize, privatize, utilize, and visualize

(Note that some words may technically be spelled with *ise*, especially in British English, but it is more common to use *ize*. Examples include *symbolize/symbolise,* and *baptize/baptise.*)

Words ending with *ceed, sede,* or *cede*
There are only three words that end with *ceed* in the English language: *exceed, proceed,* and *succeed.* There is only one word that ends with *sede*, and that word is *supersede.* Many other words that sound like *sede* actually end with *cede.* The following are examples:
- concede, recede, precede, and supercede

Words ending in *able* or *ible*
For words ending in *able* or *ible*, there are no hard and fast rules. The following are examples:
- adjustable, unbeatable, collectable, deliverable, and likeable
- edible, compatible, feasible, sensible, and credible

There are more words ending in *able* than *ible*; this is useful to know if guessing is necessary.

Words ending in *ance* or *ence*
The suffixes *ence, ency,* and *ent* are used in the following cases:
- the suffix is preceded by the letter *c* but sounds like *s* – *innocence*
- the suffix is preceded by the letter *g* but sounds like *j* – *intelligence, negligence*

The suffixes *ance, ancy,* and *ant* are used in the following cases:
- the suffix is preceded by the letter *c* but sounds like *k – significant, vacant*
- the suffix is preceded by the letter *g* with a hard sound - *elegant, extravagance*

If the suffix is preceded by other letters, there are no steadfast rules. For example: *finance, elegance,* and *defendant* use the letter *a,* while *respondent, competence,* and *excellent* use the letter *e.*

Words ending in *tion, sion,* or *cian*
Words ending in *tion, sion,* or *cian* all sound like *shun* or *zhun.* There are no rules for which ending is used for words. The following are examples:
- action, agitation, caution, fiction, nation, and motion
- admission, expression, mansion, permission, and television
- electrician, magician, musician, optician, and physician (note that these words tend to describe occupations)

Words with the *ai* or *ia* combination
When deciding if *ai* or *ia* is correct, the combination of *ai* usually sounds like one vowel sound, as in *Britain,* while the vowels in *ia* are pronounced separately, as in *guardian.* The following are examples:
- captain, certain, faint, hair, malaise, and praise (*ai* makes one sound)
- bacteria, beneficiary, diamond, humiliation, and nuptial (*ia* makes two sounds)

Plural forms of nouns

Nouns ending in *ch, sh, s, x,* or *z*
When a noun ends in the letters *ch, sh, s, x,* or *z,* an *es* instead of a singular *s* is added to the end of the word to make it plural. The following are examples:
- *church* becomes *churches*
- *bush* becomes *bushes*
- *bass* becomes *basses*
- *mix* becomes *mixes*
- *buzz* becomes *buzzes*

This is the rule with proper names as well; the Ross family would become the Rosses.

Nouns ending in *y* or *ay/ey/iy/oy/uy*
If a noun ends with a consonant and *y,* the plural is formed by replacing the *y* with *ies.* For example, *fly* becomes *flies* and *puppy* becomes *puppies.* If a noun ends with a vowel and *y,* the plural is formed by adding an *s.* For example, *alley* becomes *alleys* and *boy* becomes *boys.*

Nouns ending in *f* or *fe*
Most nouns ending in *f* or *fe* are pluralized by replacing the *f* with *v* and adding *es.* The following are examples:
- *knife* becomes *knives; self* becomes *selves; wolf* becomes *wolves.*

An exception to this rule is the word *roof; roof* becomes *roofs.*

<u>Nouns ending in *o*</u>

Most nouns ending with a consonant and *o* are pluralized by adding *es*. The following are examples:
- *hero* becomes *heroes; tornado* becomes *tornadoes; potato* becomes *potatoes*

Most nouns ending with a vowel and *o* are pluralized by adding *s*. The following are examples:
- *portfolio* becomes *portfolios; radio* becomes *radios; shoe* becomes *shoes.*

An exception to these rules is seen with musical terms ending in *o*. These words are pluralized by adding *s* even if they end in a consonant and *o*. The following are examples: *soprano* becomes *sopranos; banjo* becomes *banjos; piano* becomes *pianos.*

Exceptions to the rules of plurals

Some words do not fall into any specific category for making the singular form plural. They are irregular. Certain words become plural by changing the vowels within the word. The following are examples:
- *woman* becomes *women; goose* becomes *geese; foot* becomes *feet*

Some words become completely different words in the plural form. The following are examples:
- *mouse* becomes *mice; fungus* becomes *fungi; alumnus* becomes *alumni*

Some words are the same in both the singular and plural forms. The following are examples:
- *Salmon, species,* and *deer* are all the same whether singular or plural.

Plural forms of letters, numbers, symbols, and compound nouns with hyphens

Letters and numbers become plural by adding an apostrophe and *s*. The following are examples:
- The *L's* are the people whose names begin with the letter *L*.
- They broke the teams down into groups of *3's*.
- The sorority girls were all *KD's*.

A compound noun is a noun that is made up of two or more words; they can be written with hyphens. For example, *mother-in-law* or *court-martial* are compound nouns. To make them plural, an *s* or *es* is added to the main word. The following are examples: *mother-in-law* becomes *mothers-in-law; court-martial* becomes *court-martials.*

Commonly misspelled words

accidentally	conceive	finally
accommodate	congratulations	forehead
accompanied	conqueror	foreign
accompany	conscious	foreigner
achieved	coolly	foremost
acknowledgment	correspondent	forfeit
across	courtesy	ghost
address	curiosity	glamorous
aggravate	cylinder	government
aisle	deceive	grammar
ancient	deference	grateful
anxiety	deferred	grief
apparently	definite	grievous
appearance	describe	handkerchief
arctic	desirable	harass
argument	desperate	hoping
arrangement	develop	hurriedly
attendance	diphtheria	hygiene
auxiliary	disappear	hypocrisy
awkward	disappoint	imminent
bachelor	disastrous	incidentally
barbarian	discipline	incredible
beggar	discussion	independent
beneficiary	disease	indigestible
biscuit	dissatisfied	inevitable
brilliant	dissipate	innocence
business	drudgery	intelligible
cafeteria	ecstasy	intentionally
calendar	efficient	intercede
campaign	eighth	interest
candidate	eligible	irresistible
ceiling	embarrass	judgment
cemetery	emphasize	legitimate
changeable	especially	liable
changing	exaggerate	library
characteristic	exceed	likelihood
chauffeur	exhaust	literature
colonel	exhilaration	maintenance
column	existence	maneuver
commit	explanation	manual
committee	extraordinary	mathematics
comparative	familiar	mattress
compel	fascinate	miniature
competent	February	mischievous
competition	fiery	misspell

- 63 -

momentous
mortgage
neither
nickel
niece
ninety
noticeable
notoriety
obedience
obstacle
occasion
occurrence
omitted
operate
optimistic
organization
outrageous
pageant
pamphlet
parallel
parliament
permissible
perseverance
persuade
physically
physician
possess
possibly
practically
prairie
preceding
prejudice
prevalent
professor
pronunciation
pronouncement
propeller
protein
psychiatrist
psychology
quantity
questionnaire
rally
recede
receive

recognize
recommend
referral
referred
relieve
religious
resistance
restaurant
rhetoric
rhythm
ridiculous
sacrilegious
salary
scarcely
schedule
secretary
sentinel
separate
severely
sheriff
shriek
similar
soliloquy
sophomore
species
strenuous
studying
suffrage
supersede
suppress
surprise
symmetry
temperament
temperature
tendency
tournament
tragedy
transferred
truly
twelfth
tyranny
unanimous
unpleasant
usage
vacuum

valuable
vengeance
vigilance
villain
Wednesday
weird
wholly
yolk

> **Review Video:** <u>Spelling Tips</u>
*Visit **mometrix.com/academy** and enter **Code:** **138869***

Figurative Language

When authors want to share their message in a creative way, they use figurative language devices. Learning these devices will help you understand what you read. Figurative language is communication that goes beyond the actual meaning of a word or phrase. Descriptive language that awakens imagery in the reader's mind is one type of figurative language. Exaggeration is another type of figurative language. Also, when you compare two things, you are using figurative language. Similes and metaphors are the two main ways of comparing things. An example of a simile: *The child howled like a coyote when her mother told her to pick up the toys.* In this example, the child's howling is compared to a coyote. This helps the reader understand the sound being made by the child.

A figure of speech is a word or phrase that is not a part of straightforward, everyday language. Figures of speech are used for emphasis, fresh expression, or clearness. However, clearness of a passage may be incomplete with the use of these devices. For example: *I am going to crown you.* The author may mean:

- I am going to place a real crown on your head.
- I am going to make you king or queen of this area.
- I am going to punch you in the head with my fist.
- I am going to put a second checker's piece on top of your checker piece to show that it has become a king.

> ➤ **Review Video: <u>Figure of Speech</u>**
> *Visit **mometrix.com/academy** and enter **Code: 111295***

A metaphor is the comparison of one thing with a different thing. For example: *The bird was an arrow flying across the sky.* In this sentence, the arrow is compared to a bird. The metaphor asks you to think about the bird in another way. Let's continue with this metaphor for a bird. You are asked to view the bird's flight as the flight of an arrow. So, you may imagine the flight to be quick and purposeful. Metaphors allow the author to describe a thing without being direct. Remember that the thing being described will not always be mentioned directly by the author. Think about a forest in winter: *Swaying skeletons reached for the sky and groaned as the wind blew through them.* In this sentence, the author uses *skeletons* as a metaphor for trees without leaves.

> ➤ **Review Video: <u>Metaphor</u>**
> *Visit **mometrix.com/academy** and enter **Code: 133295***

A simile is a comparison that needs the separation words *like* or *as*. Some examples: *The sun was like an orange, eager as a beaver,* and *quick as a mountain goat.* Because a simile includes *like* or *as*, the comparison uses a different tone than a simple description of something. For example: *the house was like a shoebox.* The tone is different than the author saying that the house *was* a shoebox.

> ➤ **Review Video: <u>Simile</u>**
> *Visit **mometrix.com/academy** and enter **Code: 642949***

Reading Comprehension

Constructing Meaning

To be a careful reader, pay attention to the author's **position** and purpose. Even passages that seem fair and equal--like textbooks--have a position or bias (i.e., the author is unfair or inaccurate with opposing ideas). Readers need to take these positions into account when considering the author's message. Authors who appeal to feelings or like one side of an argument make their position clear. Authors' positions may be found in what they write and in what they don't write. Normally, you would want to review other passages on the same topic to understand the author's position. However, you are in the middle of an exam. So, look for language and arguments that show a position.

> ➤ **Review Video: <u>Author's Position</u>**
> *Visit **mometrix.com/academy** and enter **Code: 478923***

Sometimes, finding the **purpose** of an author is easier than finding his or her position. In most cases, the author has no interest in hiding his or her purpose. A passage for entertainment will be written to please readers. Most stories are written to entertain. However, they can inform or persuade. Informative texts are easy to recognize. The most difficult purpose of a text to determine is persuasion. In persuasion, the author wants to make the purpose hard to find. When you learn that the author wants to persuade, you should be skeptical of the argument. Persuasive passages try to establish an entertaining tone and hope to amuse you into agreement. On the other hand, an informative tone may be used to seem fair and equal to all sides.

An author's purpose is clear often in the organization of the text (e.g., section headings in bold font points for an informative passage). However, you may not have this organization in your passages. So, if authors make their main idea clear from the beginning, then their likely purpose is to inform. If the author makes a main argument and gives minor arguments for support, then the purpose is probably to persuade. If the author tells a story, then his or her purpose is most likely to entertain. If the author wants your attention more than to persuade or inform, then his or her purpose is most likely to entertain. You must judge authors on how well they reach their purpose. In other words, think about the type of passage (e.g., technical, persuasive, etc.) that the author has written and if the author has followed the demands of the passage type.

> ➤ **Review Video: <u>Purpose of an Author</u>**
> *Visit **mometrix.com/academy** and enter **Code: 497555***

The author's purpose will influence his or her writing approach and the reader's reaction. In a **persuasive essay**, the author wants to prove something to readers. There are several important marks of persuasive writing. Opinion given as fact is one mark. When authors try to persuade readers, they give their opinions as if they were facts. Readers must be on guard for statements that sound like facts but cannot be tested. Another mark of persuasive writing is the appeal to feelings. An author will try to play with the feelings of readers by appealing to their ideas of what is right and wrong. When an author uses strong language to excite the reader's feelings, then the author may want to persuade. Many times, a persuasive passage will give an unfair explanation of other sides. Or, the other sides are not shown.

An **informative passage** is written to teach readers. Informative passages are almost always nonfiction. The purpose of an informative passage is to share information in the clearest way. In an informative passage, you may have a thesis statement (i.e., an argument on the topic of a passage that is explained by proof). A thesis statement is a sentence that normally comes at the end of the first paragraph. Authors of informative passages are likely to put more importance on being clear. Informative passages do not normally appeal to the feelings. They often contain facts and figures. Informative passages almost never include the opinion of the author. However, you should know that there can be a bias in the facts. Sometimes, a persuasive passage can be like an informative passage. This is true when authors give their ideas as if they were facts.

Entertainment passages describe real or imagined people, places, and events. Entertainment passages are often stories or poems. So, figurative language is a common part of these passages. Often, an entertainment passage appeals to the imagination and feelings. Authors may persuade or inform in an entertainment passage. Or, an entertainment passage may cause readers to think differently about a subject.

When authors want to **share feelings,** they may use strong language. Authors may share feelings about a moment of great pain or happiness. Other times, authors will try to persuade readers by sharing feelings. Some phrases like *I felt* and *I sense* hint that the author is sharing feelings. Authors may share a story of deep pain or great joy. You must not be influenced by these stories. You need to keep some distance to judge the author's argument.

Almost all writing is descriptive. In one way or another, authors try to describe events, ideas, or people. Some texts are concerned only with **description**. A descriptive passage focuses on a single subject and seeks to explain the subject clearly. Descriptive passages contain many adjectives and adverbs (i.e., words that give a complete picture for you to imagine). Normally, a descriptive passage is informative. Yet, the passage may be persuasive or entertaining.

Topics and Main Ideas
One of the most important skills in reading comprehension is finding topics and main ideas. There is a small difference between these two. The topic is the subject of a passage (i.e., what the passage is all about). The main idea is the most important argument being made by the author. The topic is shared in a few words while the main idea needs a full sentence to be understood. As an example, a short passage might have the topic of penguins, and the main idea could be written as *Penguins are different from other birds in many ways.*

In most nonfiction writing, the topic and the main idea will be stated clearly. Sometimes, they will come in a sentence at the very beginning or end of the passage. When you want to know the topic, you may find it in the first sentence of each paragraph. A body paragraph's first sentence is often-- but not always--the main topic sentence. The topic sentence gives you a summary of the ideas in the paragraph. You may find that the topic or main idea is not given clearly. So, you must read every sentence of the passage. Then, try to come up with an overall idea from each sentence.

Note: A thesis statement is not the same as the main idea. The main idea gives a brief, general summary of a text. The thesis statement gives a clear idea on an issue that is backed up with evidence.

> **Review Video:** Topics and Main Ideas
*Visit **mometrix.com/academy** and enter **Code: 691033***

Supporting Details

The main idea is the umbrella argument of a passage. So, **supporting details** back up the main idea. To show that a main idea is correct, authors add details that prove their idea. All passages contain details. However, they are supporting details when the details help an argument in the passage. Supporting details are found in informative and persuasive texts. Sometimes they will come with terms like *for example* or *for instance*. Or, they will be numbered with terms like *first*, *second*, and *last*. You should think about how the author's supporting details back up his or her main idea. Supporting details can be correct, yet they may help the author's main idea. Sometimes supporting details can seem helpful. However, they may be useless when they are based on opinions.

> ➤ **Review Video: Supporting Details**
> *Visit* ***mometrix.com/academy*** *and enter* ***Code:*** **396297**

An example of a main idea: *Giraffes live in the Serengeti of Africa.* A supporting detail about giraffes could be: *A giraffe in the Serengeti benefits from a long neck by reaching twigs and leaves on tall trees.* The main idea gives the general idea that the text is about giraffes. The supporting detail gives a clear fact about how the giraffes eat.

Theme

A theme is an issue, an idea, or a question raised by a passage. For example, a theme of *Cinderella* is determination as Cinderella serves her step-sisters and step-mother. Passages may have many themes, and you must be sure to find only themes that you are asked to find. One common mark of themes is that they give more questions than answers. Authors try to push readers to consider themes in other ways. You can find themes by asking about the general problems that the passage is addressing. A good way to find a theme is to begin reading with a question in mind (e.g., How does this passage use the theme of love?) and to look for answers to that question.

> ➤ **Review Video: Theme**
> *Visit* ***mometrix.com/academy*** *and enter* ***Code:*** **732074**

Cause and Effect

A cause is an act or event that makes something happen. An effect is what comes from the cause. A cause and effect relationship is not always easy to find. So, there are some words and phrases that show causes: *since*, *because*, and *due to*. Words and phrases that show effects include *consequently*, *therefore*, *this lead(s) to*, *as a result*. For example, *Because the sky was clear, Ron did not bring an umbrella.* The cause is the clear sky, and the effect is that Ron did not bring an umbrella. Readers may find that the cause and effect relationship is not clear. For example, *He was late and missed the meeting.* This does not have any words that show cause or effect. Yet, the sentence still has a cause (e.g., he was late) and an effect (e.g., he missed the meeting).

Remember the chance for a single cause to have many effects (e.g., *Single cause*: Because you left your homework on the table, your dog eats the homework. *Many effects*: (1) As a result, you fail your homework. (2) Your parents do not let you see your friends. (3) You miss out on the new movie. (4) You miss holding the hand of an important person.).

Also, the chance of a single effect to have many causes (e.g.. *Single effect*: Alan has a fever. *Many causes*: (1) An unexpected cold front came through the area, and (2) Alan forgot to take his multivitamin.)

Now, an effect can become the cause of another effect. This is known as a cause and effect chain. (e.g., As a result of her hatred for not doing work, Lynn got ready for her exam. This led to her passing her test with high marks. Hence, her resume was accepted, and her application was accepted.)

Analogy
Often, authors use analogies to add meaning to their passages. An analogy is a comparison of two things. The words in the analogy are connected by a relationship. Look at this analogy: *moo is to cow as quack is to duck*. This analogy compares the sound that a cow makes with the sound that a duck makes. What could you do if the word *quack* was not given? Well, you could finish the analogy if you know the connection between *moo* and *cow*. Relationships for analogies include synonyms, antonyms, part to whole, definition, and actor to action.

Summarizing and Paraphrasing
Another helpful tool is the skill of summarizing information. This process is similar to creating an outline. First, a summary should define the main idea of the passage. The summary should have the most important supporting details or arguments. Summaries can be unclear or wrong because they do not stay true to the information in the passage. A helpful summary should have the same message as the passage.

Paraphrasing is another method that you can use to understand a passage. To paraphrase, you put what you have read into your own words. Or, you can *translate* what the author shared into your words by including as many details as you can.

Compare and Contrast
Many passages follow the compare-and-contrast model. In this model, the similarities and differences between two ideas or things are reviewed. A review of the similarities between ideas is called comparison. In a perfect comparison, the author shows ideas or things in the same way. If authors want to show the similarities between football and baseball, then they can list the equipment and rules for each game. Think about the similarities as they appear in the passage and take note of any differences.

Careful thinking about ideas and conclusions can seem like a difficult task. You can make this task easy by understanding the basic parts of ideas and writing skills. Looking at the way that ideas link to others is a good way for you to begin. Sometimes authors will write about two ideas that are against each other. Other times, an author will support a topic, and another author will argue against the topic. The review of these rival ideas is known as contrast. In contrast, all ideas should be presented clearly. If the author does favor a side, you need to read carefully to find where the author shows or hides this favoritism. Also, as you read the passage, you should write out how one side views the other.

Fact and Opinion
Readers must always be aware of the difference between fact and opinion. A fact can be proved or disproved. An opinion is the author's personal thoughts or feelings. So, an opinion cannot be proved or disproved. For example, an author writes that the distance from New York City to Boston is about two hundred miles. The author is giving a fact. We can drive to Boston from New York City and find that it took about 200 miles. However, another author writes that New York City is too crowded. This author is giving an opinion. The reason that this is an opinion is that there is no independent measurement for overpopulation. You may think that where you live is overcrowded. Yet, someone else may say that more people can live in your area.

An opinion may come with words like *believe*, *think*, or *feel*. Know that an opinion can be backed up with facts. For example, someone may give the population density (i.e., the number of people living for each square mile) of New York City as a reason for an overcrowded population. An opinion backed up with facts can seem convincing. However, this does not mean that you should accept the argument.

Use these steps to know the difference between fact and opinion. First, think about the type of source that is presenting information (e.g., Is this information coming from someone or something that is trusted by me and others?). Next, think about the information that backs up a claim (e.g., Are the details for the argument opinions or facts?). Then, think about the author's motivation to have a certain point of view on a topic (e.g., Why does this person care about this issue?). For example, a group of scientists tests the value of a product. The results are likely to be full of facts. Now, compare the group of scientists to a company. The company sells a product and says that their products are good. The company says this because they want to sell their product. Yet, the scientists use the scientific method (i.e. an independent way of proving ideas and questions) to prove the value of the product. The company's statements about the product may be true. But, the group of scientists *proves* the value of the product.

> **Review Video:** <u>Fact or Opinion</u>
Visit mometrix.com/academy and enter Code: **870899**

Extending Meaning

<u>Prediction</u>
One part of being a good reader is making predictions. A prediction is a guess about what will happen next. Readers make predictions from what they have read and what they already know. For example: *Staring at the computer screen in shock, Kim reached for the glass of water.* The sentence leaves you to think that she is not looking at the glass. So, you may guess that Kim is going to knock over the glass. Yet, in the next sentence, you may read that Kim does not knock over the glass. As you have more information, be ready for your predictions to change.

> **Review Video:** <u>Predictions</u>
Visit mometrix.com/academy and enter Code: **437248**

Test-taking tip: To respond to questions that ask about predictions, your answer should come from the passage.

<u>Inferences and Implications</u>
You will be asked to understand text that gives ideas without stating them directly. An inference is something that is implied but not stated directly by the author. For example: *After the final out of the inning, the fans were filled with joy and rushed the field.* From this sentence, you can infer that the fans were watching baseball and their team won. You should not use information outside of the passage before making inferences. As you practice making inferences, you will find that they need all of your attention.

> **Review Video:** <u>Inference</u>
Visit mometrix.com/academy and enter Code: **379203**

Test-taking tip: When asked about inferences, look for context clues. Context is what surrounds the words and sentences that add explanation or information to an unknown piece. An answer can be *true* but not *correct*. The context clues will help you find the answer that is best. When asked for the implied meaning of a statement, you should locate the statement first. Then, read the context around the statement. Finally, look for an answer with a similar phrase.

Implications are things that the author does not say directly. Yet, you can assume from what the author does say. For example, *I stepped outside and opened my umbrella. By the time I got to work, the cuffs of my pants were soaked.* The author never says that it is raining. However, you can conclude that this is information is implied. Conclusions from implications must be well supported by the passage. To draw a conclusion, you should have many pieces of proof. Yet, let's say that you have only one piece. Then, you need to be sure that there is no other possible explanation than your conclusion. Practice drawing conclusions from implications in real life events to improve your skills.

Sequence

For your exam, you must be able to find a text's sequence (i.e., the order that things happen). When the sequence is very important to the author, the passage comes with signal words: *first, then, next,* and *last*. However, a sequence can be implied. For example, *He walked through the garden and gave water and fertilizer to the plants.* Clearly, the man did not walk through the garden at the beginning. First, he found water. Then, he collected fertilizer. Next, he walked through the garden. Finally, he gave water and fertilizer to the plants. Passages do not always come in a clear sequence. Sometimes they begin at the end. Or, they can start over at the beginning. You can strengthen your understanding of the passage by taking notes to understand the sequence.

Transitional words and phrases are devices that guide readers through a passage. You may know the common transitions. Though you may not have thought about how they are used. Some transitional phrases (*after, before, during, in the middle of*) give information about time. Some hint that an example is about to be given (*for example, in fact, for instance*). Writers use transitions to compare (*also, likewise*) and contrast (*however, but, yet*). Transitional words and phrases can point to addition (*and, also, furthermore, moreover*) and understood relationships (*if, then, therefore, as a result, since*). Finally, transitional words and phrases can separate the chronological steps (*first, second, last*).

> ➤ **Review Video: Transitional Words and Phrases**
> *Visit* ***mometrix.com/academy*** *and enter* ***Code: 197796***

Evaluating a Passage

Find a Logical Conclusion

When you read informational passages, you need to make a conclusion from the author's writing. You can identify a logical conclusion (i.e., find a conclusion that makes sense) to know whether you agree or disagree with an author. Coming to this conclusion is like making an inference. You combine the information from the passage with what you already know. From the passage's information and your knowledge, you can come to a conclusion that makes sense. One way to have a conclusion that makes sense is to take notes of all the author's points. When the notes are organized, they may point to the logical conclusion. Another way to reach conclusions is to ask if the author's passage raises any helpful questions. Sometimes you will be able to draw many conclusions from a passage. Yet, these may be conclusions that were never imagined by the author. Therefore, find reasons in the passage for the conclusions that you make.

> ➤ **Review Video: Identifying a Logical Conclusion**
> *Visit mometrix.com/academy and enter Code:* **281653**

Directly Stated Information

A reader should always draw conclusions from passages. Sometimes conclusions are implied (i.e., information that is assumed) from written information. Other times the information is stated directly within the passage. You should try to draw conclusions from information stated in a passage. Furthermore, you should always read through the entire passage before drawing conclusions. Many readers expect the author's conclusions at the beginning or the end of the passage. However, many texts do not follow this format.

Text Evidence

Text evidence is the information that supports a main argument or minor argument. This evidence, or proof, can lead you to a conclusion. Information used as text evidence is clear, descriptive, and full of facts. Supporting details give evidence to back-up an argument. For example, a passage may state that winter occurs during opposite months in the Northern hemisphere (i.e., north of the equator) and Southern hemisphere (i.e., south of the equator). Text evidence for this claim may include a list of countries where winter occurs in opposite months. Also, you may be given reasons that winter occurs at different times of the year in these hemispheres (e.g., the tilt of the Earth as it rotates around the sun).

> ➤ **Review Video: Text Evidence**
> *Visit mometrix.com/academy and enter Code:* **486236**

Language

Grammar Review

Nouns

When you talk about a person, place, thing, or idea, you are talking about nouns. The two main types of nouns are common and proper nouns. Also, nouns can be abstract (i.e., general) or concrete (i.e., specific).

Common nouns are the class or group of people, places, and things (Note: Do not capitalize common nouns). Examples of common nouns:
People: boy, girl, worker, manager
Places: school, bank, library, home
Things: dog, cat, truck, car

Proper nouns are the names of a specific person, place, or thing (Note: Capitalize all proper nouns). Examples of proper nouns:
People: Abraham Lincoln, George Washington, Martin Luther King, Jr.
Places: Los Angeles, California / New York / Asia
Things: Statue of Liberty, Earth*, Lincoln Memorial

*Note: When you talk about the planet that we live on, you capitalize *Earth*. When you mean the dirt, rocks, or land, you lowercase *earth*.

General nouns are the names of conditions or ideas. **Specific nouns** name people, places, and things that are understood by using your senses.

General nouns:
Condition: beauty, strength
Idea: truth, peace

Specific nouns:
People: baby, friend, father
Places: town, park, city hall
Things: rainbow (see), cough (hear), apple (taste), silk (feel), gasoline (smell)

Collective nouns are the names for a person, place, or thing that may act as a whole. The following are examples of collective nouns: *class, company, dozen, group, herd, team,* and *public.*

Pronouns

Pronouns are words that are used to stand in for a noun. A pronoun may be grouped as personal, intensive, relative, interrogative, demonstrative, indefinite, and reciprocal.

Personal: Nominative is the case for nouns and pronouns that are the subject of a sentence. Objective is the case for nouns and pronouns that are an object in a sentence. Possessive is the case for nouns and pronouns that show possession or ownership.

Singular

	Nominative	Objective	Possessive
First Person	I	me	my, mine
Second Person	you	you	your, yours
Third Person	he, she, it	him, her, it	his, her, hers, its

Plural

	Nominative	Objective	Possessive
First Person	we	us	our, ours
Second Person	you	you	your, yours
Third Person	they	them	their, theirs

Intensive: I myself, you yourself, he himself, she herself, the (thing) itself, we ourselves, you yourselves, they themselves

Relative: which, who, whom, whose

Interrogative: what, which, who, whom, whose

Demonstrative: this, that, these, those

Indefinite: all, any, each, everyone, either/neither, one, some, several

Reciprocal: each other, one another

> ➤ **Review Video:** <u>Nouns and Pronouns</u>
> *Visit **mometrix.com/academy** and enter **Code:** 312073*

Verbs

If you want to write a sentence, then you need a verb in your sentence. Without a verb, you have no sentence. Go ahead. Try to make a sentence without using a verb.

Can't make a sentence? Okay, let's get back to work. The verb of a sentence explains action or being (i.e., the condition or status of someone or something). In other words, the verb shows the subject's movement or the movement that has been done to the subject.

Transitive and Intransitive Verbs
A transitive verb is a verb whose action (e.g., drive, run, jump) points to a receiver (e.g., car, dog, kangaroo). Intransitive verbs do not point to a receiver of an action. In other words, the action of the verb does not point to a subject or object.

Transitive: He plays the piano. | The piano was played by him.

Intransitive: He plays. | John writes well.

A dictionary will let you know whether a verb is transitive or intransitive. Some verbs can be transitive and intransitive.

Action Verbs and Linking Verbs
An action verb is a verb that shows what the subject is doing in a sentence. In other words, an action verb shows action. A sentence can be complete with one word: an action verb. Linking verbs are intransitive verbs that show a condition (i.e., the subject is described, but does no action).

Linking verbs link the subject of a sentence to a noun or pronoun, or they link a subject with an adjective. You always need a verb if you want a complete sentence. However, linking verbs are not able to complete a sentence.

Common linking verbs include *appear, be, become, feel, grow, look, seem, smell, sound,* and *taste.* However, any verb that shows a condition and has a noun, pronoun, or adjective that describes the subject of a sentence is a linking verb.

Action: He sings. | Run! | Go! | I talk with him every day. | She reads.

Linking:
Incorrect: I am.
Correct: I am John. | I smell roses. | I feel tired.

Note: Some verbs are followed by words that look like prepositions, but they are a part of the verb and a part of the verb's meaning. These are known as phrasal verbs and examples include *call off, look up,* and *drop off.*

Voice
Transitive verbs come in active or passive voice. If the subject does an action or receives the action of the verb, then you will know whether a verb is active or passive. When the subject of the sentence is doing the action, the verb is active voice. When the subject receives the action, the verb is passive voice.

Active: Jon drew the picture. (The subject *Jon* is doing the action of *drawing a picture.*)

Passive: The picture is drawn by Jon. (The subject *picture* is receiving the action from Jon.)

Verb Tenses

A verb tense shows the different form of a verb to point to the time of an action. The present and past tense are shown by changing the verb's form. An action in the present *I talk* can change form for the past: *I talked*. However, for the other tenses an auxiliary (i.e., helping) verb is needed to show the change in form. These helping verbs include *am, are, is | have, has, had | was, were, will* (or *shall*).

Present: I talk	Present perfect: I have talked
Past: I talked	Past perfect: I had talked
Future: I will talk	Future perfect: I will have talked

Present: The action happens at the current time.
Example: He *walks* to the store every morning.
To show that something is happening right now, use the progressive present tense: I *am walking*.

Past: The action happened in the past.
Example: He *walked* to the store an hour ago.

Future: The action is going to happen later.
Example: I *will walk* to the store tomorrow.

Present perfect: The action started in the past and continues into the present.
Example: I *have walked* to the store three times today.

Past perfect: The second action happened in the past. The first action came before the second.
Example: Before I walked to the store (Action 2), I *had walked* to the library (Action 1).

Future perfect: An action that uses the past and the future. In other words, the action is complete before a future moment.
Example: When she comes for the supplies (future moment), I *will have walked* to the store (action completed in the past).

Conjugating Verbs

When you need to change the form of a verb, you are conjugating a verb. The key parts of a verb are first person singular, present tense (dream); first person singular, past tense (dreamed); and the past participle (dreamed). Note: the past participle needs a helping verb to make a verb tense. For example, I *have dreamed* of this day. | I *am dreaming* of this day.

Present Tense: Active Voice

	Singular	Plural
First Person	I dream	We dream
Second Person	You dream	You dream
Third Person	He, she, it dreams	They dream

Mood
There are three moods in English: the indicative, the imperative, and the subjunctive.

The **indicative mood** is used for facts, opinions, and questions.
Fact: You can do this.
Opinion: I think that you can do this.
Question: Do you know that you can do this?

The **imperative** is used for orders or requests.
Order: You are going to do this!
Request: Will you do this for me?

The **subjunctive mood** is for wishes and statements that go against fact.
Wish: I wish that I were going to do this.
Statement against fact: If I were you, I would do this. (This goes against fact because I am not you. You have the chance to do this, and I do not the chance.)

The mood that causes trouble for most people is the subjunctive mood. If you have trouble with any of the moods, then be sure to practice.

Adjectives

An adjective is a word that is used to modify (i.e., describe or explain) a noun or pronoun. An adjective answers a question: *Which one?*, *What kind of?*, or *How many?* . Usually, adjectives come before the words that they modify.

Which one?: The *third* suit is my favorite.
What kind?: The *navy blue* suit is my favorite.
How many?: Can I look over the *four* neckties for the suit?

Articles
Articles are adjectives that are used to mark nouns. There are only three: the definite (i.e., limited or fixed amount) article *the*, and the indefinite (i.e., no limit or fixed amount) articles *a* and *an*. Note: *An* comes before words that start with a vowel sound (i.e., vowels include *a, e, i, o, u,* and *y*). For example, Are you going to get an **u**mbrella?

Definite: I lost *the* bottle that belongs to me.
Indefinite: Does anyone have *a* bottle to share?

Comparison with Adjectives
Some adjectives are relative and other adjectives are absolute. Adjectives that are relative can show the comparison between things. Adjectives that are absolute can show comparison. However, they show comparison in a different way. Let's say that you are reading two books. You think that one book is perfect, and the other book is not perfect. It is <u>not</u> possible for the book to be more perfect than the other. Either you think that the book is perfect, or you think that the book is not perfect.

The adjectives that are relative will show the different degrees of something or someone to something else or someone else. The three degrees of adjectives include positive, comparative, and superlative.

The positive degree is the normal form of an adjective.
Example: This work is *difficult.* | She is *smart.*

The comparative degree compares one person or thing to another person or thing.
Example: This work is *more difficult* than your work. | She is *smarter* than me.

The superlative degree compares more than two people or things.
Example: This is the *most difficult* work of my life. | She is the *smartest* lady in school.

> ➤ **Review Video:** <u>What is an Adjective?</u>
> *Visit **mometrix.com/academy** and enter **Code: 809578***

Adverbs

An adverb is a word that is used to modify a verb, adjective, or another adverb. Usually, adverbs answer one of these questions: *When?*, *Where?*, *How?*, and *Why?* . The negatives *not* and *never* are known as adverbs. Adverbs that modify adjectives or other adverbs strengthen or weaken the words that they modify.

Examples:
He walks quickly through the crowd.
The water flows smoothly on the rocks.

Note: While many adverbs end in *-ly*, you need to remember that not all adverbs end in *-ly*. Also, some words that end in *-ly* are adjectives, not adverbs. Some examples include: *early, friendly, holy, lonely, silly,* and *ugly.* To know if a word that ends in *-ly* is an adjective or adverb, you need to check your dictionary.

Examples:
He is *never* angry.
You talk *too* loud.

Comparison with Adverbs
The rules for comparing adverbs are the same as the rules for adjectives.

The positive degree is the standard form of an adverb.
Example: He arrives soon. | She speaks softly to her friends.

The comparative degree compares one person or thing to another person or thing.
Example: He arrives sooner than Sarah. | She speaks more softly than him.

The superlative degree compares more than two people or things.
Example: He arrives soonest of the group. | She speaks most softly of any of her friends.

> ➤ **Review Video:** <u>Adverbs</u>
> *Visit **mometrix.com/academy** and enter **Code: 713951***

Prepositions

A preposition is a word placed before a noun or pronoun that shows the relationship between an object and another word in the sentence.

Common Prepositions:

about	before	during	on	under
after	beneath	for	over	until
against	between	from	past	up
among	beyond	in	through	with
around	by	of	to	within
at	down	off	toward	without

Examples:
The napkin is *in* the drawer.
The Earth moves *around* the Sun.
The needle is *beneath* the haystack.
Can you find me *among* the words?

> ➤ **Review Video: What is a Preposition?**
> *Visit mometrix.com/academy and enter Code:* **946763**

Conjunctions

Conjunctions join words, phrases, or clauses, and they show the connection between the joined pieces. There are coordinating conjunctions that connect equal parts of sentences. Correlative conjunctions show the connection between pairs. Subordinating conjunctions join subordinate (i.e., dependent) clauses with independent clauses.

Coordinating Conjunctions
The coordinating conjunctions include: *and, but, yet, or, nor, for,* and *so*
Examples:
The rock was small, but it was heavy.
She drove in the night, and he drove in the day.

Correlative Conjunctions
The correlative conjunctions are: *either...or | neither...nor | not only... but also*
Examples:
Either you are coming, *or* you are staying. | He ran *not only* three miles, *but also* swam 200 yards.

> ➤ **Review Video: Coordinating and Correlative Conjunctions**
> *Visit mometrix.com/academy and enter Code:* **390329**

Subordinating Conjunctions

Common subordinating conjunctions include:

after	since	whenever
although	so that	where
because	unless	wherever
before	until	whether
in order that	when	while

Examples:
I am hungry *because* I did not eat breakfast.
He went home *after* everyone left.

> ➤ **Review Video: <u>Subordinating Conjunctions</u>**
> *Visit **mometrix.com/academy** and enter **Code:** 958913*

Interjections

An interjection is a word for exclamation (i.e., great amount of feeling) that is used alone or as a piece to a sentence. Often, they are used at the beginning of a sentence for an introduction. Sometimes, they can be used in the middle of a sentence to show a change in thought or attitude.

Common Interjections: Hey! | Oh,... | Ouch! | Please! | Wow!

Language and Usage

Subjects and Predicates

Subjects

Every sentence has two things: a subject and a verb. The subject of a sentence names who or what the sentence is all about. The subject may be directly stated in a sentence, or the subject may be the implied *you*.

In imperative sentences, the verb's subject is understood (e.g., |You| Run to the store). So, the subject may not be in the sentence. Normally, the subject comes before the verb. However, the subject comes after the verb in sentences that begin with *There are* or *There was*.

Direct:
John knows the way to the park.
(Who knows the way to the park? Answer: John)

The cookies need ten more minutes.
(What needs ten minutes? Answer: The cookies)

By five o' clock, Bill will need to leave.
(Who needs to leave? Answer: Bill)

Remember: The subject can come after the verb.
There are five letters on the table for him.
(What is on the table? Answer: Five letters)

There were coffee and doughnuts in the house.
(What was in the house? Answer: Coffee and doughnuts)

Implied:
Go to the post office for me.
(Who is going to the post office? Answer: You are.)

Come and sit with me, please?
(Who needs to come and sit? Answer: You do.)

The complete subject has the simple subject and all of the modifiers. To find the complete subject, ask *Who* or *What* and insert the verb to complete the question. The answer is the complete subject. To find the simple subject, remove all of the modifiers in the complete subject. When you can find the subject of a sentence, you can correct many problems. These problems include sentence fragments and subject-verb agreement.

Examples:
The small red car is the one that he wants for Christmas.
(The complete subject is *the small red car*.)

The young artist is coming over for dinner.
(The complete subject is *the young artist*.)

➢ **Review Video: Subjects**
*Visit **mometrix.com/academy** and enter **Code: 444771***

Predicates

In a sentence, you always have a predicate and a subject. A predicate is what remains when you have found the subject. The subject tells what the sentence is about, and the predicate explains or describes the subject.

Think about the sentence: *He sings.* In this sentence, we have a subject (He) and a predicate (sings). This is all that is needed for a sentence to be complete. Would we like more information? Of course, we would like to know more. However, if this all the information that you are given, you have a complete sentence.

Now, let's look at another sentence:
John and Jane sing on Tuesday nights at the dance hall.

What is the subject of this sentence?
Answer: John and Jane.

What is the predicate of this sentence?
Answer: Everything else in the sentence besides John and Jane.

Subject-Verb Agreement

Verbs agree with their subjects in number. In other words, singular subjects need singular verbs. Plural subjects need plural verbs. Singular is for one person, place, or thing. Plural is for more than one person, place, or thing. Subjects and verbs must also agree in person: first, second, or third. The present tense ending -*s* is used on a verb if its subject is third person singular; otherwise, the verb takes no ending.

➢ **Review Video: Subjects and Verbs**
*Visit **mometrix.com/academy** and enter **Code: 987207***

Number Agreement Examples:
Single Subject and Verb: *Dan calls home.*
(Dan is one person. So, the singular verb *calls* is needed.)

Plural Subject and Verb: *Dan and Bob call home.*
(More than one person needs the plural verb *call*.)

- 82 -

Person Agreement Examples:
First Person: I *am* walking.
Second Person: You *are* walking.
Third Person: He *is* walking.

Problems with Subject-Verb Agreement

- Words between Subject and Verb
  The joy of my life returns home tonight.
  (**Singular Subject**: joy. **Singular Verb**: returns)
  The phrase *of my life* does not influence the verb *returns*.

  The question that still remains unanswered is "Who are you?"
  (**Singular Subject**: question. **Singular Verb**: is)
  Don't let the phrase "*that still remains...*" trouble you. The subject *questions* goes with *is*.

- Compound Subjects
  You and Jon are invited to come to my house.
  (**Plural Subject**: You and Jon. **Plural Verb**: are)

  The pencil and paper belong to me.
  (**Plural Subject**: pencil and paper. **Plural Verb**: belong)

- Subjects Joined by *Or* and *Nor*
  Today or tomorrow is the day.
  (**Subject**: Today / tomorrow. **Verb**: is)

  Stan or Phil wants to read the book.
  (**Subject**: Stan / Phil. **Verb**: wants)

  Neither the books nor the *pen is* on the desk.
  (**Subject**: Books / Pen. **Verb**: was)

  Either the blanket or *pillows arrive* this afternoon.
  (**Subject**: Blanket / Pillows. **Verb**: arrive)

  Note: Singular subjects that are joined with the conjunction *or* need a singular verb. However, when one subject is singular and another is plural, you make the verb agree with the closer subject. The example about books and the pen has a singular verb because the pen (singular subject) is closer to the verb.

- Indefinite Pronouns: Either, Neither, and Each
  Is either of you ready for the game?
  (**Singular Subject**: Either. **Singular Verb**: is)

  Each man, woman, and child is unique.
  (**Singular Subject**: Each. **Singular Verb**: is)

- The adjective Every and compounds: Everybody, Everyone, Anybody, Anyone
  Every day passes faster than the last.
  (**Singular Subject**: Every day. **Singular Verb**: passes)

  Anybody is welcome to bring a tent.
  (**Singular Subject**: Anybody. **Singular Verb**: is)

- Collective Nouns
  The family eats at the restaurant every Friday night.
  (The members of the family are one at the restaurant.)

  The team are leaving for their homes after the game.
  (The members of the team are leaving as individuals to go to their own homes.)

- Who, Which, and That as Subject
  This is the man who is helping me today.
  He is a good man who serves others before himself.
  This painting that is hung over the couch is very beautiful.

- Plural Form and Singular Meaning
  Some nouns that are singular in meaning but plural in form: news, mathematics, physics, and economics
  > The news is coming on now.
  > Mathematics is my favorite class.

  Some nouns that are plural in meaning: athletics, gymnastics, scissors, and pants
  > Do these pants come with a shirt?
  > The scissors are for my project.

  Note: There are more nouns in plural form and are singular in meaning than plural in meaning. Look to your dictionary for help when you don't know about the meaning of a verb.

  Addition, Multiplication, Subtraction, and Division are normally singular.
  > One plus one is two.
  > Three times three is nine.

Complements

A complement is a noun, pronoun, or adjective that is used to give more information about the verb in the sentence.

Direct Objects
A direct object is a noun that takes or receives the action of a verb. Remember: a complete sentence does not need a direct object. A sentence needs only a subject and a verb. When you are looking for a direct object, find the verb and ask *who* or *what*.
> Example: I took the blanket. (Who or what did I take? *The blanket*)
> Jane read books. (Who or what does Jane read? *Books*)

Indirect Objects
An indirect object is a word or group of words that show how an action had an influence on someone or something. If there is an indirect object in a sentence, then you always have a direct object in the sentence. When you are looking for the indirect object, find the verb and ask *to/for whom or what*.
> Examples: We taught the old dog a new trick.
> (To/For Whom or What was taught? *The old dog*)
>
> I gave them a math lesson.
> (To/For Whom or What was given? *Them*)

<u>Predicate Nouns</u> are nouns that modify the subject and finish linking verbs.
   Example: My father is a lawyer.
               Father is the subject. Lawyer is the predicate noun.

<u>Predicate Adjectives</u> are adjectives that modify the subject and finish linking verbs.
   Example: Your mother is patient.
               Mother is the subject. Patient is the predicate adjective.

Pronoun Usage

Pronoun - antecedent agreement - The antecedent is the noun that has been replaced by a pronoun. A pronoun and the antecedent agree when they are singular or plural.

Singular agreement: *John* came into town, and *he* played for us.
(The word *He* replaces *John*.)

Plural agreement: *John and Rick* came into town, and *they* played for us.
(The word *They* replaces *John* and *Rick*.)

To know the correct pronoun for a compound subject, try each pronoun separately with the verb. Your knowledge of pronouns will tell you which one is correct.
Example: Bob and (I, me) will be going.
(Answer: Bob and I will be going.)

(1) *I will be going* or (2) *Me will be going*. The second choice cannot be correct because *me* is not used as a subject of a sentence. Instead, *me* is used as an object.

When a pronoun is used with a noun immediately following (as in "we boys"), try the sentence without the added noun.
Example: (We/Us) boys played football last year.
(Answer: We boys played football last year.)

(1) *We* played football last year or (2) *Us* played football last year. Again, the second choice cannot be correct because *us* is not used as a subject of a sentence. Instead, *us* is used as an object.

> **Review Video: <u>Pronoun Usage</u>**
Visit mometrix.com/academy and enter Code: 666500

Pronoun reference - A pronoun should point clearly to the antecedent. Here is how a pronoun reference can be unhelpful if it is not directly stated or puzzling.

Unhelpful: Ron and Jim went to the store, and he bought soda.
(Who bought soda? Ron or Jim?)

Helpful: Jim went to the store, and he bought soda.
(The sentence is clear. Jim bought the soda.)

Personal pronouns - Some pronouns change their form by their placement in a sentence. A pronoun that is a subject in a sentence comes in the subjective case. Pronouns that serve as objects appear in the objective case. Finally, the pronouns that are used as possessives appear in the possessive case.

Subjective case: *He* is coming to the show.
(The pronoun *He* is the subject of the sentence.)

Objective case: Josh drove *him* to the airport.
(The pronoun *him* is the object of the sentence.)

Possessive case: The flowers are *mine*.
(The pronoun *mine* shows ownership of the flowers.)

Who or whom - *Who*, a subjective-case pronoun, can be used as a subject. *Whom*, an objective case pronoun, can be used as an object. The words *who* and *whom* are common in subordinate clauses or in questions.

Subject: He knows who wants to come.
(*Who* is the subject of the verb *wants*.)

Object: He knows whom we want at the party.
(*Whom* is the object of *we want*.)

Word Confusion

Which is used for things only.
    Example: John's dog, *which was called Max*, is large and fierce.

That is used for people or things.
    Example: Is this the only book *that Louis L'Amour wrote?*
    Example: Is Louis L'Amour the author *that wrote Western novels?*

Who is used for people only.
    Example: Mozart was the composer *who wrote those operas*.

<u>Homonyms</u>
Homonyms are words that sound alike, but they have different spellings and definitions.

To, Too, and Two

To can be an adverb or a preposition for showing direction, purpose, and relationship. See your dictionary for the many other ways use *to* in a sentence.
Examples: I went to the store. | I want to go with you.

Too is an adverb that means *also, as well, very, or more than enough*.
Examples: I can walk a mile too. | You have eaten too much.

Two is the second number in the series of numbers (e.g., one (1), two, (2), three (3)...)
Example: You have two minutes left.

There, Their, and They're

There can be an adjective, adverb, or pronoun. Often, *there* is used to show a place or to start a sentence.
Examples: I went there yesterday. | There is something in his pocket.

Their is a pronoun that is used to show ownership.
Examples: He is their father. | This is their fourth apology this week.

They're is a contraction (i.e., a combination of words by deleting some letters) of *they are*.
Example: Did you know that they're in town?

Knew and New

Knew is the past tense of *know*.
Example: I knew the answer.

New is an adjective that means something is current, has not been used, or modern.
Example: This is my new phone.

Its and It's

Its is an adjective that shows ownership.
Example: The guitar is in its case.

It's is a contraction of *it is*.
Example: It's an honor and a privilege to meet you.
Note: The *h* in honor is silent. So, the sound of the vowel *o* must have the article *an*.

Your and You're

Your is an adjective that shows ownership.
Example: This is your moment to shine.

You're is a contraction of you are.
Example: Yes, you're correct.

Affect and Effect

Affect can be used as a noun for feeling, emotion, or mood. Effect can be used as a noun that means result. Affect as a verb means to influence. Effect as a verb means to bring about.
Affect: The sunshine affects plants.
Effect: The new rules will effect order in the office.

Phrases

A phrase is not a complete sentence. So, a phrase cannot be a statement and cannot give a complete thought. Instead, a phrase is a group of words that can be used as a noun, adjective, or adverb in a sentence. Phrases strengthen sentences by adding explanation or renaming something.

<u>Prepositional Phrases</u> - A phrase that can be found in many sentences is the prepositional phrase. A prepositional phrase begins with a preposition and ends with a noun or pronoun that is used as an object. Normally, the prepositional phrase works as an adjective or an adverb.

Examples:
The picnic is *on the blanket.*
I am sick *with a fever* today.
Among the many flowers, a four-leaf clover was found by John.

<u>Verbals and Verbal Phrases</u>
A verbal looks like a verb, but it is not used as a verb. Instead, a verbal is used as a noun, adjective, or adverb. Be careful with verbals. They do not replace a verb in a sentence.

Correct: Walk a mile daily.
(*Walk* is the verb of this sentence. As in, "*You* walk a mile daily.")

Incorrect: To walk a mile.
(*To walk* is a type of verbal. But, verbals cannot be a verb for a sentence.)

A verbal phrase is a verb form that does not function as the verb of a clause. There are three major types of verbal phrases: participial, gerund, and infinitive phrases.

Participles - A participle is a verbal that is used as an adjective. The present participle always ends with *-ing*. Past participles end with *-d, -ed, -n,* or *-t.*
Examples: Verb: *dance* | Present Participle: *dancing* | Past Participle: *danced*

Participial phrases are made of a participle and any complements or modifiers. Often, they come right after the noun or pronoun that they modify.

Examples:
Shipwrecked on an island, the boys started to fish for food.
Having been seated for five hours, we got out of the car to stretch our legs.
Praised for their work, the group accepted the first place trophy.

Gerunds - A gerund is a verbal that is used as a noun. Gerunds can be found by looking for their *-ing* endings. However, you need to be careful that you have found a gerund, not a present participle. Since gerunds are nouns, they can be used as a subject of a sentence and the object of a verb or preposition.

Gerund Phrases are built around present participles (i.e., *-ing* endings to verbs) and they are always used as nouns. The gerund phrase has a gerund and any complements or modifiers.

Examples:
We want to be known for *teaching the poor.* (Object of Preposition)
Coaching this team is the best job of my life. (Subject)
We like *practicing our songs* in the basement. (Object of the verb: *like*)

Infinitives - An infinitive is a verbal that can be used as a noun, an adjective, or an adverb. An infinitive is made of the basic form of a verb with the word *to* coming before the verb.

Infinitive Phrases are made of an infinitive and all complements and modifiers. They are used as nouns, adjectives, or adverbs.

Examples:
To join the team is my goal in life. (Noun)
The animals have enough food *to eat for the night*. (Adjective)
People lift weights *to exercise their muscles*. (Adverb)

<u>Appositive Phrases</u>
An appositive is a word or phrase that is used to explain or rename nouns or pronouns. In a sentence they can be noun phrases, prepositional phrases, gerund phrases, or infinitive phrases.

Examples:
Terriers, *hunters at heart*, have been dressed up to look like lap dogs.
(The phrase *hunters at heart* renames the noun *terriers*.)

His plan, *to save and invest his money*, was proven as a safe approach.
(The italicized infinitive phrase renames the plan.)

Appositive phrases can be essential or nonessential. An appositive phrase is essential if the person, place, or thing being described or renamed is too general.
Essential: Two Founding Fathers George Washington and Thomas Jefferson served as presidents.

Nonessential: George Washington and Thomas Jefferson, two Founding Fathers, served as presidents.

<u>Absolute Phrases</u>
An absolute phrase is a phrase with a participle that comes after a noun. The absolute phrase is never the subject of a sentence. Also, the phrase does not explain or add to the meaning of a word in a sentence. Absolute phrases are used independently from the rest of the sentence. However, they are still a phrase, and phrases cannot give a complete thought.

Examples:
The alarm ringing, he pushed the snooze button.
The music paused, she continued to dance through the crowd.

Note: Appositive and absolute phrases can be confusing in sentences. So, don't be discouraged if you have a difficult time with them.

Clauses

There are two groups of clauses: independent and dependent. Unlike phrases, a clause has a subject and a verb. So, what is the difference between a clause that is independent and one that is dependent? An independent clause gives a complete thought. A dependent clause does not share a complete thought. Instead, a dependent clause has a subject and a verb, but it needs an independent clause. Subordinate (i.e., dependent) clauses look like sentences. They may have a subject, a verb, and objects or complements. They are used within sentences as adverbs, adjectives, or nouns.

Examples:
Independent Clause: I am running outside.
(The sentence has a subject *I* and a verb *am running*.)

Dependent Clause: I am running <u>because I want to stay in shape</u>.

The clause *I am running* is an independent clause. The underlined clause is dependent. Remember: a dependent clause does not give a complete thought. Think about the dependent clause: *because I want to stay in shape*.

Without any other information, you think: So, you want to stay in shape. What are you are doing to stay in shape? Answer: *I am running*.

Types of Dependent Clauses
An **adjective clause** is a dependent clause that modifies nouns and pronouns. Adjective clauses begin with a relative pronoun (*who, whose, whom, which,* and *that*) or a relative adverb (*where, when,* and *why*). Also, adjective clauses come after the noun that the clause needs to explain or rename. This is done to have a clear connection to the independent clause.
Examples:
I learned the reason *why I won the award*.
This is the place *where I started my first job*.

An adjective clause can be an essential or nonessential clause. An essential clause is very important to the sentence. Essential clauses explain or define a person or thing. Nonessential clauses give more information about a person or thing. However, they are not necessary to the sentence.
Examples:
Essential: A person *who works hard at first* can rest later in life.
Nonessential: Neil Armstrong, *who walked on the moon*, is my hero.

An **adverb clause** is a dependent clause that modifies verbs, adjectives, and other adverbs. To show a clear connection to the independent clause, put the adverb clause immediately before or after the independent clause. An adverb clause can start with *after, although, as, as if, before, because, if, since, so, so that, unless, when, where,* or *while*.
Examples:
When you walked outside, I called the manager.
I want to go with you *unless you want to stay*.

A **noun clause** is a dependent clause that can be used as a subject, object, or complement. Noun clauses can begin with *how, that, what, whether, which, who,* or *why*. These words can also come with an adjective clause. Remember that the entire clause makes a noun or an adjective clause, not the word that starts a clause. So, be sure to look for more than the word that begins the clause. To show a clear connection to the independent clause, be sure that a noun clause comes after the verb. The exception is when the noun clause is the subject of the sentence.
Examples:
The fact *that you were alone* alarms me.
What you learn from each other depends on your honesty with others.

Transitions

Transitions are bridges between what has been read and what is about to be read. Transitions smooth the path between sentences and show connections to new ideas. When you think about the correct phrase for a transition, you need to think about the previous and upcoming words in a sentence. Thus, transitional phrases should be used with care. Tone is important when you want to use a transitional phrase. For example, *in summary* would be better than the informal *in short*.

<u>Restatement</u>: He wanted to walk the trails at the park, *namely* Yosemite National Park.
<u>Contrast</u>: This could be the best plan. *On the other hand*, this plan may lead to more damage.

> **Review Video: Transitions in Writing**
> *Visit mometrix.com/academy and enter Code:* **233246**

Conjunctive Adverbs
Two independent clauses can be joined by a conjunctive (a.k.a. transitional) adverb with one of the following words: *accordingly, besides, hence, however, moreover, nevertheless, then, therefore,* or *thus*. Examples: I worked for eight hours; *therefore*, I deserve a break. We ate cake all week; consequently, we are not eating cake tonight.

Sentence Structures

The four major types of sentence structure are:
1. Simple Sentences - Simple sentences have one independent clause with no subordinate clauses. A simple sentence can have compound elements (e.g., a compound subject or verb). Examples:
   Judy watered the lawn. (Singular Subject & Singular Predicate)
   Judy and Alan watered the lawn. (Compound Subject: Judy and Alan)

2. Compound Sentences - Compound sentences have two or more independent clauses with no dependent clauses. Usually, the independent clauses are joined with a comma and a coordinating conjunction, or they can be joined with a semicolon. Example:
   The time has come, and we are ready.
   I woke up at dawn; then I went outside to watch the sun rise.

3. Complex Sentences - A complex sentence has one independent clause and one or more dependent clauses. Examples:
   Although he had the flu, Harry went to work.
   Marcia got married after she finished college.

4. Compound-Complex Sentences - A compound-complex sentence has at least two independent clauses and at least one dependent clause. Examples:
   John is my friend who went to India, and he brought souvenirs for us.
   You may not know, but we heard the music that you played last night.

> **Review Video: Sentence Structure**
> *Visit mometrix.com/academy and enter Code:* **700478**

Sentence Fragments

A part of a sentence should not be treated like a complete sentence. A sentence must be made of at least one independent clause. An independent clause has a subject and a verb. Remember that the independent clause can stand alone as a sentence. Some fragments are independent clauses that begin with a subordinating word (e.g., as, because, so, etc.). Other fragments may not have a subject, a verb, or both.

A sentence fragment can be repaired in several ways. One way is to put the fragment with a neighbor sentence. Another way is to be sure that punctuation is not needed. You can also turn the fragment into a sentence by adding any missing pieces. Sentence fragments are allowed for writers who want to show off their art. However, for your exam, sentence fragments are not allowed.

Fragment: Because he wanted to sail for Rome.
Correct: He dreamed of Europe because he wanted to sail for Rome.

Run-on Sentences

Run-on sentences are independent clauses that have not been joined by a conjunction. When two or more independent clauses appear in one sentence, they must be joined in one of these ways:
1. Correction with a comma and a coordinating conjunction.
   Incorrect: I went on the trip and I had a good time.
   Correct: I went on the trip, and I had a good time.

2. Correction with a semicolon, a colon, or a dash. Used when independent clauses are closely related and their connection is clear without a coordinating conjunction.
   Incorrect: I went to the store and I bought some eggs.
   Correct: I went to the store; I bought some eggs.

3. Correction by separating sentences. This correction may be used when both independent clauses are long. Also, this can be used when one sentence is a question and one is not.
   Incorrect: The drive to New York takes ten hours it makes me very tired.
   Correct: The drive to New York takes ten hours. So, I become very tired.

4. Correction by changing parts of the sentence. One way is to turn one of the independent clauses into a phrase or subordinate clause.
   Incorrect: The drive to New York takes ten hours it makes me very tired.
   Correct: During the ten hour drive to New York, I become very tired.

Note: Normally, one of these choices will be a clear correction to a run-on sentence. The fourth way can be the best correction but needs the most work.

> ➤ **Review Video: Fragments and Run-on Sentences**
> *Visit **mometrix.com/academy** and enter **Code: 541989***

Dangling and Misplaced Modifiers

Dangling Modifiers
A dangling modifier is a verbal phrase that does not have a clear connection to a word. A dangling modifier can also be a dependent clause (the subject and/or verb are not included) that does not have a clear connection to a word.

Examples:
Dangling: *Reading each magazine article*, the stories caught my attention.
Corrected: Reading each magazine article, *I* was entertained by the stories.

In this example, the word *stories* cannot be modified by *Reading each magazine article*. People can read, but stories cannot read. So, the pronoun *I* is needed for the modifying phrase *Reading each magazine article*.

Dangling: Since childhood, my grandparents have visited me for Christmas.
Corrected: Since childhood, I have been visited by my grandparents for Christmas.

In this example, the dependent adverb clause *Since childhood* cannot modify grandparents. So, the pronoun *I* is needed for the modifying adverb clause.

Misplaced Modifiers
In some sentences, a modifier can be put in more than one place. However, you need to be sure that there is no confusion about which word is being explained or given more detail.

Incorrect: He read the book to a crowd that was filled with beautiful pictures.
Correct: He read the book that was filled with beautiful pictures to a crowd.

The crowd is not filled with pictures. The book is filled with pictures.

Incorrect: John only ate fruits and vegetables for two weeks.
Correct: John ate *only* fruits and vegetables for two weeks.

John may have done nothing else for two weeks but eat fruits and vegetables and sleep. However, it is reasonable to think that John had fruits and vegetables for his meals. Then, he continued to work on other things.

Split Infinitives
A split infinitive is when something comes between the word *to* and the verb that pairs with *to*.
Incorrect: To *clearly* explain | To *softly* sing
Correct: *To explain* clearly | *To sing* softly

Parallelism and Subordination

Parallelism
Parallel structures are used in sentences to highlight similar ideas and to connect sentences that give similar information. Parallelism pairs parts of speech, phrases, or clauses together with a matching piece. To write, *I enjoy <u>reading</u> and <u>to study</u>* would be incorrect. An infinitive does not match with a gerund. Instead, you should write *I enjoy <u>reading</u> and <u>studying</u>*.

Be sure that you continue to use certain words (e.g., articles, linking verbs, prepositions, infinitive sign (to), and the introductory word for a dependent clause) in sentences.

Incorrect: Will you bring the paper and pen with you?
Correct: Will you bring *the* paper and *a* pen with you?

Incorrect: The animals can come to eat and play.
Correct: The animals can come *to* eat and *to* play.

Incorrect: You are the person who remembered my name and cared for me.
Correct: You are the person *who* remembered my name and *who* cared for me.

Subordination

When two items are not equal to each other, you can join them by making the more important piece an independent clause. The less important piece can become subordinate. To make the less important piece subordinate, you make it a phrase or a dependent clause. The piece of more importance should be the one that readers want or will need to remember.
Example:
(1) The team had a perfect regular season. (2) The team lost the championship.
Despite having a perfect regular season, *the team lost the championship.*

Final Notes

Don't Use Your Ear

Read each sentence carefully and put the answer choices into the blanks. Don't stop at the first answer choice if you think that you have the right answer. Read through the choices and think about each choice to know which one is best. At first you may have an answer choice that you think is correct. Then, you may have a different idea after you have read each choice. Don't allow your ear to decide what sounds right. Instead, use your knowledge and think about each answer choice. You may think that some answer choices can be ruled out because they sound incorrect. However, those are the answer choices that may be correct.

Context Clues

To decide on the best answer, you can use context clues as you read through the answer choices. Key words in the sentence will allow you to decide which answer choice is the best to fill in the blank.

Watch Out for Simplicity

When your answer choices seem simple, you need to be careful with the question. Don't pick an answer choice because one choice is long or complicated. A simple or short sentence can be correct. However, not every simple or short sentence will be correct. An answer that is simple and does not make sense may not be correct.

The phrases *of which [...] are* in the below examples are wordy (i.e., too many words) and unnecessary. They should be removed. You can place a colon after the words *sport* and *following*.

Examples:
  1. There are many benefits to running as a sport, *of which the top advantages are*:
  2. The necessary school supplies were the following, *of which a few are*:

Punctuation

Capitalization

The rules for capitalization are:

1. Capitalize the first word of a sentence and the first word in a direct quotation
   Examples:
   First Word: *Football* is my favorite sport.
   Direct Quote: She asked, "*What* is your name?"

2. Capitalize proper nouns and adjectives that come from proper nouns
   Examples:
   Proper Noun: My parents are from *Europe*.
   Adjective from Proper Noun: My father is *British*, and my mother is *Italian*.

3. Capitalize the names of days, months, and holidays
   Examples:
   Day: Everyone needs to be here on *Wednesday*.
   Month: I am so excited for *December*.
   Holiday: *Independence Day* comes every July.

4. Capitalize the names on a compass for specific areas, not when they give direction
   Examples:
   Specific Area: James is from the *West*.
   Direction: After three miles, turn *south* toward the highway.

5. Capitalize the first word for each word in a title (Note: Articles, Prepositions, and Conjunctions are not capitalized.)
   Examples:
   Titles: <u>*Romeo and Juliet*</u> is a beautiful drama on love.
   Incorrect: <u>*The Taming Of The Shrew*</u> is my favorite. (Remember that prepositions and articles are not capitalized.)

   Note: Books, movies, plays (more than one act), newspapers, magazines, and long musical pieces are put in italics. The two examples of Shakespeare's plays are underlined to show their use as an example.

End Punctuation

<u>Periods</u>
Use a period to end all sentences except direct questions, exclamations, and questions.

Declarative Sentence
A declarative sentence gives information or makes a statement.
Examples: I can fly a kite. | The plane left two hours ago.

Imperative Sentence
An imperative sentence gives an order or command.
Examples: You are coming with me. | Bring me that note.

Periods for abbreviations
Examples: 3 P.M. | 2 A.M. | Mr. Jones | Mrs. Stevens | Dr. Smith | Bill Jr. | Pennsylvania Ave.
Note: an abbreviation is a shortened form of a word or phrase.

Question Marks

Question marks should be used following a direct question. A polite request can be followed by a period instead of a question mark.

Direct Question: What is for lunch today? | How are you? | Why is that the answer?

Polite Requests:
Can you please send me the item tomorrow. | Will you please walk with me on the track.

Exclamation Marks

Exclamation marks are used after a word group or sentence that shows much feeling or has special importance. Exclamation marks should not be overused. They are saved for proper exclamatory interjections.
Examples: We're going to the finals! | You have a beautiful car! | That's crazy!

Commas

The comma is a punctuation mark that can help you understand connections in a sentence. Not every sentence needs a comma. However, if a sentence needs a comma, you need to put it in the right place. A comma in the wrong place (or an absent comma) will make a sentence's meaning unclear. These are some of the rules for commas:

1. Use a comma between a coordinating conjunction joining independent clauses
   Example: *Bob caught three fish, and I caught two fish.*

2. Use a comma after an introductory phrase or an adverbial clause
   Examples:
   After the final out, we went to a restaurant to celebrate.
   Studying the stars, I was surprised at the beauty of the sky.

3. Use a comma between items in a series.
   Example: I will bring *the turkey, the pie, and the coffee.*

4. Use a comma between coordinate adjectives not joined with *and*
   Incorrect: The kind, brown dog followed me home.
   Correct: The *kind, loyal* dog followed me home.

   Not all adjectives are coordinate (i.e., equal or parallel). There are two simple ways to know if your adjectives are coordinate. One, you can join the adjectives with *and*: *The kind and loyal dog.* Two, you can change the order of the adjectives: *The loyal, kind dog.*

5. Use commas for interjections and after *yes* and *no* responses
    Examples:
    Interjection: Oh, I had no idea. | Wow, you know how to play this game.
    Yes and No: *Yes,* I heard you. | *No,* I cannot come tomorrow.

6. Use commas to separate nonessential modifiers and nonessential appositives
    Examples:
    Nonessential Modifier: John Frank, who is coaching the team, was promoted today.

    Nonessential Appositive: Thomas Edison, an American inventor, was born in Ohio.

7. Use commas to set off nouns of direct address, interrogative tags, and contrast
    Examples:
    Direct Address: You, *John,* are my only hope in this moment.
    Interrogative Tag: This is the last time, *correct*?
    Contrast: You are my friend, *not my enemy.*

8. Use commas with dates, addresses, geographical names, and titles
    Examples:
    Date: *July 4, 1776,* is an important date to remember.
    Address: He is meeting me at *456 Delaware Avenue,* tomorrow morning.
    Geographical Name: *Paris, France,* is my favorite city.
    Title: John Smith, *Ph. D.,* will be visiting your class today.

9. Use commas to separate expressions like *he said* and *she said* if they come between a sentence of a quote
    Examples:
    "I want you to know," he began, "that I always wanted the best for you."
    "You can start," Jane said, "with an apology."

> ➤ **Review Video: Commas**
> *Visit **mometrix.com/academy** and enter **Code: 644254***

Semicolons

The semicolon is used to connect major sentence pieces of equal value. Some rules for semicolons include:
1. Use a semicolon between closely connected independent clauses that are not connected with a coordinating conjunction.
    Examples:
    She is outside; we are inside.
    You are right; we should go with your plan.

2. Use a semicolon between independent clauses linked with a transitional word.
    Examples:
    I think that we can agree on this; *however,* I am not sure about my friends.
    You are looking in the wrong places; *therefore,* you will not find what you need.

3. Use a semicolon between items in a series that has internal punctuation.
   Example: I have visited *New York, New York; Augusta, Maine; and Baltimore, Maryland.*

> ➤ **Review Video:** <u>Semicolon Usage</u>
> *Visit **mometrix.com/academy** and enter **Code: 370605***

Colons

The colon is used to call attention to the words that follow it. A colon must come after an independent clause. The rules for colons are as follows:
1. Use a colon after an independent clause to make a list
   Example: I want to learn many languages: Spanish, French, German, and Italian.

2. Use a colon for explanations or to give a quote
   Examples:
   Quote: The man started with an idea: "We are able to do more than we imagine."

   Explanation: There is one thing that stands out on your resume: your responsibility.

3. Use a colon after the greeting in a formal letter, to show hours and minutes, and to separate a title and subtitle
   Examples:
   Greeting in a formal letter: Dear Sir: | To Whom It May Concern:

   Time: It is 3:14 P.M.

   Title: The essay is titled "America: A Short Introduction to a Modern Country"

Quotation Marks

Use quotation marks to close off direct quotations of a person's spoken or written words. Do not use quotation marks around indirect quotations. An indirect quotation gives someone's message without using the person's exact words. Use single quotation marks to close off a quotation inside a quotation.

Direct Quote: Nancy said, "I am waiting for Henry to arrive."

Indirect Quote: Henry said that he is going to be late to the meeting.

Quote inside a Quote: The teacher asked, "Has everyone read 'The Gift of the Magi'?"

Quotation marks should be used around the titles of short works: newspaper and magazine articles, poems, short stories, songs, television episodes, radio programs, and subdivisions of books or web sites.
Examples:
"Rip van Winkle" (short story by Washington Irving)
"O Captain! My Captain!" (poem by Walt Whitman)

Quotation marks may be used to set off words that are being used in a different way from a dictionary definition. Also, they can be used to highlight irony.
Examples:
The boss warned Frank that he was walking on "thin ice."
(Frank is not walking on real ice. Instead, Frank is being warned to not make a mistake.)

The teacher thanked the young man for his "honesty."
(Honesty and truth are not always the same thing. In this example, the quotation marks around *honesty* show that the teacher does not believe the young man.)

> ➤ **Review Video: Quotation Marks**
> *Visit **mometrix.com/academy** and enter **Code:** **118471***

Note: Periods and commas are put inside quotation marks. Colons and semicolons are put outside the quotation marks. Question marks and exclamation points are placed inside quotation marks when they are a part of a quote. When the question or exclamation mark goes with the whole sentence, the mark is left outside of the quotation marks.
Examples:
Period and comma: We read "Peter Pan," "Alice in Wonderland," and "Cinderella."

Semicolon: They watched "The Nutcracker"; then, they went home.

Exclamation mark that is a part of a quote: The crowd cheered, "Victory!"

Question mark that goes with the whole sentence: Is your favorite book "The Hobbit"?

Apostrophes

An apostrophe is used to show possession or the deletion of letters in contractions. An apostrophe is not needed with the possessive pronouns *his, hers, its, ours, theirs, whose,* and *yours.*

Singular Nouns: David's car | a book's theme | my brother's board game
Plural Nouns with -*s*: the scissors' handle | boys' basketball
Plural Nouns without -*s*: Men's department | the people's adventure

> ➤ **Review Video: Apostrophes**
> *Visit **mometrix.com/academy** and enter **Code:** **213068***

Paragraph Development

Unrelated and Supporting Sentences

The sentences of a paragraph are shaped by the purpose of the paragraph. If the purpose of a paragraph is to explain a task or tell a story, then each sentence should be connected or related to that purpose. In casual conversation, you might add a few personal comments that are loosely related to your subject. In writing, sentences that are unrelated can be confusing and discredit an author.

Example: Unrelated Sentence
Today, we live in a digital age. Information can be sent and received quickly and easily. The Internet allows this ease of exchange in information. More newspapers, journals, and books are made available everyday on the Internet. With more information being spread digitally, many forests will be saved.

The unrelated sentence in this paragraph is the last sentence. The paragraph covers the idea of digital information being spread with ease. So, the final sentence in this paragraph may be a fact, but it is unrelated to the idea of passing on more information.

Example: Supporting Sentence
Intercity passenger rail is used widely in Europe and Japan. In the United States, it could have many benefits to society by complementing other heavily used modes of transportation.

_____ Rail transport can compete in markets comprised of nearby cities as well as along routes that parallel heavily traveled highways.

Which of the following should be a supporting sentence in the paragraph?

A. As everyone knows, traffic between overpopulated cities is growing worse every year, and Americans could use an alternative method of transportation.

B. Potential benefits include controlling increases in air and highway traffic, decreasing pollution caused by aircraft and automobiles, reducing fuel consumption, and increasing passenger safety.

C. Of course, Congress would have to approve the funding for the Department of Transportation to carry out all the aspects of this project.

D. Many people in the United States value the freedom of driving themselves, but this could be a benefit for tourism.

The best answer is choice B. The reason is that the supporting sentence should explain the potential benefits of passenger rail after mentioning that there are "many benefits to society" by installing intercity rail.

Development of a Topic Sentence

A paragraph should be unified around a main point. Normally, a good topic sentence summarizes the paragraph's main point. A topic sentence is a general sentence that gives an introduction to the paragraph. The sentences that follow are a support to the topic sentence. You may use the topic sentence as the final sentence to the paragraph if the earlier sentences give a clear explanation of the topic sentence. Overall, you need to stay true to the main point. This means that you need to remove unnecessary sentences that do not advance the main point.

Example: Topic Sentence
In the late 19th century, the first practical telephone was invented.

Which of the following should come after the topic sentence?

A. Many advancements with the phone continue with other changes in technology.
B. Telephones have come a long way since the 1800s.
C. The inventor of this telephone was Alexander Graham Bell.
D. We would not be where we are today without this invention.

The best answer is choice C. The reason is that it supports the topic sentence with information about the inventor of the device in the 19th century.

Ways to Develop Paragraphs
A common way to develop paragraphs can be done with **examples**. These examples are the supporting details to the main idea of a paragraph or passage. When an audience may be confused by an author's idea, the author can give an example to show his or her point. When authors write about something that is not easily accepted, they can also give examples to prove their point.

Analogies make comparisons between items that appear to have nothing in common. Analogies are employed by writers to provoke fresh thoughts about a subject. They may be used to explain the unfamiliar, to clarify an abstract point, or to argue a point. Although analogies are effective literary devices, they should be used carefully. Two things may be alike in some respects but completely different in others.

Cause and effect is an excellent device used when the cause and effect are accepted as true. One way of using cause and effect is to state the effect in the topic sentence of a paragraph and add the causes in the body of the paragraph. With this method, your paragraphs can have structure which always strengthens writing.

Practice Tests

Language Practice Questions

For Questions 1-4, select the correct punctuation mark for the sentence.

1. I knew the price of housing was going to increase but I had no idea that it would go up so much!
    A. ;
    B. :
    C. ,
    D. None

2. As a matter of fact everything she said was true.
    A. ;
    B. –
    C. ,
    D. None

3. Michael had been studying for this exam for two weeks but still could not pass.
    A. ;
    B. :
    C. ,
    D. None

4. Are you sure that Mark said, "the plants will arrive on Saturday".
    A. :
    B. !
    C. ?
    D. None

For Questions 5-7, choose the best word or phrase to complete the sentence.

5. This tree _____ a lot since I started watering it more.
    A. grew
    B. is growing
    C. has grown
    D. grows

6. Barney did really _____ and finished in the top three in the competition.
    A. excellent
    B. well
    C. good
    D. fine

7. My mother gave the tickets to my brother and ____.
    A. I
    B. they
    C. she
    D. me

For Questions 8-18, select the complete sentence that is written correctly.

8.
    A. A group of six people are affected.
    B. This box of papers belong in the desk
    C. A collection of stamps is selling for a dollar.
    D. Two hundred cars, every hour, cross the bridge.

9.
    A. The water is fall to the ground.
    B. She and her mother went to church.
    C. The sheriff were waiting for them.
    D. Not, another word out of you.

10.
    A. He applied for a loan.
    B. One of a kind.
    C. They struggled, for nearly an hour.
    D. Coming out of the country.

11.
    A. Renting a movie is less fun than the excitement of being there.
    B. Her native language, French was easier for her to speak than English.
    C. In a challenging environment, she found the best in herself.
    D. We went shopping for a new camera, most were digital models.

12.
    A. Here today gone tomorrow
    B. It wouldn't have happened if I hadn't went there.
    C. A stitch in time, saves nine.
    D. Give me a dollar.

13.
    A. Not an option.
    B. Holiday shopping.
    C. Can you open this for me, please?
    D. This one is mine, that one is her's.

14.
    A. It's no wonder that his friends nicknamed him Goth.
    B. He ain't done nothing but sleep.
    C. He was a habitual scoundrel; one who would beat the check in restaurants.
    D. Cold soup don't taste good.

15.
  A. The plaintiff, who plans to appeal appeared unfazed.
  B. She'll get paid, I hope, within a few weeks.
  C. Of the three she was the tallest.
  D. I couldn't hardly wait for the sequel.

16.
  A. Do you know the poem "Wait Until Later?"
  B. "Of all the stories in this book," she said, "this is my favorite."
  C. Jack mentioned the poem Ode to a Nightingale in his letter.
  D. Mike's father asked him "what was wrong."

17.
  A. In the local currency yen everything seemed to be more expensive.
  B. My new car a Honda.
  C. I don't understand why she keeps calling me?
  D. Is there anyone here with change of a dollar?

18.
  A. Got a couple of friends to help me.
  B. "Canada" is a country in North America.
  C. She was feeling weak and almost fainted.
  D. When boating I always wear a life vest.

For Questions 19-22, select the answer that best combines the underlined sentences into one.

19. I spent $25,000 on a new car.
  I don't have enough money left for maintenance.
  A. After spending $25,000 on a new car, I don't have enough money left for maintenance.
  B. I spent $25,000 on a new car because I don't have enough money left for maintenance.
  C. I spent $25,000 on a new car when I don't have enough money left for maintenance.
  D. When I spent $25,000 on a new car I don't have enough money left for maintenance.

20. She was the first female president of the company.
  Her success met with derision from many people in the community.
  A. When her success met with derision from many people in the community, she was the first female president of the company.
  B. She was the first female president of the company, but her success met with derision from many people in the community.
  C. She was the first female president of the company, whenever her success met with derision from many people in the community.
  D. She was the first female president of the company whose success met with derision from many people in the community

21. The center fielder broke the season record for home runs.
  He was handsomely rewarded.
  A. The handsome center fielder was rewarded for breaking the season record for home runs.
  B. The center fielder was handsomely rewarded, breaking the season record for home runs.
  C. The center fielder was handsomely rewarded for breaking the season record for home runs.
  D. The handsomely rewarded center fielder broke the season record for home runs.

22. <u>The mechanic performed a number of diagnostic tests on the car.</u>
    <u>The mechanic used a computer to perform the diagnostic tests.</u>
    A. While performing a number of diagnostic tests on the car, the mechanic used a computer to perform the tests.
    B. Although the mechanic used a computer, he performed a number of diagnostic tests on the car.
    C. Because he used a computer, the mechanic performed a number of diagnostic tests on the car.
    D. The mechanic used a computer to perform a number of diagnostic tests on the car.

For Questions 23-28, choose the best sentence to fill in the blank in the paragraph.

23. _____. This letter tells the employer why you are qualified for the job you are applying for. Effective application letters explain the reasons for your interest in the specific organization and identify your most relevant skills or experiences.
    A. A letter of application should be sent with your resume to provide additional information.
    B. It is not enough merely to send a resume in with your job application.
    C. The resume and letter of application demonstrate your qualifications to prospective employers.
    D. When applying for a job, always request a personal interview.

24. _____. Books may be thrown from shelving. Roofs, rooms and buildings may collapse, burying collections under furniture, beams, dirt and debris, or leaving collections exposed and vulnerable to wind, rain and snow. Structural collapse may cause broken gas and power lines, leading to fire damage to collections as well as water damage from fire hoses and sprinklers.
    A. People are frequently killed by earthquakes.
    B. The Loma Prieta earthquake did a lot of damage to libraries and their collections.
    C. Earthquakes can damage library collections in many ways.
    D. Never go into a library during an earthquake.

25. Sunscreens are lotions that help prevent the sun's ultraviolet rays from reaching the skin. _____. UVB is the main cause of sunburn, whereas the more penetrating UVA rays are the cause of wrinkling and sagging of the skin. They also add to the carcinogenic effects of UVB rays. Sunscreens vary in their ability to protect against UVA and UVB.
    A. You can get a sunburn on cloudy days as well as on sunny ones.
    B. There are two types of ultraviolet radiation, UVA and UVB, that damage skin and increase the risk of skin cancer.
    C. The sun is particularly damaging at high altitudes.
    D. A day without coffee is like a day without sunshine.

26. Most banks offer checking accounts for their customers. Usually, they require an initial deposit before establishing a new account, along with identification and proof of address. You may opt for a no-frills checking account, which doesn't charge fees, or choose one that pays interest but requires maintaining a high minimum balance. _____.
    A. A bank is an institution that provides financial services to its customers.
    B. Banks are licensed by the government.
    C. There may also be surcharges for ATM usage and other services.
    D. Banking is a rewarding profession.

27. The Florida Everglades cover thousands of square miles between the east and west coasts of Florida. Everglades National Park is the centerpiece of the region, but there are other great places to explore. _____. The weather is mild, birds are abundant, and there are fewer mosquitoes than at other times of year.

    A. The best time to visit is during the winter, from November through early April.

    B. The park is run by the National Parks Service.

    C. Many visitors come to see the alligators.

    D. One way to see the Everglades is by boat.

28. Organic food standards are defined by a 2002 federal law. _____. Use of pesticides and other synthetic chemicals is forbidden. As a result of this law, wherever you go in the fifty states you can be certain that produce carrying an organic label was grown in accordance with the same standards. That fact has helped increase organic food sales.

    A. You can now buy organic foods at most markets.

    B. Many other laws were passed in 2002.

    C. Organic foods are sometimes more expensive.

    D. It outlines how products must be grown in order to be certified organic.

For Questions 29 and 30, choose the best sentence to follow and develop the topic sentence that is given.

29. Tooth enamel is the hardest part of the human body.

    A. Most people have 32 teeth.

    B. It is made almost entirely of minerals, with a small amount of organic material.

    C. Dentures, bridges and fillings are common dental appliances.

    D. You should visit your dentist regularly to take care of you teeth.

30. More than 200 people were rescued after an Egyptian ferry sank in the Red Sea.

    A. The Red Sea is a popular tourist destination in the Middle East.

    B. Egypt is the most populous country in North Africa.

    C. Authorities blamed rough seas and overloading of the ferry.

    D. January is the coldest month in these waters.

For questions 31 and 32, select the sentence that does not belong in the paragraph.

31. In 1957 Fortune magazine ran an article about Jean Paul Getty. (a) It suggested that Getty was the richest man in the world. (b) A museum is built on his estate today. (c) An interviewer asked Getty how much he thought he could really get in cash if he were to sell his oil, realty, art and other holdings. (d) A note of gone-are-the-better-days crept into his response. "I would hope to realize several billions," he said. "But, remember, a billion dollars isn't worth what it used to be."

    A. a

    B. b

    C. c

    D. d

32. (a) Vegetable oil can be used in as fuel in diesel-powered automobiles. (b) There are almost 250 million automobiles in the U.S. (c) It can even be used as is, without being converted to biodiesel. (d) The difficulty is that straight vegetable oil is much more viscous than conventional diesel fuel or biodiesel: studies have found that it can damage engines. But it can be used if you get a professional engine conversion.

    A. a
    B. b
    C. c
    D. d

For Questions 33-55, read the passage and select the correctly written answer to replace each underlined sentence or phrase.

Passage I

Settlement of Costa Rica began in 1522. For nearly three centuries, Spain administered the region under a military governor. The Spanish optimistically called the country "Rich Coast." **33.** <u>Although they found little gold or other valuable minerals in Costa Rica, however, the Spanish turned to agriculture</u>.

34. <u>An equalness tradition arose in Costa Rica during the early years of Spanish colonization.</u> This tradition survived the widened class distinctions brought on by the 19th-century introduction of banana and coffee cultivation and consequent accumulations of local wealth.

Costa Rica joined other Central American provinces in 1821 in a joint declaration of independence from Spain. **35.** <u>The newly independent provinces formed a federation when border disputes broke out among them</u>. **36.** <u>Costa Rica's northern Guanacaste Province was annexed from Nicaragua in one such dispute</u>. In 1838, Costa Rica formally withdrew from the Federation and proclaimed itself sovereign.

33.
    A. Finding little gold or other valuable minerals in Costa Rica, however, the Spanish turned to agriculture.
    B. Because of not finding gold or other valuable minerals in Costa Rica, then, the Spanish turned to agriculture.
    C. There turned out to be no gold or other valuable minerals in Costa Rica, however, the Spanish turned to agriculture.
    D. Finding out about gold or other valuable minerals in Costa Rica, however, the Spanish turned to agriculture.

34.
    A. A tradition where everyone is equal arose in Costa Rica during the early years of Spanish colonization.
    B. A democratic tradition arose in Costa Rica during the early years of Spanish colonization.
    C. An egalitarian tradition arose in Costa Rica during the early years of Spanish colonization.
    D. A commensurate tradition rose up in Costa Rica during the early years of Spanish colonization.

35.

    A. The newly independent provinces formed a Federation, because border disputes broke out among them.

    B. Although the newly independent provinces formed a Federation, border disputes breaking out among them.

    C. The newly independent provinces formed a Federation with the border disputes that broke out among them.

    D. Although the newly independent provinces formed a Federation, border disputes broke out among them.

36.

    A. Costa Rica's northern Guanacaste Province, was annexed from Nicaragua in one such dispute.

    B. Costa Rica's northern Guanacaste Province was annexed, from Nicaragua, in one such dispute.

    C. Costa Rica's northern Guanacaste Province was annexed in one such dispute from Nicaragua.

    D. Costa Rica's northern Guanacaste Province was annexed from Nicaragua in one such dispute.

Passage II

It's easy to patch a bicycle inner tube! **37.** <u>The technology has been round a long time, and is quite reliable</u> if the job is done properly. Here's how:

38. <u>First select a patch slightly larger than the size of the hole.</u>

Next, use sandpaper to **39.**<u>rough the surface of the tube at an area somewhat larger than the patch.</u>

40.<u>Buff the tube so that it don't shine any more.</u> If there is a molding line in the area where the patch is to be applied, sand it down completely or it will leak.

41.<u>Apply a dab of rubber cement then spread a thin coat.</u> Work quickly.

Allow the cement to dry completely.

Peel the foil from the patch and press the patch onto the tube firmly.

Squeeze the patch tightly onto the tube. **42.**<u>Now, re-inflate the tire and you finished!</u>

This procedure should give you a tire that is as good as new.

37.

    A. The technology has been round a long time and is quite reliable

    B. The technology has been around a long time, and is quite reliable

    C. The technology has been around for a long time, and is quite reliable

    D. The technology has been around for a long time and is quite reliable

38.

    A. First select a patch slightly larger than the size of the hole.

    B. First, select a patch slightly larger than the size of the hole.

    C. First select a patch, slightly larger than the size of the hole.

    D. First select a patch: slightly larger than the size of the hole.

39.

    A. roughen the surface of the tube at an area somewhat larger than the patch.

    B. rough up the surface of the tube at an area somewhat larger than the patch.

    C. roughen a portion of the tube surface with an area somewhat larger than the patch.

    D. roughen the surface of the tube with an area somewhat larger than the patch.

40.
    A. Buff the tube so that it don't shine no more.
    B. Buff the tube so that it doesn't shine any more.
    C. Buff the tube so that it doesn't shine no more.
    D. Buff the tube so that it don't shine.

41.
    A. Applying a dab of rubber cement then spread a thin coat.
    B. Apply a dab of rubber cement then spreads a thin coat.
    C. Apply a dab of rubber cement, and then spread a thin coat.
    D. Apply a dab of rubber cement and, then, spread a thin coat.

42.
    A. Now, re-inflate the tire and you're finished!
    B. Now re-inflate the tire and your finished!
    C. Now, re-inflate the tire and your finished!
    D. Now re-inflate the tire and you've finished!

Passage III

43. Norway's economy relies heavy upon oil and gas. Exports of these commodities account for roughly half of all export earnings. **44.** Other exports include metals ships and fish. Norway is one of the world's top 10 fishing nations. **45.** Agriculture is diversified and is a great deal of livestock, though **46.** more than half of the country's food needs are imported.

43.
    A. Norway's economy relies upon heavy oil and gas.
    B. Norway's economy relies heavily upon oil and gas.
    C. Norways economy relies heavy upon oil and gas.
    D. Norways economy relies heavily upon oil and gas.

44.
    A. Other exports include metal ships and fish.
    B. Other exports includes metals ships and fish.
    C. Other exports include metals ships and fishes.
    D. Other exports include metals, ships, and fish.

45.
    A. Agriculture is diversified and there is a great deal of livestock
    B. Agriculture is diversified and with a great deal of livestock
    C. Agriculture is diversified and includes a great deal of livestock
    D. Agriculture is diversified and has a great deal of livestock

46.
    A. more than half of the country's food is imported
    B. more than half of the countries food needs are imported
    C. more than half the country's food needs are imported
    D. more than half of the countries foods are imported

Passage IV

47. <u>Patient's with tennis elbow are having pain outside of the elbow</u>. It is made worse when grasping objects or drawing back the wrist. The most common symptoms of tennis elbow are pain over the outside of the elbow and pain when lifting objects. **48.** <u>The pain is often radiating down the forearm to the hand.</u>

The pain associated with tennis elbow **49.** <u>usually came on gradually but it could also be sudden</u>. Most patients are between the ages of 35 and 65. **50.** <u>The syndrome affects men and women the same</u>, usually occurring in the dominant arm. **51.** <u>Anyone can be affected, but mostly they were either manual laborers or active sports participants.</u>

47.
  A. Patient's with tennis elbow experience pain outside of the elbow.
  B. Patients with tennis elbow have pain outside of the elbow.
  C. Patients with tennis elbow experience pain on the outside of the elbow.
  D. Patients with tennis elbow pain have it on the outside elbow.

48.
  A. The pain often radiates down the forearm to the hand.
  B. The pain often radiated down the forearm to the hand.
  C. The pain is often goes and radiates down the forearm to the hand.
  D. The pain is often radiation down the forearm to the hand.

49.
  A. usually came on gradually but could also be sudden
  B. usually comes on gradually but may also be sudden
  C. usually comes on gradually, but could also be sudden
  D. usually comes on gradually but is also sudden

50.
  A. The syndrome affects men and women too,
  B. The syndrome affects men and women also,
  C. The syndrome affects men and women similarly,
  D. The syndrome affects men and women the same,

51.
  A. Anyone can be affected, but mostly manual laborers or active sports participants.
  B. Anyone can be affected, but mostly it's either manual laborers or active sports participants.
  C. Anyone can be affected, but most patients were either manual laborers or active sports participants.
  D. Anyone can be affected, but most patients are either manual laborers or active sports participants.

Passage V

The traditional form of home mortgage loan is the fixed rate variety. The term "fixed rate" mortgage refers to the fact that **52.** <u>the interest rate ain't going to change over the life of the loan.</u> The major advantage of this type of loan is that **53.** <u>it is predictable, the payments remain the same over the</u> <u>duration of the loan.</u> Compare this to an adjustable rate mortgage (ARM): **54.** <u>In these loans the interest rate and therefore the payment change regularly</u> based upon market conditions. **55.** <u>When interest rates are low, an adjustable rate mortgage may seem like an</u> <u>attractive option however when interest rates go up so will your monthly mortgage payment.</u>

52.
- A. the interest rate don't change over the life of the loan.
- B. the interest rate doesn't change over the life of the loan.
- C. the interest rate won't be going to change over the life of the loan.
- D. the interest rate won't be changing over the life of the loan.

53.
- A. it is predictable, the payments remain the same over the duration of the loan.
- B. it is predictable (the payments remain the same over the duration of the loan).
- C. it is predictable: the payments remain the same over the duration of the loan.
- D. it is predictable; the payments remain the same over the duration of the loan.

54.
- A. in these loans the interest rate and so the payment change regularly
- B. in these loans the interest rate and also the payment change regularly
- C. in these loans the interest rate and even the payment change regularly
- D. in these loans the interest rate, and therefore the payment, change regularly

55.
- A. When interest rates are low, an adjustable rate mortgage may seem like an attractive option. However, when interest rates go up so will your monthly mortgage payment.
- B. When interest rates are low, an adjustable rate mortgage may seem like an attractive option, however, when interest rates go up so will your monthly mortgage payment.
- C. When interest rates are low, an adjustable rate mortgage may seem like an attractive option however when they go up so will your monthly mortgage payment.
- D. When interest rates are low, an adjustable rate mortgage may seem like an attractive option, when interest rates go up so will your monthly mortgage payment.

Reading Skills Practice Questions

Look at the chart below, which shows average reading scores from five rural public schools in standardized tests administered in 2006 and 2007. Then, answer Questions 1-3.

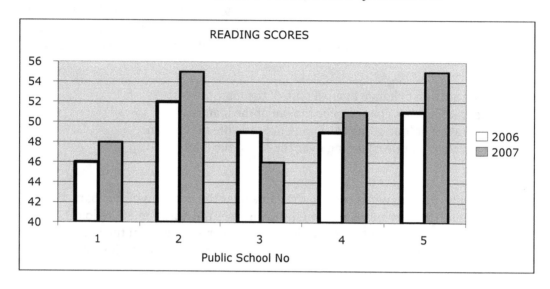

1. Which public school had the lowest average reading score in 2007?
   A. School 1
   B. School 3
   C. School 4
   D. School 5

2. Which public school registered the greatest improvement in reading scores from 2006 to 2007?
   A. School 1
   B. School 2
   C. School 4
   D. School 5

3. What was the highest average reading score obtained by any of the schools during 2006?
   A. 52
   B. 53
   C. 54
   D. 55

Find the answers to Questions 4-8 by reading the chart.

Table 1. Consumer Price Index for All Urban Consumers (CPI-U): U.S. city average, by expenditure category and commodity and service group

(1982-84=100, unless otherwise noted)

Item and group	Relative importance, December 2008	Unadjusted indexes		Unadjusted percent change to June 2009 from—		Seasonally adjusted percent change from—		
		May 2009	June 2009	June 2008	May 2009	Mar. to Apr.	Apr. to May	May to June
Expenditure category								
All items	100.000	213.856	215.693	-1.4	0.9	0.0	0.1	0.7
All items (1967=100)	-	640.616	646.121	-	-	-	-	-
Food and beverages	15.757	218.076	218.030	2.2	.0	-.2	-.2	.1
Food	14.629	217.826	217.740	2.1	.0	-.2	-.2	.0
Food at home	8.156	215.088	214.824	.8	-.1	-.6	-.5	.0
Cereals and bakery products	1.150	252.714	253.008	3.0	.1	-.7	-.2	.0
Meats, poultry, fish, and eggs	1.898	203.789	204.031	.6	.1	.0	-.9	-.2
Dairy and related products [1]	.910	196.055	194.197	-7.1	-.9	-1.3	-.5	-.9
Fruits and vegetables	1.194	274.006	272.608	-1.9	-.5	.0	-1.0	1.1
Nonalcoholic beverages and beverage materials	.982	162.803	162.571	2.7	-.1	-1.0	-.1	.1
Other food at home	2.022	191.144	191.328	4.1	.1	-.8	-.1	.0
Sugar and sweets	.300	196.403	197.009	6.2	.3	-.5	.0	.2
Fats and oils	.241	200.679	201.127	2.5	.2	-1.4	-.7	.6
Other foods	1.481	205.587	205.654	3.9	.0	-.8	.0	-.2
Other miscellaneous foods [1,2]	.433	122.838	122.224	3.2	-.5	.4	.0	-.5
Food away from home [1]	6.474	223.023	223.163	3.8	.1	.3	.1	.1
Other food away from home [1,2] ...	.314	155.099	155.841	4.0	.5	.4	.0	.5
Alcoholic beverages	1.127	220.005	220.477	3.1	.2	-.1	.3	.2
Housing	43.421	216.971	218.071	.1	.5	-.1	-.1	.0
Shelter	33.200	249.779	250.243	1.3	.2	.2	.1	.1
Rent of primary residence [3]	5.957	249.069	249.092	2.7	.0	.2	.1	.1
Lodging away from home [2]	2.478	135.680	138.318	-6.9	1.9	.5	.1	.3
Owners' equivalent rent of primary residence [3,4]	24.433	256.875	256.981	1.9	.0	.1	.1	.1
Tenants' and household insurance [1,2]	.333	120.728	121.083	1.7	.3	-.1	.0	.3
Fuels and utilities	5.431	206.358	212.677	-8.1	3.1	-1.7	-1.3	-.8
Household energy	4.460	183.783	190.647	-10.8	3.7	-2.2	-1.8	-1.0
Fuel oil and other fuels	.301	225.164	232.638	-40.3	3.3	-2.1	-3.1	2.0
Gas (piped) and electricity [3]	4.159	189.619	196.754	-7.8	3.8	-2.2	-1.7	-1.2
Water and sewer and trash collection services [2]	.971	159.517	159.831	6.2	.2	.6	.6	.4
Household furnishings and operations ..	4.790	129.644	129.623	1.6	.0	.0	.0	.0
Household operations [1,2]	.781	149.468	149.995	1.3	.4	-.1	-.9	.4
Apparel	3.691	121.751	118.799	1.5	-2.4	-.2	-.2	.7
Men's and boys' apparel	.923	117.146	112.849	.7	-3.7	-1.7	.4	-.5
Women's and girls' apparel	1.541	109.460	106.455	2.1	-2.7	.2	-.1	1.6
Infants' and toddlers' apparel	.183	114.142	113.915	2.1	-.2	1.3	-1.6	2.2
Footwear	.688	127.519	125.515	1.6	-1.6	.4	.1	.2
Transportation	15.314	175.997	183.735	-13.2	4.4	-.4	.8	4.2
Private transportation	14.189	171.757	179.649	-13.3	4.6	-.3	.9	4.5
New and used motor vehicles [2]	6.931	92.701	93.020	-.6	.3	.4	.5	.4
New vehicles	4.480	135.162	135.719	.9	.4	.4	.5	.7
Used cars and trucks	1.628	122.650	124.323	-8.6	1.4	-.1	1.0	.9
Motor fuel	3.164	193.609	225.021	-35.2	16.2	-2.6	2.7	17.2
Gasoline (all types)	2.964	193.727	225.526	-34.6	16.4	-2.8	3.1	17.3
Motor vehicle parts and equipment [1]	.382	134.347	134.270	5.0	-.1	.1	-.2	-.1
Motor vehicle maintenance and repair [1]	1.188	242.488	242.683	4.1	.1	.2	-.1	.1
Public transportation	1.125	228.878	232.540	-12.1	1.6	-.8	-1.0	-.5

4. Which of the following expense categories decreased in the year prior to June 2009?
   A. Rent of primary residence
   B. Boys' and men's apparel
   C. Transportation
   D. Meats, fish, and eggs

5. On a seasonally adjusted basis, which of the following decreased by the greatest percentage between April and May of 2009?
   A. Gasoline
   B. Fuel oil and other fuels
   C. Infants' and toddlers' apparel
   D. Fruits and vegetables

6. In the month prior to June 2009, which of the following prices did not change at all?
    A. Public transportation
    B. Used cars and trucks
    C. Food
    D. Housing

7. According to the organization of the table, which of the following expense categories is not considered to be a component of the "Food at Home" category?
    A. Cereals and bakery products
    B. Fats and oils
    C. Other miscellaneous foods
    D. Alcoholic beverages

8. Which expenditure category was the most important in December of 2008?
    A. Housing
    B. Food and Beverages
    C. Apparel
    D. Transportation

Read this article on food storage, then answer Questions 9-14.

Food Storage Containers

Plastic is one of the most common materials used for food storage. Plastic containers, bags and boxes, are inexpensive, lightweight, and convenient. But is plastic safe? The answer to this question may not be a simple one, as there are many different varieties of plastic, manufactured by different processes. Some of these processes employ phthalates, a type of chemical used to soften the plastic so that it may be molded. And, there is mounting evidence that phthalates may be toxic.

The most common phthalate is *bis*-phenol A, commonly known as BPA. BPA has been declared safe for food storage by the Food and Drug Administration, but the FDA relied on information supplied by the chemical industry to reach that conclusion. Recent evidence has called its decision into doubt, and the agency has announced that it will review its earlier determination.

The concern about BPA's toxicity is widespread, especially when food is stored for young children. Its use in baby bottles has been banned in Canada and in several states in the U.S., and Connecticut has prohibited it in all reusable food containers.

Traces of BPA can be found in foods that have been stored in containers made of polycarbonate and other plastic materials. But these are not limited to baby bottles or to reusable plastic food-storage containers. Canned foods are also found to be contaminated, since plastic linings are often used in food cans to protect the product from taking on the flavor of the metal. The use of plastics in the food industry is widespread, and calls for its elimination have led to predictable protests.

A particular concern is the use of plastic storage containers to microwave food that is to be warmed before serving. BPA has been found to leach from polycarbonates and form other plastics during this process. Caroline Baier-Anderson, a health scientist and an assistant professor in the Department of Epidemiology and Preventive Medicine at the University of Maryland, Baltimore, told the Washington Post: "It is best not to microwave plastics, particularly since alternatives are widely available."

So how can you avoid the potential problems with plastic food storage? You have three major options when it comes to selecting our food storage containers.

1. Use glass containers. Many of these are available with either glass or plastic lids. Some of the plastic lids are BPA-free, but since the lid comes into only limited contact with the product, the presence of BPA is a lesser concern here.

2. Use stainless steel containers. While glass and steel are expensive, they can be used over many times, so that the cost is eventually amortized. They are heavier than plastic, however.

3. Use safer plastic containers. Some manufacturers have responded to consumer concerns by marketing plastics that are BPA-free. There have been some misleading claims however, so that consumers are advised to seek third-party reviews of particular products. One source of information is thegreenguide.com, a website presented by the National Geographic. It has reviews of specific brands of plastic storage products that have been tested for the presence of BPA.

9. What is the main purpose of this article?
    A. To describe the use of plastic in storing food.
    B. To warn readers about a potential danger in using plastic containers for food storage.
    C. To list a variety of different containers that can be used to store food.
    D. To tell readers not to microwave food in plastic containers.

10. Which of the following statements is true, according to the text?
    A. Canada has banned the use of plastics in baby bottles.
    B. Canada has banned the use of plastics in reusable food containers.
    C. Canada has banned the use of BPA in plastics.
    D. Canada has banned the use of BPA in reusable baby bottles.

11. Which of the following statements best reflects the author's point of view in writing this article?
    A. The author feels that all BPA-containing plastics should be banned.
    B. The author feels that BPA-containing plastics should be banned from use in food containers.
    C. The author wants to offer consumers alternatives to using BPA-containing food storage containers.
    D. The author feels that stainless steel food storage containers are the best for all uses.

12. Phthalates are used in manufacturing plastics
    A. to facilitate molding
    B. to make them toxic
    C. to allow them to be microwaved
    D. to make them safer

13. To avoid potential problems with food storage containers, the author suggests
    A. avoiding all plastics
    B. carefully selecting materials
    C. never using plastics in microwave ovens
    D. avoiding plastic baby bottles

14. Which of the following would the author most likely recommend?
    A. Discarding plastic food storage containers after a single use.
    B. Avoiding canned foods.
    C. Moving to Canada or Connecticut if you have a new baby.
    D. Writing to your congressperson for more information about BPA

Read this article on leatherback turtles, then answer Questions 15-19.

Leatherback Turtle Populations Recover

The Pacific leatherback turtle arrives in California during the late summer to feed on offshore jellyfish populations. In recent years, egg poaching and accidental capture of adults by fishing nets have led to severe reductions of leatherback populations throughout the Pacific. Conservation of remaining populations of this endangered species became a priority for the U.S. Fish and Wildlife Service.

Since leatherbacks nest on tropical beaches, it was long thought that the California visitors originated from nearby colonies in Mexico and Central America. But research during the past decade has shown that these populations actually come from nesting colonies in the western Pacific.

The western populations were also shown to be comprised of several groups with distinct feeding and migratory patterns. Although they are genetically identical, some groups feed on California beaches, while others visit beaches in the eastern and southern Pacific. These results have caused the Fish and Wildlife service to alter its approach to conserving the species.

"To help protect the leatherbacks, we have expanded our central California work to include a variety of conservation and research initiatives in western Pacific island nations," said Jeff Seminoff, head of the Southwest Fisheries Center Marine Turtle Ecology and Assessment Team. "We recently conducted aerial surveys in Papua New Guinea, Papua (Indonesia) and the Solomon Islands, confirming that large numbers of nesting leatherbacks remain only on a few beaches in Papua. This underscores the need to protect these last remaining rookeries before it is too late."

A program of sustained beach conservation efforts is now in progress in Papua and throughout the western Pacific. This project coordinates contributions from local organizations, government and university biologists, World Wildlife Fund researchers and fishery management organizations. Local residents are being trained to monitor the nesting beaches and to evaluate hatching success. Early results have inspired a cautious optimism: leatherback turtle populations seem to be recovering.

An important part of local folklore, the leatherback is known by many names throughout the western Pacific: trousel, tabob, penyubelimbing, leddebak. Once an important food source, it figures in the legends of many island peoples. With the new awareness that the turtles travel broadly across the ocean, the new partnership is now working within the international community to ensure survival of the leatherback for future generations.

Continued success of these conservation efforts will require a more complete understanding of the entire ecosystem in which the turtles live. These highly mobile marine reptiles move freely across one third of the globe, roaming the entire Pacific Ocean. An effective program necessitates a broad approach that includes the restoration of feeding grounds, nesting beaches, and the migratory routes that connect them.

As leatherback turtles journey from one edge of the Pacific to the other, these gentle marine ambassadors are bringing governments, communities and people together to share a common cause of preserving vibrant marine ecosystems for future generations.

15. The passage is primarily concerned with
    A. beach conservation efforts in the western Pacific
    B. the occurrence of leatherback turtles in the legends of island peoples
    C. the geographic origins of California leatherback populations
    D. international efforts to protect leatherback habitats

16. The author's tone in this passage is best described as
    A. hectoring
    B. factual
    C. mobilizing
    D. dismissive

17. California's leatherbacks were thought to come from beaches in Mexico because
    A. these beaches are relatively close
    B. they prefer warm water
    C. they are poor swimmers
    D. they are genetic variants

18. The article tells us that leatherback turtle populations are presently
    A. recovering rapidly due to conservation efforts
    B. an important source of food for many native populations
    C. highly mobile
    D. recovering on a small scale

19. The article implies that effective measures to protect the leatherback turtle will require an understanding of
    A. native myths
    B. the diet of Third World people
    C. a combination of interacting factors
    D. foreign governments

Read this passage about teaching children about money, then answer Questions 20-24.

Have you ever bought your child a toy to calm a tantrum? Most parents experience moments like this, moments where money comes into play. But money doesn't always buy happiness, especially when it comes to kids.

Kids start learning about money from a very early age. In fact, today's children have more money than ever: extra income spent on snacks, toys, and clothing. It is estimated that more than 10 million youths between the ages of 10 and 18 receive regular allowances from their parents, averaging over $50 per week.

While today's young people may have more money to spend than ever before, their understanding of savings and values hasn't improved. For example, most young people don't know how to calculate the interest earned on a savings account. For the most part, they don't understand how to manage debt or invest for future expenses like college tuition.

Educators say that parents should teach their children about financial responsibility. Early lessons will go a long way toward fostering positive attitudes and habits later in life. Young children learn about money through everyday activities like grocery shopping, and watching their parents pay bills and withdraw cash from the ATM. Family discussions can also help. Take the time to explain the basics to your child: that there is a certain amount of money that comes into the household and a certain amount of money that goes out, and that essential expenses-food, utilities, and clothing-must be paid from that money.

Most children have no idea where money comes from. Ask them, and they will say, "From the ATM machine." Take the time to explain to your children that you must work to earn your money, that you must put it into the bank before you can withdraw it from the ATM machine. Giving a child an allowance tied to the performance of certain family chores is an excellent way to teach this concept.

Here are some ideas for interacting with your children on the subject of money:

Talk money. Routinely discuss how money is earned and spent. Explain your purchasing decisions: "We are buying apples because they are on sale" or "We need electricity so I have to pay the bill."

Model behavior. Children develop their attitudes from what they see you do, not what they hear you say. A lesson on the value of money might also involve family activities: "Let's rent a movie instead of all going to the theater. We can save for our family vacation."

Set limits. Even if you can buy everything your child asks for, consider the wisdom of setting some boundaries. Learn to say no to your child and be firm.

Provide freedom. As your children grow up and learn more, let them make their own decisions about money and personal finances. Support their decision-making with advice, but gradually cede the final decision.

Teach saving. For young children, a personal piggy bank is a good way to introduce concepts of money and savings. Early opportunities to save help develop a lifelong respect for the value of money. Money can be set aside for a favorite toy, as well as for future goals like college or a car.

20. This passage is best described as
    A. humorous
    B. factual
    C. advising
    D. dramatic

21. The purpose of the first paragraph is to
    A. capture attention by relating the topic to something in the reader's personal experience.
    B. introduce the topic of tantrums.
    C. suggest that rich children are not happy.
    D. show how money can be used to induce children to behave well.

22. The article argues that
   A. young children should not be trusted with money.
   B. parents should discuss money with children from an early age.
   C. children should be given ATM cards.
   D. parents should buy children whatever they can afford.

23. One suggestion in the article about allowances is that they
   A. should be generous.
   B. should not be given.
   C. should be tied to some responsibilities.
   D. should be given on a monthly basis.

24. The author is of the opinion that
   A. children should be given no say in money matters.
   B. children should be allowed to spend their own money however they wish.
   C. children should not be given money at all.
   D. children should be given increasing freedom to make their own decisions about how to spend money.

Read the following paragraph, then answer Questions 25-28.

The Nigerian Letter Fraud

Nigerian letter frauds are variations of advance fee schemes in which a letter, mailed from Nigeria, offers the recipient the "opportunity" to share in millions of dollars that the author, a self-proclaimed government official, is trying to transfer illegally out of Nigeria. The victim receives a letter or email asking him to send personal information: blank letterhead stationery, bank name and account numbers and other identifying information. Eventually, the scheme attempts to get the willing victim, who has demonstrated a propensity for larceny by responding to the invitation, to send money to the author of the letter in Nigeria in several installments of increasing amounts for a variety of reasons. Payment of taxes, bribes to government officials, and legal fees are often described in great detail with the promise that all expenses will be reimbursed as soon as the funds are spirited out of Nigeria. In reality, the millions of dollars do not exist and the victim gets nothing. In fact, once the victim stops sending money, the perpetrators have been known to use the personal information that they received to impersonate the victim, draining bank accounts and credit card balances. While such an invitation strikes most of us as a laughable hoax, millions of dollars in losses are caused by these schemes annually.

25. This paragraph is best described as
   A. factual reporting
   B. humor
   C. fiction
   D. poetry

26. A "propensity for larceny" is
   A. a desire for compensation
   B. a proclivity for theft
   C. a talent for robbery
   D. a disinclination for pilferage

27. The hoax described in the paragraph attempts to get the victim to send money to the perpetrator in order to
    A. show good faith
    B. pay Nigerian taxes
    C. buy stationery
    D. help the perpetrator escape persecution

28. According to the text, the Nigerian letter gambit is
    A. a laughable attempt to defraud people that has little chance of success
    B. a good reason not to open email attachments
    C. sometimes legitimate
    D. surprisingly successful

Read the following passage, then answer Questions 29-32.

(Adapted from "Roughing It", by Mark Twain).

After fifteen days of hiking along the Humboldt River, we reached Unionville. People who are used to the Mississippi grow accustomed to associating the term "river" with a great deal of watery grandeur. Consequently, such a person may feel rather disappointed to find that he can jump across the Humboldt until he is overheated, then drink it dry.

Unionville consists of eleven cabins built in a deep crevice on a bleak mountainside. The mountain walls rise so steeply around it that the sun only touches the rooftops for an hour out of each day. We built a small, rude cabin in the side of the crevice and roofed it with canvas, leaving a corner open to serve as a chimney, through which the cattle used to tumble occasionally, at night, and mash our furniture and interrupt our sleep. It was very cold weather and fuel for the fire was scarce. We shivered and bore it.

I confess that I had expected to see the mountains glittering with gold. I expected it to litter the ground, waiting to be picked up. Some suspicion that this might be an exaggerated notion kept me from sharing my expectation with my friends, yet I was perfectly satisfied in my own mind that, within a few days at the most, I would gather up gold enough to make me satisfactorily wealthy. And so, at the first opportunity, I sauntered nonchalantly away from the cabin, keeping an eye on the boys and stopping to contemplate the sky when they seemed to look at me.. then, as soon as the coast was clear, I fled away as guiltily as a thief might have done and never halted till I was far beyond sight and call. Then, I began my feverish search for the riches of the mountains.

By and by, in the bed of a shallow rivulet, I found a deposit of shining yellow scales, and my breath almost forsook me. A gold mine! Picking up a bright fragment, I hid behind a boulder and polished it and scrutinized it with a nervous eagerness. It shone brightly in the light of the sun. I set about scooping out more, and for an hour I toiled down the windings of the stream and robbed its bed. But at last the descending sun warned me to give up the quest, and I turned homeward laden with wealth.

The boys were as hungry as usual, but I could eat nothing. Neither could I talk. I was full of dreams and far away. Their conversation kept interrupting my thoughts, annoying me at first, but presently I became amused.

Here they were, talking of privations and small economies that must be made, when our very own gold mine lay but a mile away. I decided to break the news to them calmly and to watch the play of emotions on their faces. I said:

"Where have you all been?"

"Prospecting."

"What did you find?"

"Nothing."

"Nothing? What do you think of the country?"

"Can't tell, yet," said Mr. Ballou, who was an experienced gold-miner. "It's fair enough here, maybe, but overrated. We won't starve, but we aren't going to get rich, here, either."

"So you think the prospects are pretty poor, eh?"

"I guess that's so, but we'll try it for a bit."

"Suppose, now," I put forth, "suppose you could find a ledge that would yield, say, a hundred and fifty dollars a ton—would that satisfy you?"

"Try us once!" from the whole party.

"Or suppose—merely a supposition, of course— suppose you were to find a ledge that would yield two thousand dollars a ton—would that satisfy you?"

"Here—what do you mean? What are you coming at? Is there some mystery behind all this?"

"Gentlemen," said I, "I am but a mere novice, of course, and don't know anything—but all I ask of you is to cast your eye on this and tell me what you think of it!" and I tossed my treasure before them.

There was an eager scrabble for it, and a closing of heads together over it under the candle-light. Then old Ballou said:

"Think of it? I think it is nothing but a lot of granite rubbish and nasty glittering mica that isn't worth ten cents an acre!"

So vanished my dream. So melted my wealth away. So toppled my airy castle to the earth and left me stricken and forlorn.

Moralizing, I observed, then, that "all that glitters is not gold."

So I learned then that gold in its native state is but dull, un-ornamental stuff, and that only low-born metals excite the admiration of the ignorant with an ostentatious glitter. However, like the rest of the world, I still go on underrating men of gold and glorifying men of mica.

29. Which of the following best describes the nature and tone of the passage?
    A. adventure
    B. history
    C. drama
    D. caricature

30. In the second paragraph, the author describes cattle falling through the chimney of the cabin from the steep hillside above. This is an example of
    A. burlesque
    B. illustrative detail
    C. character development
    D. denouement

31. Mr. Ballou is able to recognize that the author's find has no value because
    A. he is a mineralogist
    B. he has mined gold before
    C. he compares it to a gold watch
    D. he bites down on it to see if it is hard

32. The author concludes the passage with
    A. a lament about lost riches
    B. a comparison of minerals and men
    C. an angry denunciation of mica
    D. the hope that he will find gold the next day

Read the work instruction below, then answer questions 33-37.

JOB HAZARDS ANALYSIS

1.0 PURPOSE AND SCOPE
This procedure describes the Job Hazard Analysis (JHA) process for identifying, evaluating, controlling, and communicating potential hazards and environmental impacts associated with operations or work by the Tank Operations Contractor (TOC). It applies to all TOC work activities, including the performance of field work involving general plant maintenance, operations, and environmental remediation. This procedure applies to subcontractors who do not have an approved job hazard analysis process.

Everyone is required to work safely and to maintain a safe work environment. Training procedures have been reviewed to ensure that workers are trained to the general hazards associated with work at the tank farms. Visitors should be briefed on the general safety hazards they may be exposed to and controls expected of them as part of their orientation.

2.0 IMPLEMENTATION
This procedure is effective on the date shown in the header.

3.0 RESPONSIBILITIES
Responsibilities are contained within Section 4.0.

4.0 METHODS FOR IMPLEMENTATION OF CONTROLS
In order to effectively implement necessary controls to mitigate or eliminate hazards to the workers, the following guidelines should be used:

4.1. The following hierarchy of methods to eliminate or mitigate hazards shall be used in descending order, when feasible and appropriate:
   a. Eliminate the hazard or substitution (e.g., different chemical cleaning agent)
   b. Utilize engineering controls (e.g., ventilation)
   c. Administrative controls (e.g., dose monitoring)
   d. Personal protective equipment (PPE) (e.g., self-contained breathing apparatus)

4.2. Controls within the qualification or training of the worker that are often used do not need to be discussed in the work instructions. Examples: Use of leather gloves, safety glasses of the proper type that the worker normally uses.

4.3. Controls within the qualification or training of the worker that are seldom used, and are applicable to the entire work activity, should be placed in the precautions as a reminder that the hazard exists and the workers are expected to take the appropriate actions. Examples: Use of hearing protection due to a noisy environment at the job site, or observation of overhead lines when they are present at the job site.

4.4. Controls within the qualification and training of the workers, but for hazards that are introduced at specific steps or by specific actions during the job, should have a warning or caution statement immediately prior to the step but require no detailed mitigation instructions in the work instructions. Example: a warning for the release of pressure when breaching a system that may have residual pressure.

4.5. Controls not within the qualification and training of the workers for hazards should have detailed instructions for how the workers are to mitigate the hazard and should be in the work instructions or procedure in a way that is prominent and prevents or mitigates the hazard. Example: the steps required to successfully release the pressure on a system in an operation which is not normally performed.

33. This document is
   A. a government request for proposals
   B. a process for making rules for working safely
   C. a portion of a contract
   D. a set of rules for working efficiently

34. According to the procedure, if a worker is exposed to a hazardous chemical, which of the following is the last thing that should be tried to prevent injury or illness?
   A. Use a different chemical.
   B. Install fans to keep fumes away from the worker.
   C. Measure the amount of exposure of each affected worker.
   D. Give the worker protective clothing.

35. Welders must always use goggles and are taught to use them as part of their basic training. According to the text, the use of goggles during specific welding operations should
   A. be prominently displayed at the beginning of the work instruction.
   B. be displayed as a caution prior to the welding step described in the work instruction.
   C. be described in detail in the work instruction.
   D. not be discussed in the work instruction.

36. This passage would normally need to be read and understood by
    A. managers at the site.
    B. laborers at the site.
    C. visitors to the site.
    D. workers making deliveries to the site.

37. Which of the following requires the most comprehensive description within the work instructions?
    A. Controls that are part of the worker's training and are used routinely
    B. Controls that are part of the worker's training but that are seldom used
    C. Controls that are part of the worker's training and that are required for specific steps in the work procedure
    D. Controls that are not part of the worker's training

Read the following instructions, then answer Questions 38-39.

Application Instructions: American Institute for the Written Arts, Grants and Awards Program (excerpt)

WORK SAMPLES

Manuscripts must be submitted by applicants in Screenwriting, Playwriting, and Literature (poetry, fiction, and creative nonfiction).

Manuscripts should include a title page with your name, address, and year the work was completed. All pages must be numbered. All writing samples, including previously published work, must be submitted in 12-point.

Photocopied excerpts from books or periodicals in published form are not accepted. Instead, publication, performance, or production information must be restricted to the résumé.

Fiction and creative nonfiction writers must submit 10-20 pages from several short works, or a portion from no more than two larger works, and they must be labeled fiction or nonfiction. If your work is an excerpt, include a one-page statement in the manuscript about where it fits into the whole to orient the reviewers. Poets must submit 10-15 pages of poetry. Shorter poems should be printed one to a page.

Fellowship and Writer-in-Residence applicants must submit one copy of work with applicant name throughout and one copy without applicant name. There should be no identifying marks on the anonymous copy.

Writer-in-Residence applicants must also include one standard size audiotape or CD with up to ten minutes of the applicant reading aloud from his or her own work. The case must be labeled with applicant's name, title of work, and date written. Do not use your name on the audio portion of your reading. (Work samples will not be returned.)

Screenwriters and playwrights must submit 10 to 20 pages from one or two works. Applicants are encouraged to include a one-page synopsis. If screenwriters and playwrights are submitting produced works, they must submit a videotape work sample.

38. Information describing publication or other production of the work samples must be
   A. included with the sample.
   B. prominently displayed.
   C. kept separate from the sample.
   D. submitted as an audio tape.

39. Excerpts must be accompanied by
   A. an anonymous copy.
   B. a videotape work sample.
   C. a label indicating whether the work is fiction or nonfiction.
   D. a statement indicating where the text fits into the larger work.

Read the following paragraphs, then answer Questions 40-44.

Forest Manager: Salvage logging is removing dead or dying forest stands that are left behind by a fire or disease. This practice has been used for several decades. These dead or dying trees become fuel that feeds future fires. The best way to lower the risk of forest fires is to remove the dead timber from the forest floor. Salvage logging followed by replanting ensures the reestablishment of desirable tree species.

For example, planting conifers accelerates the return of fire resistant forests. Harvesting timber helps forests by reducing fuel load, thinning the forest stands, and relieving competition between trees. Burned landscapes leave black surfaces and ash layers that have very high soil temperatures. These high soil temperatures can kill many plant species. Logging mixes the soil. So, this lowers surface temperatures to more normal levels. The shade from material that is left behind by logging also helps to lower surface temperatures. After an area has been salvage logged, seedlings in the area start to grow almost immediately. However, this regrowth can take several years in areas that are not managed well.

Ecology professor: Salvage logging moves material like small, broken branches to the forest floor. These pieces can become fuel for more fires. The removal of larger, less flammable trees leaves behind small limbs and increases the risk of forest fires. In unmanaged areas, these pieces are found more commonly on the tops of trees where they are unavailable to fires. Logging destroys old forests that are more resistant to wildfires. So, this creates younger forests that are more open to fires. In old forests, branches of bigger trees are higher above the floor where fires may not reach.

Replanting after wildfires creates monoculture plantations where only a single crop is planted. This monoculture allows less biological diversity. Also, it allows plants to be less resistant to disease. So, this increases the chance of fire. Salvage logging also upsets natural forest regrowth by killing most of the seedlings that grow after a wildfire. It breaks up the soil and increases erosion. Also, it removes most of the shade that is needed for young seedlings to grow.

40. According to the professor, how are unmanaged areas helpful in spreading small, woody materials after a fire?
   A. They are left on the forest floor and bring nutrients to the soil.
   B. They are left on the forest floor and serve as fuel for fires.
   C. They are left on the tops of trees where fires cannot reach.
   D. They are spread more evenly across the forest floor.

41. A study compared two plots of land that were managed differently after a fire. Plot A was salvage logged. Plot B was left unmanaged. After a second fire, they compared two plant groups between Plots A and B. They found that both plant groups burned worse in Plot A than in Plot B. Which viewpoint do these results support?
    A. only the manager
    B. only the professor
    C. both the manager and professor
    D. neither the manager nor the professor

42. What is the main idea of the forest manager's argument?
    A. Salvage logging is helpful because it removes dead or dying timber from the forest floor. So, this lowers the risk of future fires.
    B. Salvage logging is helpful because it has been practiced for many decades.
    C. Salvage logging is harmful because it raises soil temperatures above normal levels. So, this threatens the health of plant species.
    D. Salvage logging is helpful because it gives shade for seedlings to grow after a wildfire.

43. According to the professor, young forests are more open to harsh fires than old growth forests. Which of the following statements does not support this view?
    A. In younger forests, small branches are closer to the forest floor and more available for fires.
    B. Old growth forests have larger and taller trees. So, branches are high up and fires cannot reach.
    C. Younger forests have less biological diversity and less disease-resistant trees.
    D. Larger trees are common in old growth forests and serve as the main fuel source for severe fires.

44. Whose viewpoints would be proven by a future study looking at the spreading out and regrowth of seedlings for many years after a wildfire in managed and unmanaged forests?
    A. only the manager
    B. only the professor
    C. both the manager and professor
    D. neither the manager nor professor

Read the following passage, then answer Questions 45-47.

Section 1: Improving Diets

A healthier diet is something that many people want for themselves. However, this can be a struggle to put into practice for many people. This does not mean that just because it's hard and frustrating doesn't mean that people should stop trying.

A powerful and easy approach to improving diets is to know that some foods are so good for us that we can almost think of them as medicine. Some foods help to fight heart disease, cancer, or depression. Other foods help to lower cholesterol or blood pressure. Broccoli is high in vitamin K and vitamin C which help build strong bones and fight off cancers. Avocadoes can lower cholesterol and help reduce the risk of heart disease. Sweet potatoes are full of cancer-fighting and immune system-boosting vitamin A. Garlic can slow down the growth of bacteria and has been shown to lower cholesterol and blood pressure. Spinach is a great cancer fighter and has immune-boosting antioxidants important for eye health. Beans help lower risk of heart disease and breast cancer.

At some point, people want to give themselves the full treatment: diet, exercise, and general health overhaul. In the meantime, they can take the baby step of adding in one or more healthy food a week. This step is quick, easy, and painless. It couldn't be simpler to implement. Also, it will make their switch to healthy eating much easier to accomplish when they finally get there.

Section 2: Dietary Guidelines for Americans

The Dietary Guidelines for Americans is put together by the U.S. Department of Health and Human Services and the U.S. Department of Agriculture. The guidelines offer advice to people about food choices that advance good health and lower the risk of certain diseases (e.g., hypertension, anemia, and osteoporosis). In addition, this form offers a detailed outline on the kinds of foods that people should have in their diets. The outline is given so that additional supplements or vitamins may not be necessary. The form also has information on the types of exercise that are necessary for someone to stay healthy. Also, there is information on to handle and prepare certain foods to lower the risk of foodborne illness.

The Food Pyramid gave recommendations for the number of daily servings from each group. The USDA's Food Pyramid was heavily criticized for being unclear and confusing. In 2011, MyPlate replaced the Food Pyramid. MyPlate is much easier to understand because it has a picture of a dinner plate that is divided into four sections. So, this shows how our daily diet should be spread out among the different food groups. Vegetables and grains each take up 30% of the plate. Fruits and proteins each make up 20% of the plate. In the corner of the image is a cup that is marked as Dairy.

Most experts consider MyPlate to be a great improvement over the Food Pyramid. However, some it has still come under criticism from some quarters. Many believe too much emphasis is placed on protein, and some say the dairy recommendation should be eliminated altogether. The Harvard School of Public Health created its own Healthy Eating Plate to address what it sees as shortcomings in MyPlate. Harvard's guide adds healthy plant-based oils to the mix, stresses whole grains instead of merely grains, recommends drinking water or unsweetened coffee or tea instead of milk, and adds a reminder that physical activity is important.

Section 3: Preparing Better Meals in the Food Industry

People in the food industry that want to prepare a healthy meal for their customers should first decide on the nutritional goals of their menu. Once these goals have been set up, you should continue to plan by researching foods. These foods need to meet your goals without going beyond the available time and resource limits. Then, you can put together a meal plan that list several details. These details should have what foods will be included, the average time it takes to prepare and cook each of these meals, and the cost of preparing these meals. The next step is to decide on the best way of preparing the food for these meals. Think about which foods should be prepared first and the best ways to handle or prepare your food to lower the risk of illness. Also, think about methods that can be used to lower the cooking time. Finally, you can prepare the meal according to your plans.

When you need to decide on what foods to prepare, you need to think about several things. You should consider the food's nutritional value, the time it takes to prepare each food, the number of people to be served, and the cost of preparing each food. Each food has its own cooking time and has different nutrients. So, it is important to prepare foods that meet people's nutritional goals without using too much time for cooking the meal. Since you will likely have a budget for the meal, you need to review the number of people to be served and the cost of preparing each food. If the cost is too high, some meals may not be good choices to serve to large groups. For example, you are interested in serving a good source of protein for a meal. So, steak may be a good option for a small group of people. However, that would probably be too expensive for a larger group.

45. What is the main idea of Section 1?
    A. Making a change to your diet is a quick process.
    B. Some foods are healthier than others.
    C. With discipline and smart decisions, you can make positive changes to your diet.
    D. There are some people who can make dietary changes and some who cannot.

46. What is the purpose of including Section 2 in this passage?
    A. To highlight the main argumentative points of the Food Pyramid and MyPlate
    B. To cover the government's influence on the dietary recommendations for Americans
    C. To show that there is no perfect system for coming up with dietary recommendations
    D. To share information on generally accepted nutrition guidelines for future workers in the food industry

47. What is the tone of the three sections?
    A. Condemning
    B. Informative
    C. Serious
    D. Pretentious

Questions 48–50 are based upon the following figure and text:

THE WATER CYCLE

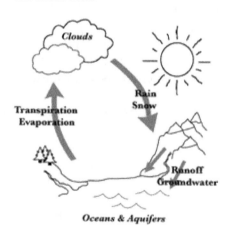

Oceans & Aquifers

Energy from the sun heats the water in the oceans and causes it to evaporate, forming water vapor that rises through the atmosphere. Cooler temperatures at high altitudes cause this vapor to condense and form clouds. Water droplets in the clouds condense and grow, eventually falling to the ground as precipitation. This continuous movement of water above and below ground is called the hydrologic cycle, or water cycle, and it is essential for life on our planet. All the Earth's stores of water, including that found in clouds, oceans, underground, etc., are known as the *hydrosphere.*

Water can be stored in several locations as part of the water cycle. The largest reservoirs are the oceans, which hold about 95% of the world's water, more than 300,000,000 cubic miles.

Water is also stored in polar ice caps, mountain snowcaps, lakes and streams, plants, and below ground in aquifers. Each of these reservoirs has a characteristic *residence time*, which is the average amount of time a water molecule will spend there before moving on. Some typical residence times are shown in the table.

Average reservoir residence times of water.

Reservoir	Residence Time
Atmosphere	9 days
Oceans	3,000 years
Glaciers and ice caps	100 years
Soil moisture	2 months
Underground aquifers	10,000 years

The water cycle can change over time. During cold climatic periods, more water is stored as ice and snow, and the rate of evaporation is lower. This affects the level of the Earth's oceans. During the last ice age, for instance, oceans were 400 feet lower than today. Human activities that affect the water cycle include agriculture, dam construction, deforestation, and industrial activities.

48. Another name for the water cycle is
    A. the hydrosphere.
    B. the atmosphere.
    C. the residence cycle.
    D. the hydrologic cycle.

49. Other than atmospheric water, water molecules spend the least time in
    A. aquifers.
    B. oceans.
    C. glaciers.
    D. soil.

50. Which of the following statements is NOT true?
    A. Cutting down trees affects the water cycle.
    B. Ocean levels rise during an ice age.
    C. Oceans hold most of the world's water.
    D. Clouds are formed because of cold temperatures.

Mathematics Computation Practice Questions

1. 4.73 – 2.13 =
    A. 6.96
    B. 2.60
    C. 2.50
    D. 2.63
    E. None of these

2. Solve the equation for x: $x + 7 = 11$
    A. x = 3
    B. x = 4
    C. x = -4
    D. x = -3
    E. None of these

3. 1.02 + 0.0003 =
    A. 1.0007
    B. 1.023
    C. 1.0203
    D. 1.23
    E. None of these

4. $68 \times \dfrac{1}{4} =$

    A. $\dfrac{69}{4}$

    B. 272

    C. $\dfrac{4}{69}$

    D. 17

    E. None of these

5. 20% of 19 =
    A. 1.9
    B. 2.9
    C. 3.8
    D. 9.5
    E. None of these

6. $\frac{18}{4} \div 0.3 =$
    A. 1.5
    B. 15
    C. $\frac{15}{4}$
    D. $\frac{1.8}{12}$
    E. None of these

7. $\frac{8}{7} \div \frac{12}{7} =$
    A. 1
    B. $\frac{3}{2}$
    C. 0.5
    D. $\frac{3}{4}$
    E. None of these

8. $4 - (3 - 1)^2 =$
    A. 0
    B. 1
    C. 2
    D. 3
    E. None of these

9. $\frac{-27}{-3} =$
    A. 30
    B. – 30
    C. 9
    D. – 9
    E. None of these

10. $\sqrt{36} =$
    A. 3
    B. 6
    C. 9
    D. 12
    E. None of these

11. 5 x 0 =
   A. 5
   B. 50
   C. 0
   D. 0.5
   E. None of these

12. $6\frac{5}{8} + 3\frac{7}{8} =$
   A. $9\frac{5}{8}$
   B. $11\frac{1}{8}$
   C. $10\frac{5}{8}$
   D. $10\frac{1}{2}$
   E. None of these

13. 16 + (- 4) -7 =
   A. 13
   B. 27
   C. 11
   D. 5
   E. None of these

14. 4.302 + 6.71 =
   A. 11.12
   B. 11.012
   C. 12.11
   D. 10.1012
   E. None of these

15. 7.19 – (-3.2) =
   A. 10.39
   B. 3.99
   C. 9.99
   D. 9.39
   E. None of these

16. $8.65 + \frac{1}{4} =$
   A. 10.9
   B. 8.6525
   C. 8.9
   D. 8.654
   E. None of these

- 132 -

17. 36 is ___% of 60.
   A. 40%
   B. 50%
   C. 55%
   D. 60%
   E. None of these

18. Solve for k if $\dfrac{1}{2}k + 6 = 9$
   A. k = 12
   B. k = 3
   C. k = 6
   D. k = 9
   E. None of these

19. $\dfrac{3^7}{3^5} =$
   A. 3
   B. 6
   C. 9
   D. 27
   E. None of these

20. $7 - (-4) - 4 =$
   A. – 1
   B. 1
   C. 15
   D. 11
   E. None of these

21. $6\dfrac{3}{13} + 2\dfrac{4}{13} =$
   A. $8\dfrac{7}{26}$
   B. $8\dfrac{7}{13}$
   C. $7\dfrac{8}{13}$
   D. $8\dfrac{1}{13}$
   E. None of these

22. 30% of 1000 =
   A. 30
   B. 60
   C. 300
   D. 3
   E. None of these

23. $\dfrac{8}{18} \div \dfrac{4}{18} =$

A. 2

B. 4

C. $\dfrac{2}{18}$

D. $\dfrac{6}{18}$

E. None of these

24. $81.09 \div 0.9 =$

A. 9.01

B. 9.1

C. 90.01

D. 90.1

E. None of these

25. $4^2 + 4 =$

A. 43

B. 12

C. 16

D. 20

E. None of these

26. $\dfrac{7}{3} \times \dfrac{2}{3} =$

A. $\dfrac{14}{9}$

B. $\dfrac{14}{3}$

C. $\dfrac{9}{3}$

D. $\dfrac{9}{6}$

E. None of these

27. $(6 - 4) \times 2 =$

A. -2

B. 2

C. 4

D. -4

E. None of these

28. $6^2 + 6^0 =$
    A. 6
    B. 36
    C. 7
    D. 37
    E. None of these

29. $23.01 - 2.999 =$
    A. 20.11
    B. 20.011
    C. 21.01
    D. 21.001
    E. None of these

30. $(5 \times 20) \div 4 =$
    A. 20
    B. 22
    C. 25
    D. 33
    E. None of these

31. $-15 - (6 \times 3) =$
    A. 3
    B. 33
    C. -33
    D. -3
    E. None of these

32. Solve for x if $32 = x^2 - 4$
    A. x = 6
    B. x = 36
    C. x = 4
    D. x = 8
    E. None of these

33. $6\frac{1}{3} - 4\frac{2}{9} =$
    A. $2\frac{2}{9}$
    B. $2\frac{1}{9}$
    C. $2\frac{2}{6}$
    D. $-2\frac{1}{6}$
    E. None of these

34. 30% of _____ = 18
    A. 54
    B. 60
    C. 66
    D. 75
    E. None of these

35. $\sqrt{81} - \sqrt{25} =$
    A. $\sqrt{56}$
    B. 56
    C. 2
    D. 4
    E. None of these

36. 6 – 7 x 2 - 1 =
    A. - 9
    B. - 3
    C. - 15
    D. - 14
    E. None of these

37. $9 \div (9 - 6)^2 =$
    A. $\dfrac{1}{5}$
    B. $\dfrac{9}{5}$
    C. 1
    D. 3
    E. None of these

38. – 12 (– 4 + 3) =
    A. 144
    B. -144
    C. 12
    D. – 12
    E. None of these

39. $\dfrac{85}{18} \div \dfrac{17}{18} =$
    A. $\dfrac{1}{5}$
    B. 5
    C. $\dfrac{34}{9}$
    D. $\dfrac{51}{9}$
    E. None of these

40. 23% of 10,000 =
    A. 23
    B. 230
    C. 2300
    D. 460
    E. None of these

Applied Mathematics Practice Questions

1. Bob buys the newspaper every day for $1.50. If he subscribes, he pays only $3.50 per week for seven issues. How much will his weekly savings be if he subscribes?
    A. $2.00
    B. $4.50
    C. $5.00
    D. $7.00

2. Thirty-five boys went out for the soccer team. Of these, $\frac{5}{7}$ made the team. Of the boys who made the team, $\frac{4}{5}$ showed up for practice on Wednesday. How many boys were at the Wednesday practice?
    A. 18
    B. 20
    C. 22
    D. 25

3. Jamal hosts a dinner in a restaurant for a number of his customers and the bill comes to $1128.08. The restaurant always adds an 18% tip for large groups, and this is included in the total. How much was the total before the tip was added?
    A. $1010.08
    B. $925.02
    C. $956.00
    D. $988.05

4. Which of the following is listed in order from *greatest to least*?
A. $2\frac{1}{4}, \frac{32}{5}, \frac{4}{5}, -5, -2$

B. $\frac{32}{5}, 2\frac{1}{4}, \frac{4}{5}, -2, -5$

C. $-5, -2, \frac{32}{5}, \frac{4}{5}, 2\frac{1}{4}$

D. $\frac{32}{5}, 2\frac{1}{4}, \frac{4}{5}, -5, -2$

Question 5 pertains to the following information:

Joshua has to earn more than 92 points on the state test in order to qualify for an academic scholarship. Each question is worth 4 points, and the test has a total of 30 questions. Let x represent the number of test questions.

5. Which of the following inequalities can be solved to determine the number of questions Joshua must answer correctly?
A. $4x < 30$
B. $4x < 92$
C. $4x > 30$
D. $4x > 92$

6. Gitta brings $2,082 on a business trip. The trip will last 7 days. Which of the following is the best estimate for the amount of money she has to spend per day?
A. $200
B. $320
C. $240
D. $300

7. Evaluate $x^2 - (2y - 3)$ if $x = 4$ and $y = 3$.
   A. 12
   B. 13
   C. 10
   D. 8

8. During a 60 minute television show, the entertainment portion lasted 15 minutes less than 4 times the advertising portion. How long was the entertainment portion?
   A. 30 minutes
   B. 40 minutes
   C. 45 minutes
   D. 50 minutes

9. Which number is missing in the numerical sequence 18, 15, ___, 9, 6 ?
   A. 12
   B. 14
   C. 10
   D. 8

In the figure below, lines $L1$ and $L2$ are parallel to each other. Look at the figure and answer Questions 10 – 13.

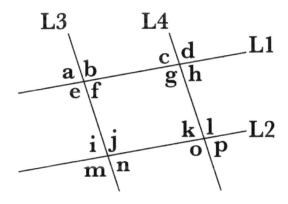

10. If angle $\angle a$ has a measure of 70°, what is the measure of angle $\angle b$?
   A. 30°
   B. 90°
   C. 100°
   D. 110°

11. If angle ∠***a*** has a measure of 70°, what is the measure of angle ∠***i***?
    A. 30°
    B. 60°
    C. 70°
    D. 110°

12. If angle ∠***n*** is congruent to angle ∠***p***, which of the following statements must be true?
    A. Line L3 is perpendicular to line L4
    B. Line L3 is parallel to line L4
    C. Line L3 must eventually intersect line L4
    D. Line *L*3 is parallel to line *L*1

13. If line *L*3 is parallel to line *L*4, which of the following statements must be true?
    A. Angle ∠f is congruent to angle ∠k, and angle ∠a is congruent to angle ∠p.
    B. Angle ∠f is congruent to angle ∠k, and angle ∠g is congruent to angle ∠p.
    C. Angle ∠f is congruent to angle ∠k, and angle ∠g is congruent to angle ∠h.
    D. Angle ∠*f* is congruent to angle ∠k, and angle ∠*g* is congruent to angle ∠*n*.

14. A jar contains 200 marbles. Thirty of them are blue, 80 are red, and the remainder are yellow. If Natasha reaches blindly into the jar and withdraws a marble at random, what is the probability that it will be blue?
    A. 30%
    B. 20%
    C. 15%
    D. 12%

Look at the following table, which shows the results of a qualification exam given to applicants for public service jobs in Montgomery County. Then, answer Questions 15 – 17.

Score	Under 65	65 – 74	75 – 85	85 – 94	95 - 100	Totals
Men	3	16	24	12	0	55
Women	3	18	20	20	2	63
Totals	6	34	44	32	2	118

15. Approximately what percentage of men passed the exam if 75 is considered to be the cutoff passing grade?
    A. 55%
    B. 65%
    C. 75%
    D. 85%

16. Approximately what percentage of applicants received a grade of 85 or higher?
    A. 25%
    B. 34%
    C. 29%
    D. 32%

17. Based on the table, how many women received a grade that was higher than that of the highest-scoring man?

    A. 0

    B. At least 2

    C. At least 4

    D. 22

18. Morgan plans to replace the floor in his bedroom with square tiles that have a side of 12 inches. The bedroom is 15 feet wide and 18 feet long, and Morgan can lay 9 tiles per hour. How long will the job take?

    A. 30 hours

    B. 18 hours

    C. 10.5 hours

    D. 12 hours

19. Tamara has 5 pair of socks in her drawer. Each pair is a different color. If she pulls out two socks at random, one at a time, what is the probability that they will be of matching colors?

    A. $\dfrac{1}{5}$

    B. $\dfrac{1}{25}$

    C. $\dfrac{1}{10}$

    D. $\dfrac{1}{9}$

20. The first three members of a 4-man swimming team swim their laps in 22.4 seconds, 23.8 seconds, and 21.9 seconds, respectively. How fast must the fourth man swim his lap for the team to average 22 seconds?

    A. 21.0 seconds

    B. 19.9 seconds

    C. 19.5 seconds

    D. 20.2 seconds

21. Which set of figures is congruent?

A.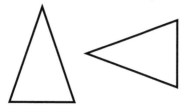

C.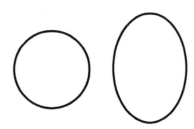

B.

D.

22. Which pair of figures below is similar?

A.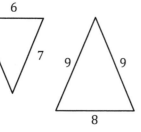

C.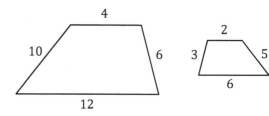

B.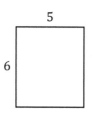

D.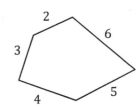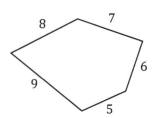

23. Two hikers start at a ranger station and leave at the same time. One hiker heads due west at 3 miles/hour. The other hiker heads due north at 4 miles/hour. How far apart are the hikers after 2 hours of hiking?
A. 5 miles
B. 7 miles
C. 10 miles
D. 14 miles

24. Sunil uses his cell phone an average of 1200 minutes per month. Which of the following cell phone monthly payment plans will be the least expensive for him?
    A. 10¢ per minute with no base fee
    B. $50 base fee for 600 minutes; 12¢ for each additional minute
    C. $75 base fee for 900 minutes; 14¢ for each additional minute
    D. $100 for 1000 minutes; 18¢ for each additional minute

25. Evaluate the following expression if $u = 3$ and $v = 4$: $\dfrac{1}{3}u^2 + \dfrac{3v}{4} =$
    A. 21
    B. 18
    C. 12
    D. 6

26. Rouenna has to drive 500 miles to Portland. Her car gets 25 miles per gallon and gasoline costs $3 per gallon. What will the trip cost?
    A. $20
    B. $60
    C. $75
    D. $150

Look at the following table, which shows the prices of five company stocks at the close of trading on the stock market one day in April. then, answer Questions 27-28.

Company	Price
IBM	127
Intel	21
Cisco	24
Apple	193
Microsoft	30

27. What is the mean share price of the stocks shown in the table?
    A. 21
    B. 193
    C. 79
    D. 30

28. What is the median share price of the stocks shown in the table?
    A. 21
    B. 193
    C. 79
    D. 30

Look at the chart below, which shows the average amounts that Americans spend on various expense categories. Then, answer Questions 29-30.

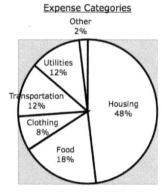

Expense Categories

29. Which category represents the greatest expense for the average American?
   A. Food
   B. Housing
   C. Transportation
   D. Clothing

30. If an average American spends a total of $40,000 per year, how much would he or she spend on clothing, according to the chart?
   A. $32,000
   B. $3,200
   C. $320
   D. $2,400

31. Solve the following proportion for x: $\dfrac{-3}{x} = \dfrac{2}{8}$.
   A. x = 3
   B. x = 12
   C. x = -2
   D. x = -12

32. A culture of yeast cells doubles in number every half hour. After 3 hours, there are 6400 yeast cells in the culture. How many were there when the culture was started?
   A. 100
   B. 200
   C. 400
   D. 800

33. Mischa drives from Town A to Town B at 90 kilometers per hour. Brenda drives the same route at 60 kilometers per hour and it takes her 3 hours longer. How far apart are Town A and Town B?
   A. 540 km
   B. 600 km
   C. 480 km
   D. 510 km

- 144 -

34. A bag of coffee costs $9.85 and contains 16 ounces of coffee. Which of the following best represents the cost per ounce?

    A. $0.67
    B. $0.64
    C. $0.65
    D. $0.62

35. Kevin pays $12.95 for a text messaging service plus $0.07 for each text message he sends. Which of the following equations could be used to represent the total cost, y, when x represents the number of text messages sent?

    A. $y = \$12.95x + \$0.07$
    B. $y = \$13.02x$
    C. $y = \frac{\$12.95}{\$0.07}x$
    D. $y = \$0.07x + \$12.95$

36. Martin's bed is 7 feet, in length. Which of the following represents the length of the bed, in centimeters?

    A. 209.42 cm
    B. 213.36 cm
    C. 215.52 cm
    D. 217.94 cm

37. Alfredo works 40 hours per week at an hourly wage of $20. For any overtime, he makes $30 per hour. This week Alfredo made $950. How many hours did he work?

    A. 40
    B. 42
    C. 45
    D. 48

38. What is the next term in the number series 3, 6, 12, 24, ____?

    A. 30
    B. 36
    C. 42
    D. 48

39. The price-earnings (PE) ratio of a stock is the ratio of the share price divided by the annual earnings per share. Company A has issued 3 million shares of stock, which are selling at $6.00 per share. If the PE ratio is 12, how much did Company A earn in the past year?

    A. $1.5 million
    B. $3.0 million
    C. $4.5 million
    D. $6.0 million

Look at the table below, which compares the orbits of the planets in our solar system. Then, answer Questions 40-43.

Property	Mercury	Venus	Earth	Mars	Jupiter	Saturn	Uranus	Neptune
Diameter (km)	4,878	12,104	12,756	6,787	142,800	120,000	51,118	49,528
Mass (Earth=1)	0.055	0.815	1	0.107	318	95	15	17
Average distance from Sun (Earth = 1)	0.39	0.72	1	1.52	5.20	9.54	19.18	30.06
Orbital period (Earth years)	0.24	0.62	1	1.88	11.86	29.46	84.01	164.8
Average orbital speed (km/sec)	47.89	35.03	29.79	24.13	13.06	9.64	6.81	5.43
Gravity (Earth=1)	0.38	0.9	1	0.38	2.64	0.93	0.89	1.12

40. Which of the following statements is true?
    A. The greater a planet's mass, the longer its orbital period.
    B. The larger a planet's diameter, the greater its gravity.
    C. The further a planet is from the Sun, the longer its orbital period.
    D. The greater a planet's mass, the greater its gravity.

41. The mass of the Earth is approximately 6×10^{24} kilograms. What is the mass of Venus?
    A. 4.9×10^{24} kilograms
    B. 4.9×10^{23} kilograms
    C. 0.81×10^{24} kilograms
    D. 8.1×10^{24} kilograms

42. Which of the following statements is true?
    A. The greater a planet's orbital period, the faster its orbital speed.
    B. The closer a planet is to the Sun, the faster its orbital speed.
    C. The smaller a planet's diameter, the faster its orbital speed.
    D. The smaller a planet's mass, the faster its orbital speed.

43. The average distance from the Earth to the Sun is 149,600,000 km. What is the average distance from Mercury to the Sun?
    A. 5.8×10^6 km
    B. 5.8×10^7 km
    C. 3.9×10^6 km
    D. 0.39×10^6 km

Look at the Figure below, which shows a circle with center at point O and several line segments. Then, answer Questions 44-47.

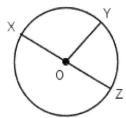

44. Which of the following represents the radius of the circle?
    A. YZ
    B. XZ
    C. OX
    D. YOX

45. Line segment XOZ is the
    A. diameter
    B. center
    C. radius
    D. chord

46. If line segment XOZ is 6 cm in length, then the area of the circle is approximately
    A. 36 cm²
    B. 113 cm²
    C. 9 cm²
    D. 28 cm²

47. Kelsey is having a pool party and brought beach balls for the guests to use in the pool. When inflated, each beach ball is 12 inches in diameter. How much air is needed to inflate each beach ball?
    A. 904.8 in³
    B. 2,714.3 in³
    C. 7,238.2 in³
    D. 21,714.7 in³

48. An elevator leaves the first floor of a 25-story building with 3 people on board. It stops at every floor. Each time it comes to an even-numbered floor, 3 people get on and one person gets off. Each time it comes to an odd-numbered floor, 3 people get on and 4 people get off. How many people are on board when it arrives at the 25th floor?
    A. 13
    B. 16
    C. 15
    D. 12

- 147 -

49. Lauren must travel a distance of 1,480 miles to get to her destination. She plans to drive approximately the same number of miles per day for 5 days. Which of the following is a reasonable estimate of the number of miles she will drive per day?

    A. 240 miles

    B. 260 miles

    C. 300 miles

    D. 340 miles

50. A shipping clerk can process 180 orders per hour. He has an assistant who can process 180 orders in 90 minutes. How many minutes will it take the two of them, working together, to process 115 orders?

    A. 36

    B. 23

    C. 27

    D. 30

Answer Explanations

Language Answers

1. C: One of the basic applications of the comma is to separate two sentences, or independent clauses. Both clauses of this sentence are independent, having both subject and verb, so it is appropriate to separate them with a comma.

2. C: Commas are used to set off introductory elements or phrases, such as "As a matter of fact".

3. D: A comma is not used to separate two clauses in a sentence if one of the clauses is dependent. In this sentence, the clause following the conjunction "but" lacks a subject and therefore depends upon the subject of the first clause.

4. D: The sentence needs a question mark, not a period. The question mark does not go inside the quotation marks because the question mark applies to whole sentence.

5. C: Use the progressive form of a verb to indicate that an action that has started continued for some time or is still continuing. In this case, the tree began to grow when the watering increased, and is still growing. The simple past tense "grew" indicates that the action took place in the past and was completed or stopped happening.

6. B: The word in place of the blank must modify the verb "did". An adverb must be used to modify a verb, not an adjective. Of the choices presented, only "well" is an adverb. All the others are adjectives.

7. D: Since the tickets were given to the person referred to by the pronoun replacing the blank, the objective pronoun must be used. Choices A, B, and C are subjective pronouns that are used when the person referred to is the subject of the verb. Only "me" is in the objective case.

8. C: In choices A and B the subject is singular ("group" of "box"), so that a singular verb is called for, not the plural verb shown.

9. B: Choices A and C exhibit poor agreement between subject and verb, and choice D has an incorrect comma.

10. A: This is a simple declarative sentence with subject, verb and indirect object. Choices B and D lack a verb. Choice C does not require a comma.

11. C: In this sentence, an introductory clause is correctly set off by a comma. Choice A lacks parallel construction, since the act of renting a movie should be compared with the act of going to one, rather than with "excitement". Choice B has an unnecessary comma. Choice D should be broken into two sentences.

12. D: Choice D is a simple imperative sentence. Choice A lacks a comma, Choice C has a comma where none belongs, and in Choice B the verb is in the wrong tense.

13. C: In a question, a comma can be used to set off the adverb "please." Choices A and B are not complete sentences. The apostrophe in Choice D does not belong there.

14. A: Choice B is slang. In Choice C, the semi-colon should be replaced by a comma. Choice D makes use of the wrong verb tense.

15. B: In this sentence, a parenthetical phrase is properly offset by commas. Choices A and C lack commas. Choice D improperly uses a negative verb.

16. B: In Choice A, the question mark should be outside of the quotation marks, since it is not part of the title. In Choice C, the title of the poem should be in quotation marks. Choice D should not use quotation marks since it is an indirect question.

17. D: In Choice A, "yen" should be offset by commas. Choice B lacks a verb and is not a complete sentence. Choice C should not have a question mark.

18. C: This is a compound sentence with one subject and two verbs. Choice A lacks a subject. The country name in Choice B requires no quotation marks. A comma should be used to set off the subordinate clause at the beginning of Choice D.

19. A: The two sentences imply a cause and effect: spending $25,000 on the car has left the writer with insufficient funds for maintenance. Choice B implies the opposite causality.

20. B: Use of the conjunction "but" serves to emphasize the contrast between the two clauses: the success described in the first clause and the derision described in the second.

21. C: This choice makes explicit that the center fielder was rewarded because he broke the season record. Choice B suggests that breaking the record was itself a reward. Choice D suggests that he was being well rewarded (i.e., well paid) even before breaking the record.

22. D: This choice makes it clear that the mechanic used the computer in order to perform the tests. Choice A makes the use of the computer appear incidental, while Choice C suggests that the mechanic was obliged to perform the tests because he used a computer.

23. A: This sentence introduces the concept of the letter of application that is developed in the remainder of the paragraph. Choice C is inappropriate since it describes both the letter and the resume: since the second sentence refers to "this letter", and not "the letter", it is clear that the first sentence must be about the letter alone.

24. C: This sentence clearly introduces the topic of the paragraph, which is the damage that may be sustained by library book collections as the result of an earthquake. Since deaths or injury are not discussed in the paragraph, Choices A and D are inappropriate. Also, the paragraph describes the types of damage that may occur, not specific damage that did occur during one earthquake, so that Choice B is inappropriate.

25. B: The remainder of the paragraph describes the differences between UVA and UVB rays. This sentence first tells the reader that these two types of ultraviolet ray exist, introducing the remainder of the text.

26. C: This paragraph describes checking accounts and their related services. Choice C continues that description by discussing ATM services and the charges that may accompany them. The other choices are also about banking, but they do not continue the description of checking account services.

27. A: This sentence, which suggests a visit in winter, leads naturally into the last sentence, which describes the weather conditions and wildlife activity at that time of year. The other choices are also about the Everglades, but bring up points that have nothing to do with the time of year.

28. D: This paragraph describes the law and the effects that it has had on the organic food market. Choice D follows the first sentence by beginning a description of the content of the law and leads naturally into the third sentence, which continues that description in more detail.

29. B: This sentence gives more information about tooth enamel, and explains why it is hard. The other choices are about teeth in general, but do not continue the discussion of tooth enamel.

30. C: This sentence gives more information about the accident that led to the sinking of the ferry. The other choices give information about the area, but they do not continue the theme of the ferry sinking that is introduced in the topic sentence.

31. B: This paragraph is about the Fortune magazine article on Getty and his answer to a question about his wealth. The information about the museum is unrelated to the other information presented in the paragraph and does not belong here.

32. B: This paragraph describes the use of vegetable oil as a diesel fuel, the problems involved in using it, and how to solve those problems with an engine conversion. The fact that there are many automobiles in the U.S. is not integral to this topic and does not belong in this paragraph.

33. A: Use of the conjunction "however" in this sentence contrasts the first and second clauses, showing the second to be a consequence of the first. Since the failure to find gold was unexpected, use of "then", as in Choice B, is inappropriate. In choice C, the conjunction should be followed by "so", to show that the second clause is a result of the first.

34. C: The adjective "egalitarian" means that all are considered to be equal. It is distinct from the adjective "democratic", which indicates a political system in which all have equal voting rights (Choice B). Choice A is slang, and "commensurate" in Choice D is nonsensical in this context.

35. D: The conjunction "although" contrasts the formation of a federation, which implies unity, with the development of border disputes. The federation could hardly have been caused by the border disputes, as implied in Choice A. Choices B and C simply string together the formation of the federation and the occurrence of the disputes without developing the relationship between them.

36. D: The phrase "Costa Rica's northern Guanacaste Province" constitutes the subject of this sentence and should not be set off by commas.

37. D: "Round" is a shape. "Around" means "in the vicinity", which is the phrase required here. Also, the comma is inappropriate in this compound sentence as the second verb does not have a separate subject.

38. B: In this sentence, a comma is used to set off an introductory phrase or word. The adjectival phrase "slightly larger than the size of the hole", which modifies the word "patch", should not be set off by commas or other punctuation.

39. C: The correct verb to use is "roughen", which means "to render something coarse". Since "area larger than the hole" is a phrase that must describe only the portion to be roughened, not the entire tube, Choice C is correct and Choice D is not.

40. B: The subject is in the third person, so use the contraction "doesn't" in place of "does not". Choices A and C, using the phrase "no more", are slang.

41. C: The two clauses are independent and should be separated by a comma. Since the sentence is imperative, there is no subject given for either clause.

42. A: The correct contraction is "you're", which is short for "you are". The word "your" is a possessive and is incorrect in this context. Additionally, the introductory word "now" should be offset by a comma.

43. B: It is necessary to use the adverb "heavily" rather than the adjective "heavy" to modify the verb. Also, the possessive form "Norway's" is called for, since "Norways" would be a plural and incorrect.

44. D: When separating the items of a list of 3 or more items with commas, use a comma after each item in the list. Note that Choice A changes the meaning of the sentence and indicates that the ships are made of metal.

45. C: Since the livestock comprises a portion of the diversified agriculture described by the sentence, the word "includes" provides the most precise meaning. The phrasings in the other choices are incorrect or awkward.

46. A: It is not the needs that are imported, but rather the foods to fill the needs. Choice D is incorrect because it uses the plural form "countries", rather than the possessive "country's".

47. C: The plural form "patients" must be used rather than the possessive. The present progressive form "are having" must be replaced by the simple present: "have" is acceptable, but the verb "experience" is more likely to be used in a medical diagnosis. The location of the pain is on the outside of the elbow, not "outside the elbow", which suggests it is outside of the body, entirely.

48. A: To radiate means to spread from the source. In this case the pain spreads from the elbow to the hand. Since this happens regularly, the simple present tense is called for.

49. B: This paragraph is written in the present tense, and so the tense of this sentence should be the same. Since the second clause is dependent, having no subject, it should not be set off by a comma, as it is in Choice C. Choice D contains an internal contradiction and makes no sense.

50. C: Choices A and B indicate that both men and women are affected, whereas the meaning of the original goes further: it tells us that both genders suffer the same effects. This is properly conveyed in choice C. Since the word "similarly" modifies the verb "affects", use the adverbial form as shown, not the adjective "same".

51. D: This paragraph is written in the present tense, and so the tense of this sentence should be the same. Choice A lacks a verb for the second clause and makes no sense. Choice B is slang and is less precise than the correct answer, Choice D.

52. B: The form in the original is slang. The present tense is called for in this paragraph, which is written in that tense. The forms in Choices C and D, which are in the future progressive, are also slang.

53. C: Use a colon to separate two clauses which could be separate sentences, but which are linked by some relationship in meaning. In the present usage (syntactical-deductive), the colon introduces a clause which describes a logical consequence of the preceding clause. The semi-colon may be used where such a logical consequence is not involved.

54. D: Commas may be used to set off a parenthetical clause which provides additional detail or modifies a component of the main sentence.

55. A: The original is a run-on sentence, with two completely independent clauses. Choice A breaks it cleanly into two separate sentences, which is the best way to correct it.

Reading Skill Answers

1. C: The scores for 2007 correspond to the grey bars. In 2007, school 3 had an average score of 46, lower than any of the others. It was the only school that experienced a decline in scores.

2. D: The change in reading scores corresponds to the difference between the white and grey bars for each school. School 5 scores increased from 51 to 55 over this interval, greater than the increase for any other school.

3. A: The scores for 2006 correspond to the white bars. The highest score for 2006 was obtained by school 2 and was a 52.

4. C: This should be read from the column labeled "Unadjusted percent change to June 2009 from June 2008", a period of one year. For transportation, the index is down 13.2%. This is the only negative change among the choices given.

5. B: Read this answer in the second column from the right. Fuel oil and other fuels decreased by 3.1% during this period. Gasoline increased by 3.1%. The other commodities decreased, but by lesser amounts.

6. C: This should be read from the column labeled "Unadjusted percent change to June 2009 from May 2009", a period of one month. The number in this column of the table on the row corresponding to Food is a zero, indicating that there was no change in the price of food during this period.

7. D: In the table, components of each category are shown by indentation under the name of the category itself. There may be sub-categories within each category that are further indented. All of the Choices are indented under "Food at Home" except for "Alcoholic Beverages", which is a separate category.

8. A: Read this from the second column in the table, "Relative Importance December 2008". These numbers represent the average percentage of household budgets that are spent on the expenditure category. The greatest number, 43.421%, is on the row corresponding to housing.

9. B: The article informs the reader that most plastic food containers contain BPA, that BPA has been detected in stored foods, and that it is a material that may be toxic. Several alternative container types are listed to enable the reader to avoid containers with BPA.

10. D: The second paragraph tells us that, due to concern about its toxicity, Canada has banned the use of BPA, but not all plastics, in baby bottles. It has not banned the use of BPA in plastic products other than baby bottles, as suggested by Choice C.

11. C: While the author states that certain countries and states have banned BPA for these applications, he does not take a stand on this issue in the article. Nor is it suggested that stainless steel is the best material: it is merely listed as one of several alternatives. The author simply provides the reader with several different types of container that can be used.

12. A: According to the text, phthalates, including BPA, are used to soften plastics so that they may be molded. They do not make the plastics safer, nor do they permit the use of plastic containers in microwave ovens.

13. B: At the end of the text, the author provides a list of three ways to avoid potential problems with food storage containers. These involve selecting containers made of glass, stainless steel, or BPA-free plastics.

14. B: According to the text, canned foods have been found to be contaminated with BPA, because plastic liners are used in the cans. Since the author counsels the avoidance of BPA, he would most likely also recommend the avoidance of canned foods.

15. D: The text describes how the migratory patterns of these turtles move them around the entire Pacific. As a result, researchers from the Fish and Wildlife service were obliged to expand their conservation efforts beyond the beaches of California to encompass sites in the western Pacific as well.

16. B: The author refrains from trying to enlist the reader's efforts in work to protect the leatherbacks, and does not appear to seek support. Rather, the text is a factual report about the conservation efforts that are already taking place.

17. A: This can be inferred from the second paragraph, which says that it was thought that the California populations originated from "nearby" beaches. There is no mention in the text of a preference for warm waters and, if anything, the text implies that they swim extremely well. Finally, the text tells us that the various populations of leatherbacks are genetically identical.

18. D: At the end of the fifth paragraph, the author states: "Early results have inspired a cautious optimism: leatherback turtle populations seem to be recovering." This does not describe a rapid recovery, so Choice A is incorrect.

19. C: According to the author, "success of these conservation efforts will require a more complete understanding of the entire ecosystem in which the turtles live." The article goes on to state that this will necessitate "a broad approach that includes the restoration of feeding grounds, nesting beaches, and the migratory routes that connect them."

20. C: The article provides guidance for parents and guardians about educating children on the subject of money. After providing some background in the initial paragraphs, it ends with five paragraphs that suggest specific steps that can be taken for this purpose.

21. A: This is an example of a "hook", an introductory paragraph designed to intrigue the reader and encourage him to read further. Since most parents have experienced occasions when their child throws a tantrum in order to be given something he or she desires, they may wish to read on. The last sentence in this paragraph suggests that the relationship between money and a child's happiness is not so simple, and will be explored further in the text.

22. B: The article tells parents to take the time to explain the basics of money to their children. It tells us that children learn about money by observing their parents using it, and that parents should explain the reasons for their actions to children from an early age.

23. C: The author says that giving a child an allowance tied to the performance of certain family chores is an excellent way to teach the concept that money must be earned.

24. D: The author advises that, as children grow up and learn more, they should be allowed to make their own decisions about money and personal finances. Their decision-making should be supported with parental advice, but gradually the final decisions should be ceded to them.

25. A: The article provides information about a scheme to defraud internet users of money. It describes the mechanics of the fraud scheme and explains how the perpetrators intend to make money.

26. B: A *propensity* is a tendency to do something. Proclivity is a synonym for this. *Larceny* is a synonym for theft. Note that *pilferage* and *robbery* are also synonyms for theft, but that *talent,* which is a latent ability, does not mean the same thing as propensity, while *disinclination* has the opposite meaning.

27. B: According to the paragraph, the perpetrators cite many reasons for the need to send them money, among them payment of taxes, bribes to government officials, and legal fees.

28. D: Despite what might seem the unlikely nature of the come-on, according to the text the Nigerian letter scheme succeeds in bilking people out of millions of dollars annually.

29. D: A caricature is a picture that ludicrously exaggerates the defects of a thing or of a person. The author first mocks the Humboldt River for being so small, suggesting that it might be possible to drink the whole thing dry. He goes on to mock his own greed, with his exaggerated stalking of gold minerals.

30. A: Burlesque is a form of humor that makes use of ludicrous exaggeration. The description is obviously absurd and meant to exaggerate the inconveniences presented by the steep hillsides surrounding the town.

31. B: Mr. Ballou is described as "an experienced gold miner". His role in the passage is to provide a grounding in reality and to puncture the author's illusions about the ease of getting rich by finding gold.

32. B: In the final paragraph, the author compares gold and lower minerals such as mica to men of quality and lesser men, and bemoans the fact that they are just as hard to tell apart as are real gold and fool's gold, as illustrated by his story.

33. B: As set out in section 1.0, Purpose and Scope, the document describes a procedure for identifying hazards associated with one or more jobs (in this case Tank Operations) or encountered by visitors and for instituting controls to mitigate (or minimize) the dangers that they present.

34. D: The methods to be used to mitigate hazards are given in section 4.1 of the text, which indicates that they are specified in descending order of use. Protective clothing is an example of the last method listed, personal protective equipment, so this is the last strategy to be tried to protect the workers from the hazardous chemical.

35. D: Section 4.2 indicates that safety procedures ("controls") that fall within the scope of normal training for workers do not need to be discussed in the work instructions for operations that are performed frequently.

36. A: The document is intended as a guide for those writing work instructions for jobs to be performed at the site. These work instructions are prepared by management. Workers and laborers would read those documents as part of their training.

37. D: Section 4.5 indicates that safety procedures that are not within the qualification and training of the workers for hazards should have detailed instructions for how the workers are to mitigate the hazard.

38. C: The text indicates that all such information should be restricted to the resume, and that photocopies of book pages, for example, from which publication information could be deduced, are not acceptable.

39. D: The instructions state that applicants submitting excerpts must include a one-page statement in the manuscript about where it fits into the whole to orient the reviewers.

40. C: The professor argues that small, woody material is left on the tops of trees where a fire cannot reach. So, the material cannot be fuel for future fires.

41. B: Plot A was salvage logged and burned worse than the unmanaged plot (Plot B). So, this study supports the professor's view that salvage logging raises the risk and energy of the fire.

42. A: The forest manager thinks that less fuel is open to future fires by removing dead or dying material through salvage logging.

43. D: The professor says that larger trees found in old growth forests are better at holding back fires than small, younger trees.

44. C: A study looking at the regrowth of seedlings in logged and unmanaged forests would help to explain and/or prove both arguments. The reason is that the manager and the professor talk on the importance of seedling growth after a fire.

45. C: The first section covers how people want to change and the options that are available to them. As people move towards a healthier lifestyle, they can work at small steps on their way to better health. Choice A is not correct because the process takes a lot of time to change habits and choose healthier options. Although there is a paragraph on benefits of certain foods, the focus of the section is on making better choices with food. Choice D is incorrect because the passage mentions that the process is a struggle for many, not an impossible task.

46. D: The overall passage is information for someone who is interested in the food industry. So, choice A is not correct. The reason is that there is not much of a comparison or contrast between the Food Pyramid and MyPlate. Choice B is incorrect because the focus of the passage is not on government involvement. Choice C is wrong as well. It is true that there is not a perfect system of dietary recommendations. However, that is not the purpose of including that section in the passage.

47. B: Each section of the passage has the tone of educating readers. So, choice A is wrong because the tone is not blaming readers. Choice C is close, but it is not the best answer choice. Overall, the

passage is more serious than entertaining. However, the main tone of the passage is informative. Choice D is wrong because the tone of the material is not snobbish or cocky.

48. D: The term *hydrologic cycle* is defined in the first paragraph. It is described as being equal to the *water cycle*. It comes from the Greek root *hydros* which means "water."

49. D: According to the table, the average residence time of water in soil is only two months. Only its residence time in the atmosphere (9 days) is shorter. *Residence time* is the average amount of time that a water molecule spends in each of the reservoirs before it moves on to the next reservoir of the water cycle.

50. B: According to the final paragraph, ocean levels actually fall during an ice age. The reason is that more water is stored in ice caps and glaciers when the temperatures are very cold. So, there is less water that stays in the oceans as liquid water.

Mathematics Computation Answers

1. B: Set up the subtraction as shown, and subtract each digit beginning at the right:

    4.73
    -2.13
    2.60

2. B: Isolate the variable, x, on the left side of the equation by subtracting 7 from each side. This leaves $x = 11 - 7 = 4$.

3. C: The 2 in the first number is in the hundredths position, and the 3 in the second number is in the ten-thousandths position. This is carried over into the sum. Set up the addition as follows and carry the digits down, adding them beginning at the right:

    1.02
    +0.0003
    1.0203

4. D: 4 goes into 68 17 times. To see that this is true, multiply the result, 17, by 4:

    17
    x 4
    68

5. C: "Percent" means "parts per 100". Divide the number 19 by 100 and then multiply by 20 to obtain the result: $\frac{19}{100} = 0.19$; 0.19 x 20 = 3.8.

6. B: Since $0.3 = \frac{3}{10}$, the division is equivalent to $\frac{18}{4} \div \frac{3}{10}$. To divide by a fraction, multiply by its inverse. This gives $\frac{18}{4} \times \frac{10}{3} = \frac{180}{12} = \frac{45}{3} = 15$.

7. E: To divide a fraction by another fraction, multiply by the inverse. Following this procedure, $\frac{8}{7} \div \frac{12}{7} = \frac{8}{7} \times \frac{7}{12}$. The two numbers 7 will cancel, leaving $\frac{8}{12}$. This can be simplified by dividing both numerator and denominator by 4, leaving $\frac{2}{3}$ as the final answer. Since this is not one of the choices given, E is correct.

8. A: Perform the operation within the grouping symbols first. This yields 3 – 1 = 2. Since $2^2 = 4$, the equation reduces to 4 – 4, and this equals zero, or Choice A.

9. C: Since both the numerator and denominator are negative, the minus signs cancel. Consider that both are products of (- 1), so that the division is equivalent to $\frac{(-1)27}{(-1)3} = \frac{27}{3} = 9$.

- 159 -

10. B: The symbol shown is a *radical*, and calls for the square root of the number under the symbol, the *radicand*. The square root is a number which, multiplied by itself, yields the radicand. Since 6 x 6 = 36, Choice B is correct.

11. C: The product of zero and any other number is equal to zero. Conversely, if the product of two numbers is equal to zero, then at least one of those two numbers must be zero (zero product property).

12. D: Convert both mixed numbers to fractions with the same denominator, i.e., 8. Since 6 x 8 = 48, then $6\frac{5}{8} = \frac{48+5}{8} = \frac{53}{8}$. Also, since 3 x 8 = 24, then $3\frac{7}{8} = \frac{24+7}{8} = \frac{31}{8}$. Therefore, the addition becomes $6\frac{5}{8} + 3\frac{7}{8} = \frac{53}{8} + \frac{31}{8} = \frac{84}{8} = 10\frac{4}{8} = 10\frac{1}{2}$. Another way to add mixed numbers is to add the whole numbers and add the fractions, then combine the answers.
$$6\frac{5}{8} + 3\frac{7}{8} = (6+3) + (\frac{5}{8} + \frac{7}{8}) = 9 + \frac{12}{8} = 9 + 1\frac{4}{8} = 10\frac{4}{8} = 10\frac{1}{2}$$

13. D: The addition of a negative number is equivalent to the subtraction of that number, so that + (-4) is the same as – 4. The problem is therefore the same as 16 – 4 – 7. Subtracting each number in turn yields 16 – 4 = 12; 12 – 7 = 5, so that choice D is correct.

14. B: The 2 in the first number is in the thousandths position, the zero in the hundredths position, and the 3 in the tenths position. The 1 in the second number is in the hundredths position and the 7 in the tenths position. Set up the addition as follows and add like digits from the right, carrying over as necessary:
    4.302
    +6.71
    11.012

15. A: To subtract a negative number from another number, add its absolute value. The subtraction becomes 7.19 + 3.2 = 10.39.

16. C: Convert the fraction into decimal notation: $\frac{1}{4} = 0.25$. The addition becomes

$8.65 + 0.25 = 8.90$.

17. D: 10% of 60 is 6. 50% (or one half) of 60 is 30. The sum of these 30 + 6 = 36 is therefore 50% + 10% = 60% of 60. Another way to see this is to divide $\frac{36}{60} = 0.6 = 60\%$.

18. C: First, isolate the variable on one side of the equal sign. This gives $\frac{1}{2}k = 9 - 6 = 3$. Next, multiply both sides of this equality by 2 to solve for *k*: $k = 2 \times 3 = 6$.

19. C: To divide two powers of the same number, subtract the exponents. The problem becomes $\frac{3^7}{3^5} = 3^{7-5} = 3^2 = 3 \times 3 = 9$.

- 160 -

20. E: Subtracting a negative number is equivalent to adding its absolute value, so the problem becomes 7 + 4 – 4 = 7. Since this is not one of the choices given, Choice E must be selected.

21. B: To add mixed numbers such as these, add the whole numbers and add the fractions separately. To add two fractions with the same denominator, add the numerators and retain the denominator. This gives 6 + 2 = 8, and $\frac{3}{13} + \frac{4}{13} = \frac{7}{13}$. Since the fraction is less than 1, we need not simplify, and the answer is Choice B.

22. C: "Percent" means "parts per 100". Divide the number 1000 by 100 and then multiply by 30 to get 30%. This gives $1000 \times \frac{30}{100} = 300$.

23. A: To divide by a fraction, multiply by its inverse. This gives $\frac{8}{18} \div \frac{4}{18} = \frac{8}{18} \times \frac{18}{4} = \frac{8}{4} = 2$.

24. D: Since $0.9 = \frac{9}{10}$, the division may be performed by multiplying by the inverse of this fraction. This gives $81.09 \times \frac{10}{9} = \frac{810.9}{9}$. To perform this division mentally, note that 810 = 10 x 81, and that 81 = 9 x 9. Therefore, $\frac{810}{9} = \frac{9 \times 9 \times 10}{9} = 90$. To deal with the decimal, note that $\frac{0.9}{9} = \frac{1}{10} = 0.1$. Combining these two operations gives 90 + 0.1 = 90.1.

25. D: The square of a number is equal to the product of the number and itself, so that 4^2 = 4 x 4 = 16. Since 16 + 4 = 20, Choice D is correct. Choice A indicates the cube of the number, which is equal to the number multiplied by itself three times, or 4^3 = 4 x 4 x 4 = 64.

26. A: To multiply two fractions, multiply the numerators and the denominators separately. In this case, for the numerators 7 x 2 = 14, and for the denominators 3 x 3 = 9. Combining yields $\frac{7}{3} \times \frac{2}{3} = \frac{14}{9}$.

27. C: The operation enclosed in the grouping symbols should be performed first. Since 6 – 4 = 2, this yields 2 x 2 = 4.

28. D: Any number raised to the zero power is equal to 1. Since 6^0 = 1, and 6^2 = 6 x 6 = 36, the problem is equivalent to 36 + 1 = 37.

29. B: Since 23.01 is equivalent to 23.010, set up the subtraction as follows:
   23.010
   - 2.999
   20.011

30. C: The operation in the grouping symbols should be performed first. Since 5 x 20 = 100, this reduces the problem to $\frac{100}{4} = 25$.

31. C: The operation in the grouping symbols should be performed first. Since 6 x 3 = 18, this reduces the problem to – 15 – 18. To subtract a number from a negative number, add their absolute values and retain the negative sign. Thus, - 15 – 18 = - (15 + 18) = - 33.

32. A: Isolate the variable by adding 4 to both sides of the equation. This yields x^2 = 36. Now, take the square root of both sides of the equation to solve for x: $x = \sqrt{36} = 6$.

33. B: Convert the fractions so that they have the same denominators by multiplying both the numerator and denominator of the first fraction by 3. This gives $6\frac{3}{9} - 4\frac{2}{9}$. The whole numbers and fractions of the mixed numbers may now be subtracted independently. Since 6 – 4 = 2, and $\frac{3}{9} - \frac{2}{9} = \frac{1}{9}$, combining these yields $6\frac{1}{3} - 4\frac{2}{9} = 2\frac{1}{9}$.

34. B: "Percent" means "parts per 100". Setting the unknown number equal to x, this gives $\frac{30}{100}x = 18$. To solve this, isolate the variable by multiplying both sides of the equation by 100 and dividing both sides by 30, resulting in $x = (18)(\frac{100}{30}) = \frac{1800}{30} = 60$.

35. D: Since 9 x 9 = 81, $\sqrt{81} = 9$. Similarly, 5 x 5 = 25, and $\sqrt{25} = 5$. Combining these yields 9 – 5 = 4.

36. A: Following normal order of operations, perform the multiplication before adding or subtracting terms that are not enclosed within grouping symbols. Since 7 x 2 = 14, the expression reduces to 6 – 14 – 1 = -9.

37. C: Perform the operation inside the grouping symbols first, then raise to the power indicated. Since 9 – 6 = 3, this equals 3^2 = 9, and the expression reduces to 9 ÷ 9 = 1.

38. C: Perform the operation inside the grouping symbols first. This yields – 4 + 3 = - 1. Then, perform the multiplication. Since the product of two negative numbers is positive, this yields – 1 x – 12 = 12.

39. B: To divide by a fraction, multiply by its inverse. The problem becomes $\frac{85}{18} \div \frac{17}{18} = \frac{85}{18} \times \frac{18}{17} = \frac{85}{17} = 5$.

40. C: "Percent" means "parts per 100", so the problem can be re-stated as $\frac{23}{100} \times 10000 = 23 \times 100 = 2300$.

Applied Mathematics Answers

1. D: If Bob buys the paper every day for $1.50, in 7 days he will spend 7 x $1.50 = $10.50. If he subscribes, he spends only $3.50. Therefore, his savings is the difference $10.50 - $3.50 = $7.00.

2. B: Since $\frac{4}{5}$ of $\frac{5}{7}$ of 35 boys were at the practice, this is $35 \times \frac{5}{7} \times \frac{4}{5} = 35 \times \frac{4}{7} = 5 \times 4 = 20$.

3. C: Since an 18% tip was added, the amount paid was equal to 118% of the total before the tip was added. Therefore, that total is calculated as $\$1128.08 \times \frac{100}{118} = \$956.00$.

4. B: The rational numbers for Choice B can be compared by either converting all of them to decimals or finding common denominators and comparing the newly written fractions. Using the first approach, the rational numbers shown for Choice B in order from left to right can be written as 6.4, 2.25, and 0.80. These numbers are indeed written in order from greatest to least. Also, the integer −2 is greater than −5. Thus, the numbers, $\frac{32}{5}, 2\frac{1}{4}, \frac{4}{5}, -2, -5$, are listed in order from greatest to least.

5. D: In order to determine the number of questions Joshua must answer correctly, consider the number of points he must earn. Joshua will receive 4 points for each question he answers correctly, and x represents the number of questions. Therefore, Joshua will receive a total of 4x points for all the questions he answers correctly. Joshua must earn more than 92 points. Therefore, to determine the number of questions he must answer correctly, solve the inequality $4x > 92$.

6. D: The total amount she brought on the trip should be rounded to a reasonable (and compatible) amount; $2,082 can be reasonably rounded to $2,100. $2,100 can easily be divided by 7 days, which gives $300 per day.

7. B: Substitute each of the given values for x and y into the equation. This yields $(4)^2 - (2 \times 3 - 3) = 16 - 3 = 13$.

8. C: Write two equations to express the problem. Since the entertainment portion (E) lasted 15 minutes less than 4 times the advertising portion (A), the first equation is $E = 4A - 15$. Since both sections add up to the total show length, 60 minutes, the second equation is $E + A = 60$. Substituting the first equation into the second yields $4A - 15 + A = 60$, which is equivalent to 5A = 75. Dividing both sides of this equation by 5 shows that A = 15 minutes. Now, since E + A = 60, it follows that E = 60 – 15 = 45 minutes.

9. A: This is an arithmetic sequence in which each term is equal to the preceding term plus (-3). To find the missing term, add (-3) to the preceding term: 15 + (-3) = 15 – 3 = 12. To verify this result, add (-3) to this term: this results in the following term: 12 + (– 3) = 12 – 3 = 9.

10. D: Two adjacent angles that form a straight line are called supplementary angles. In order to form a straight line, the sums of their measures must be 180°. Since the angle $\angle a$ is equal to 70°, then $\angle b$ = 180 – 70 = 110°.

11. C: When two parallel lines are intersected by a third straight line (called a transversal), the angles in matching corners are called corresponding angles and are congruent to one another. Lines $L1$ and $L2$ are parallel and are intersected by the transversal $L3$ to form corresponding angles $\angle a$ and $\angle i$. Since the measure of $\angle a$ is equal to 70°, then the measure of $\angle i$ must also be equal to 70°.

12. B: Angles $\angle n$ and $\angle p$ are corresponding angles for the transversal line $L2$ intersecting lines $L3$ and $L4$. If the corresponding angles are congruent, the lines must be parallel.

13. A: Angles $\angle a$ and $\angle c$ are corresponding angles and must be congruent. Angles $\angle c$ and $\angle k$ are corresponding angles and must be congruent. Therefore, $\angle a$ and $\angle k$ must be congruent. Furthermore, angles $\angle k$ and $\angle p$ are vertical angles (formed by two intersecting straight lines), so that $\angle k$ is congruent to $\angle p$. Similarly, $\angle a$ is congruent to $\angle f$. Therefore, all four angles are congruent to one another and statement A is true.

14. C: There are 200 possible outcomes to this experiment, one for each of the marbles in the jar. Each outcome is equally likely. Thirty of the possible outcomes are for a blue marble to be drawn. Therefore, the probability of this outcome is $\dfrac{30}{200} = 0.15 = 15\%$.

15. B: Thirty-six out of a total of 55 men received a grade of 75 or higher (24 + 12). The percentage of men with passing grades is calculated as $\dfrac{36}{55} \times 100 = 0.65 = 65\%$, approximately.

16. C: Thirty-four out of 118 total applicants received a grade of 85 or higher (32+2). The percentage is calculated as $\dfrac{34}{118} \times 100 = 0.29 = 29\%$, approximately.

17. B: Two women scored in the range 95 and above. None of the men did. So, at least these two women scored higher than any of the men. It is possible that some of the women who scored in the range 84 – 95 also scored higher than any of the men (if none of the men had scores at the top of this range), but it is not possible to show this from the data in the table.

18. A: Since 12 inches equals 1 foot, each tile is 1 square foot in area. The area of the bedroom floor is 15 x 18 = 270 square feet. Therefore, the number of tiles that must be laid is 270. Since Morgan can lay 9 tiles per hour, the time required will be $\dfrac{270}{9} = 30$ hours.

19. D: Tamara can pull any sock out the first time, since the color does not matter. For the second time, there is only one remaining sock out of 9 that matches the color of the sock she drew the first time, so the probability of drawing that one is $\dfrac{1}{9}$.

20. B: The average is the total number of seconds divided by the total number of events. If there are four events (four swimmers), the average will be $22 = \dfrac{Total}{4}$. Solving for the total yields $Total = 88$ seconds. The total for the first three swimmers is 22.4 + 23.8 + 21.9 = 68.1 seconds. Therefore, the last swimmer must swim his lap in 88.0 – 68.1 = 19.9 seconds.

21. A: In order for two figures to be congruent, they must have the same size and shape. The two triangles in Answer A have the same size and shape, even though the second triangle is rotated counterclockwise compared to the first triangle. The rectangles in Answer B are the same shape, but they are not the same size. In Answer C, the second circle has been vertically stretched, so the figures are not the same shape or size. In Answer D, the second trapezoid has been horizontally stretched so it is not the same size as the first trapezoid.

22. C: In order for figures to be similar, all sets of corresponding sides need to be proportional. All corresponding sides in Answer C are at a 2:1 ratio. In Answer A, the corresponding sides are 2 more for the second figure, instead of being 2 times larger. In Answer B, one set of corresponding sides is at a 1:2 ratio, while the other set of corresponding sides is at a 2:1 ratio. In Answer D, the corresponding sides are 3 more for the second figure, instead of being 3 times larger.

23. C: Hiking due west at 3 miles/hour, the first hiker will have gone 6 miles after 2 hours. Hiking due north at 4 miles/hour, the second hiker will have gone 8 miles after 2 hours. Since one hiker headed west and the other headed north, their distance from each other can be drawn as:

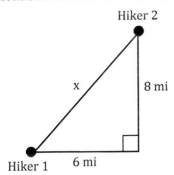

Since the distance between the two hikers is the hypotenuse of a right triangle and we know the lengths of the two legs of the right triangle, the Pythagorean Theorem ($a^2 + b^2 = c^2$) is used to find the value of x. Therefore, $6^2 + 8^2 = x^2$, $36 + 64 = x^2$, $100 = x^2$, $10 = x$. Answer A is the distance between the hikers after only 1 hour of hiking. Answer B incorrectly added the distances hiked after 1 hour. Answer D incorrectly added the distances hiked after 2 hours.

24. C: The cost for plan A is 1200 x $0.10 = $120; for plan B it is $50 + (600 x $0.12) = $122; for plan C it is $75 + (300 x $0.14) = $117; for plan D it is $100 + (200 x $0.18) = $136.

25. D: Substitute the given values into the expression, yielding $\frac{1}{3}(3)^2 + \frac{3 \times 4}{4} = 3 + 3 = 6$.

26. B: At 25 miles per gallon, Rouenna will need $\frac{500}{25} = 20$ gallons of gasoline. At $3 per gallon, this will cost 3 x 20 = $60.

27. C: To calculate the mean, or average, add the stock prices and divide by the number of stocks. This yields $\frac{127 + 21 + 24 + 193 + 30}{5} = 79$.

28. D: The median is the middle value of a group of numbers. In this case, there are two prices greater than 30, and two prices less than 30. Therefore, 30 is the middle value.

29. B: According to the chart, housing expenses average 48% of the total expenses for the American population. The next largest expense is food which, at 18%, is much lower.

30. B: Since clothing expenses are 8% of the total, on average, according to the chart, for a household spending $40,000 clothing would comprise 0.08 x 40,000 = $3,200.

31. D: Solve by setting up the cross product: $2x = (-3) \times 8 = -24$. Divide both sides of this equation by 2 to isolate the variable: $x = -12$.

32. A: To solve this problem, work backwards. Since there are 6400 yeast cells present at 3 hours and the culture doubles every half hour, there were 6400 x $\frac{1}{2}$ = 3200 cells present at 2.5 hours. At time t = 0, there were 6400 x $\frac{1}{2}$ x $\frac{1}{2}$ x $\frac{1}{2}$ x $\frac{1}{2}$ x $\frac{1}{2}$ x $\frac{1}{2}$ = 6400 x $\frac{1}{64}$ = 100 cells in the culture.

33. A: Let d represent the distance between the two towns. Then $\frac{d}{90}$ is the time it takes Mischa to drive the distance, and $\frac{d}{60}$ is the time it takes Brenda to drive the same distance. Since this is 3 hours longer than Mischa's time, $\frac{d}{90} + 3 = \frac{d}{60}$. To solve this equation for d, first gather the terms with the variable on one side: $\frac{d}{60} - \frac{d}{90} = 3$. Isolate the variable to yield $d(\frac{1}{60} - \frac{1}{90}) = 3$. The least common multiple for the denominators is 180, so this is equivalent to $d\left(\frac{3-2}{180}\right) = \frac{d}{180} = 3$. This yields d = 3 x 180 = 540 km.

34. D: The cost per ounce can be calculated by dividing the cost of the bag by the number of ounces the bag contains. Thus, the cost per ounce can be calculated by writing $9.85 ÷ 16, which equals approximately $0.62 per ounce.

35. D: The constant amount Kevin pays is $12.95; this amount represents the y-intercept. The variable amount is represented by the expression $0.07x, where x represents the number of text messages sent and $0.07 represents the constant rate of change or slope. Thus, his total cost can be represented by the equation $y = \$0.07x + \$12.95$.

36. B: Since 7 feet equals 84 inches, and 1 inch equals 2.54 centimeters, the following proportion can be written: $\frac{84}{x} = \frac{1}{2.54}$. Solving for x gives: $x = 213.36$. Thus, the bed is 213.36 centimeters, in length.

37. C: Alfredo's weekly base is 40 x $20 = $800. This week he made $950 - $800 = $150 from overtime. At $30 per hour, this corresponds to $\frac{150}{30}$ = 5 hours of overtime. Added to his normal workweek, he worked 40 + 5 = 45 hours in all.

38. D: This is a geometric series, in which a constant ratio is maintained between each term and the next. From the first two terms, for example, it can be seen that the ratio is $\frac{6}{3} = 2$. This holds for all other sequential terms. To calculate the next term in the series, multiply the preceding term by this ratio. This yields 24 x 2 = 48.

39. A: From the definition of the PE ratio, $\frac{Price}{Earnings\ per\ share} = 12$. Therefore, earnings per share must be equal to $\frac{Price}{12} = \frac{\$6.00}{12} = \$0.50$. Since there are 3 million shares issued, the total earnings must be $0.50 x 3,000,000 = $1.5 million.

40. C: To see that Choice A is incorrect, note that Saturn's mass is less than that of Jupiter, but its orbital period is longer. To see that Choice B is incorrect, note that Saturn's diameter is greater than that of Earth, but its gravity is less. To see that Choice D is incorrect, note that Saturn's mass is greater than that of Earth, but its gravity is less.

41. A: According to the table, the mass of Venus is 0.815 times that of Earth. Since 0.815 x 6 x 10^{24} = 4.9 x 10^{24}, Choice A is correct.

42. B: To see that Choice A is incorrect, note that Neptune's orbital period is greater than that of Jupiter, but its orbital speed is less. To see that Choice C is incorrect, note that Saturn's diameter is less than that of Jupiter, and its orbital speed is less. To see that Choice D is incorrect, note that Saturn's mass is greater than that of Earth, but its orbital speed is less.

43. B: In scientific notation, the distance 149,600,000 km is written as 1.496 x 10^8 km. According to the table, Mercury is 0.39 times as far from the Sun as is the Earth. Since 0.39 x 1.496 x 10^8 = 5.8 x 10^7, Choice B is correct.

44. C: The radius is a straight line segment reaching from the center of a circle to its circumference. For this question, line segment OX is the only choice that illustrates a radius.

45. B: The line segment XOZ represents the diameter of the circle.

46. D: The line segment XOZ is a diameter of the circle, since it passes through the center, O. The radius, OY, of the circle is half the length of the diameter. Since XOZ= 6 cm, then OY = 3 cm. The area of a circle is given by the formula $Area = \pi R^2 = \pi (3)^2 = 9 \times 3.14 = 28.26$.

47. A: A beach ball is the shape of a sphere and the amount of air needed to inflate each beach ball can be expressed as the volume of the beach ball. The formula for the volume of a sphere is $V = \frac{4}{3}\pi r^3$, where r is the radius of the sphere. Since each beach ball has a diameter of 12 inches, the radius is half of the diameter, or 6 inches. Therefore, by substitution, $V = \frac{4}{3}\pi r^3$ becomes $V = \frac{4}{3}\pi(6\ in)^3$ = 904.8 in³. Answer B forgot to divide by 3. Answer C used the diameter instead of the radius. Answer D forgot to divide by 3 and used the diameter instead of the radius.

48. B: There are 12 even-numbered floors between floors 1 and 25. At each one, the elevator gains 2 people, for a net gain of 24. There are 11 odd-numbered floors between floors 1 and 25 (not

counting floors 1 and 25). At each one, the elevator loses 1 person, for a net loss of 11. The elevator leaves the first floor with 3 people, so the total arriving at the 25th floor is 3 + 24 – 11 = 16.

49. C: The number of miles Lauren must drive can be rounded to 1,500; 1,500 miles divided by 5 days equals 300 miles per day. Thus, a reasonable estimate for the number of miles driven per day is 300.

50. B: At 180 orders per hour, the clerk processes 3 orders per minute, since there are 60 minutes in an hour ($\frac{180}{60} = 3$). His assistant processes 2 orders per minute ($\frac{180}{90} = 2$). Together, they can process 3 + 2 = 5 orders per minute. Therefore, 115 orders will take $\frac{115}{5} = 23$ minutes.

Special Report: TABE Secrets in Action

Sample Question from the English Section

Louisa May Alcott's _____ the philosophical brilliance of her father's intellect was _____ by her impatience with his unworldliness

A. exasperation with . . contradicted
B. concealment of . . supplanted
C. respect for . . augmented
D. rebellion against . . qualified
E. reverence for . . tempered

Let's look at a couple of different methods of solving this problem.

1. Understand What to Expect

Before you have read any of the answer choices and begin to stumble over some of the complicated vocabulary words used in the answer choices, see if you can predict what the answer might be, based on the information provided to you in the problem sentence. You aren't trying to guess the exact word that might be in the correct answer choice, but only the type of word that you should expect. Is it a positive word, negative word, etc.

Ask yourself what sort of words would likely fill the blanks provided. Consider the first blank, which comes directly before a description of the intellectual brilliance of Louisa's father. It is likely that she loved her father and thought highly of him, particularly with regards to his intelligence. Therefore, you should expect a verb with a positive meaning to fill the first blank.

The second blank comes directly before a description of her impatience with her father over his unworldliness. Her father's brilliance is a positive attribute, the unworldliness is a negative. The missing word is a verb that allows a transition between these two, somehow reconciling the positive and negative aspects of her father's character.

Now that you have an idea of what to expect in a correct answer choice, review the choices provided. Choices C and E both have a positive word to fill the first blank, "respect" and "reverence" respectively, so either could be correct. Moving to the second word to clarify which is the correct answer, you encounter the words "augmented" and "tempered". Augmenting deals with increasing or supporting. It doesn't make sense that a positive attribute of her father's would increase her impatience, making choice C incorrect. Tempering deals with modifying or adjusting. It does make sense that her perception of a positive attribute of her father's would be modified or adjusted by a negative attribute, making choice E correct.

2. Group the Answers

Review the answer choices and try to identify the common aspects of each answer choice. Are any of the words synonyms or antonyms?

Without ever having looked at the problem, but simply reviewing the answer choices can tell you a lot of information. Classify the words in the answer choice as positive or negative words and group them together. For example, you can tell that both answer choice A and D deal with "anger", using the words "exasperation" and "rebellion". Answer choices C and E deal with "appreciation", using the words "respect" and "reverence". Answer choice B stands alone, and in many cases can be immediately eliminated from consideration.

Grouping answers makes it easy to accept or reject more than one answer at a time. By reviewing the context of the sentence, "appreciation" makes more sense than "anger" in describing a woman's perception of her father's intellectual brilliance. Therefore, answer choices A and D can both be rejected simultaneously. Because "appreciation" is a likely description of Louisa's perception of her father's brilliance, choice B can be dismissed temporarily. If on further inspection answer choice C and E do not continue to make sense, then you can easily return to choice B for consideration.

Once again, in comparing the remaining words in choice C and E, "augmented" and "tempered", the meaning of the root word "temper" as a modifying agent makes it the better answer, and choice E correct.

3. Make it Easier

As you go through and read the sentence and answer choices, don't allow a complicated wording to confuse you. If you know the meaning of a phrase and it is over complicated, be sure to mentally substitute or scratch through and write above the phrase an easier word that means the same thing.

For example, you can rewrite "Louisa May Alcott's -------- the philosophical brilliance of her father's intellect was ------- by her impatience with his unworldliness" as "Louisa May Alcott's -------- her father's intelligence was ------- by her impatience with his simplicity."

Using words that are simpler and may make it easier for you to understand the true context of the sentence will make it easier for you to identify the correct answer choice. Similarly, you can use synonyms of difficult words as a mental replacement of the words in the answer choices to make it easier for you to understand how the word fits into the sentence.

For example, if you know the meaning of the word "supplanted" in choice B, but have difficulty understanding how it fits into the sentence, mentally replace it with the word "displaced." Displaced means the same thing and may be easier for you to read and understand in the context of the sentence.

Sample Question from the Mathematics Section

For a certain board game, two dice are thrown to determine the number of spaces to move. One player throws the two dice and the same number comes up on each of the dice. What is the probability that the sum of the two numbers is 9?

A. 0
B. 1/6
C. 2/9
D. 1/2

Let's look at a few different methods and steps to solving this problem.

1. Create an Algebra Problem

While you might think that creating an algebra problem is the last thing that you would want to do, it actually can make the problem extremely simple.

Consider what you know about the problem. You know that both dice are going to roll the same number, but you don't know what that number is. Therefore, make the number "x" the unknown variable that you will need to solve for.

Since you have two dice that both would roll the same number, then you have "2x" or "two times x". Since the sum of the two dice needs to equal nine, that gives you "2x = 9".

Solving for x, you should first divide both sides by 2. This creates 2x/2 = 9/2. The twos cancel out on the left side and you are have x = 9/2 or x = 4.5

You know that a dice can only roll an integer: 1, 2, 3, 4, 5, or 6, therefore 4.5 is an impossible roll. An impossible roll means that there is a zero possibility it would occur, making choice A, zero, correct.

2. Run through the Possibilities for Doubles

You know that you have to have the same number on both dice that you roll. There are only so many combinations, so quickly run through them all.

You could roll:

Double 1's = 1 + 1 = 2
Double 2's = 2 + 2 = 4
Double 3's = 3 + 3 = 6
Double 4's = 4 + 4 = 8
Double 5's = 5 + 5 = 10
Double 6's = 6 + 6 = 12

Now go through and see which, if any, combinations give you a sum of 9. As you can see here, there aren't any. No combination of doubles gives you a sum of 9, making it a zero probability, and choice A correct.

3. Run through the Possibilities for Nine

Just as there are only so many possibilities for rolling doubles, there are also only so many possibilities to roll a sum of nine. Quickly calculate all the possibilities, starting with the first die.

If you rolled a 1 with the first die, then the highest you could roll with the second is a 6. Since 1 + 6 = 7, there is no way that you can roll a sum of 9 if your first die rolls a 1. If you rolled a 2 with the first die, then the highest you could roll with the second is a 6. Since 2 + 6 = 8, there is no way that you can roll a sum of 9 if your first die rolls a 2.

If you rolled a 3 with the first die, then you could roll a 6 with your other die and have a sum of 9. Since 3 + 6 = 9, this is a valid possibility.

If you rolled a 4 with the first die, then you could roll a 5 with your other die and have a sum of 9. Since 4 + 5 = 9, this is a valid possibility.

If you rolled a 5 with the first die, then you could roll a 4 with your other die and have a sum of 9. Since 5 + 4 = 9, this is a valid possibility.

If you rolled a 6 with the first die, then you could roll a 3 with your other die and have a sum of 9. Since 6 + 3 = 9, this is a valid possibility.

Now review all the possibilities that give you a combination of 9. You have: 3 + 6, 4 + 5, 5 + 4, and 6 + 3. These are the only combinations that will give you a sum of 9, and none of them are doubles. Therefore, there is a zero probability that doubles could give you a sum of 9, and choice A is correct.

4. Calculate the Odds

Quickly calculate the odds for just rolling a 9, without setting any restrictions that it has to be through doubles or anything else. You've seen in Method 3 that there are 4 ways that you can roll a sum of 9. Since you have two dice, each with 6 sides, there are a total of 36 different combinations that you could roll (6*6 = 36). Four of those thirty-six possibilities give you a sum of 9. Four possibilities of rolling a 9 out of thirty-six total possibilities = 4/36 = 1/9. So that means there is a 1/9 chance that would roll a 9, without any restrictions. Once you add restrictions, such as having to roll doubles, then your odds are guaranteed to go down and be less than 1/9. Since the odds have to be less than 1/9, the only answer choice that satisfies that requirement, is choice A, which is zero, making choice A correct.

Sample Question from the English Section

Alice Fletcher, the Margaret Mead of her day, assisted several American Indian nations that were threatened with removal from their land to the Indian Territory. She helped them in petitioning Congress for legal titles to their farms. When no response came from Washington, she went there herself to present their case.

According to the statement above, Alice Fletcher attempted to:

A. imitate the studies of Margaret Mead
B. obtain property rights for American Indians
C. protect the integrity of the Indian Territory
D. persuade Washington to expand the Indian Territory

Let's look at a couple of different methods of solving this problem.

1. Identify the key words in each answer choice. (These are the nouns and verbs that are the most important words in the answer choice.)

A. imitate, studies
B. obtain, property rights
C. protect, integrity
D. persuade, expand

Now try to match up each of the key words with the passage and see where they fit. You're trying to find synonyms between the key words in the answer choices and key words in the passage.

A. imitate – no matches; studies – no matches
B. obtain – no matches; property rights – matches with "legal titles" in sentence 2.
C. protect – no matches; integrity – no matches
D. persuade – matches with "petitioning" in sentence 2; expand – no matches

At this point there are only two choices that have any matches, choice B and D, and they both have matches with sentence 2. This is a good sign, because TABE will often write two answer choices that are close. Having two answer choices pointing towards sentence 2 as containing the key to the passage (and no other answer choices pointing to any other sentences) is a strong indicator that sentence 2 is the most likely sentence in which to find the answer.

Now let's compare choice B and D and the unmatched key words. Choice B still has "obtain" which doesn't have a clear match, while choice D has "expand" which doesn't have a clear match. To get into the mindset of Alice Fletcher, ask yourself a quick series of questions related to sentence 2.

Sentence 2 states "She helped them in petitioning Congress for legal titles to their farms."

Ask yourself, "Why did she do that?"

Answer: The American Indian nations wanted legal title to their farms and didn't already have it.

Then ask yourself: "So what did Alice Fletcher do?"

Answer: "She tried to help them get the legal title to their farms they wanted."

Now you've suddenly got that match. "Obtain" matches with "get", so your above answer could read, "She tried to help them get (or obtain) the legal title to their farms they wanted."

2. Use a process of elimination.

A. imitate the studies of Margaret Mead – Margaret Mead is only mentioned as a point of historical reference. The passage makes no mention of Mead's studies, only that Alice Fletcher is similar to her.

B. obtain property rights for American Indians – The passage discusses how American Indians were threatened with removal from their land, but Alice Fletcher helped them get legal title, going all the way to Washington to press their case. This is the correct answer. "Obtain property rights for American Indians" is exactly what she fought for.

C. protect the integrity of the Indian Territory – Protecting the integrity of a territory or area deals with maintaining a status quo of a boundary or border. Yet boundaries and borders aren't even mentioned in this passage, only property rights. It wasn't a boundary that Alice Fletcher was fighting to maintain, but rather the right for the American Indians to even live on the land at all.

D. persuade Washington to expand the Indian Territory – At first, this sounds like a good answer choice. Alice Fletcher was trying to persuade Washington. The difference though is that she wasn't trying to persuade them to expand the Indian Territory but legitimize it, i.e. grant legal title. "Expand" suggests dealing with an increase in square mileage, not the ownership at stake – remember the American Indians were threatened with removal from the land, not fighting to increase the amount of land under their control.

Sample Question from the English Section

Sentence Correction Problem – Choose which of four ways of rewriting the sentence is correct.

As a consumer, one can accept the goods offered to us or we can reject them, but we cannot determine their quality or change the system's priorities.

A. As a consumer, one can accept
B. We the consumer either can accept
C. Either the consumer accepts
D. As consumers, we can accept

Let's look at a couple of different methods and steps to solving this problem.

1. Agreement in Pronoun Number

All pronouns have to agree in number to their antecedent or noun that they are representing. In the underlined portion, the pronoun "one" has as its antecedent the noun "consumer".

Go through and match up each of the pronouns in the answer choices with their antecedents.

A. consumer, one – correctly matches singular antecedent to singular pronoun
B. We, consumer – incorrectly matches plural antecedent to singular pronoun
C. consumer – no pronoun
D. consumers, we – correctly matches plural antecedent to plural pronoun

Based on pronoun number agreement, you can eliminate choice B from consideration because it fails the test.

2. Parallelism

Not only do the pronouns and antecedents in the underlined portion of the sentence have to be correct, but the rest of the sentence has to match as well. The remainder of the sentence has to be parallel to the underlined portion. In part of the sentence that is not underlined is the phrase "we can reject them," and another phrase, "but we cannot determine." Notice how both of these phrases use the plural pronoun "we". This means that the underlined portion of the sentence has to agree with the rest of the sentence and have matching plural pronouns and nouns as well.

Quickly review the answer choices and look for whether the nouns and pronouns in the answer choices are singular or plural.

A. consumer, one – singular noun and singular pronoun
B. We, consumer – plural pronoun and singular noun
C. consumer – singular noun
D. consumers, we – plural noun and plural pronoun

Only choice D has both a plural noun and a plural pronoun, making choice D correct.

Sample Question from the Mathematics Section

Table 1

Length of 0.10 mm diameter aluminum wire(m)	Resistance (ohms) at 20° C
1	3.55
2	7.10
4	14.20
10	35.50

Based on the information in Table 1, one would predict that a 20 m length of aluminum wire with a 0.10 mm diameter would have a resistance of:

A. 16 ohms
B. 25 ohms
C. 34 ohms
D. 71 ohms

Let's look at a few different methods and steps to solving this problem.

1. Create a Proportion or Ratio

The first way you could approach this problem is by setting up a proportion or ratio. You will find that many of the problems on the TABE can be solved using this simple technique. Usually whenever you have a given pair of numbers (this number goes with that number) and you are given a third number and asked to find what number would be its match, then you have a problem that can be converted into an easy proportion or ratio.

In this case you can take any of the pairs of numbers from Table 1. As an example, let's choose the second set of numbers (2 m and 7.10 ohms).

Form a question with the information you have at your disposal: 2 meters goes to 7.10 ohms as 20 meters (from the question) goes to which resistance?

From your ratio: 2m/7.10 ohms = 20m/x
"x" is used as the missing number that you will solve for.

Cross multiplication provides us with 2*x = 7.10*20 or 2x = 142.

Dividing both sides by 2 gives us 2x/2 = 142/2 or x = 71, making choice D correct.

2. Use Algebra

The question is asking for the resistance of a 20 m length of wire. The resistance is a function of the length of the wire, so you know that you could probably set up an algebra problem that would have 20 multiplied by some factor "x" that would give you your answer.

So, now you have 20*x = ?

But what exactly is "x"? If 20*x would give you the resistance of a 20 meter piece of wire, than 1*x would give you the resistance of a 1 meter piece of wire. Remember though, the table already told you the resistance of a 1 meter piece of wire – it's 3.55 ohms.

So, if 1*x = 3.55 ohms, then solving for "x" gives you x = 3.55 ohms.

Plugging your solution for "x" back into your initial equation of 20*x = ?, you now have 20*3.55 ohms = 71 ohms, making choice D correct.

3. Look for a Pattern

Much of the time you can get by with just looking for patterns on problems that provide you with a lot of different numbers. In this case, consider the provided table.

```
1 – 3.55
2 – 7.10
4 – 14.20
10 – 35.50
```

What patterns do you see in the above number sequences. It appears that when the number in the first column doubled from 1 to 2, the numbers in the second column doubled as well, going from 3.55 to 7.10. Further inspection shows that when the numbers in the first column doubled from 2 to 4, the numbers in the second column doubled again, going from 7.10 to 14.20. Now you've got a pattern, when the first column of numbers doubles, so does the second column.

Since the question asked about a resistance of 20, you should recognize that 20 is the double of 10. Since a length of 10 meant a resistance of 35.50 ohms, then doubling the length of 10 should double the resistance, making 71 ohms, or choice D, correct.

4. Use Logic

A method that works even faster than finding patterns or setting up equations is using simple logic. It appears that as the first number (the length of the wire) gets larger, so does the second number (the resistance).

Since the length of 10 (the largest length wire in the provided table) has a corresponding resistance of 35.50, then another length (such as 20 in the question) should have a length greater than 35.50. As you inspect the answer choices, there is only one answer choice that is greater than 35.50, which is choice D, making it correct.

Special Report: How to Find a Great Job in a Horrible Economy

If you've been laid off, or if you're in an industry where layoffs are possible, you really need to be thinking ahead of the curve. Get a job now in a safe industry while the getting is good and before the market is flooded with applicants. What are the most vulnerable industries? Take a look at the list below:

The Most Vulnerable Industries in a Downturn

- **Airlines and transportation**- in a slow economy, fewer goods are sold, business activity stalls or declines, and those who operate on the edge of growth and economic activity are exceptionally vulnerable. Most business travel can be postponed or done with increasingly sophisticated technology that makes travel somewhat obsolete. This makes the bread-and-butter of the airlines a very risky bet. The "premium" airlines that rely on juicy business rates are the riskiest- American Airlines, Delta, etc. Smaller economy airlines such as Southwest and Air Tran are better bets.
- **Manufacturers and marketers of durable goods**- a "durable good" is any purchase that can be postponed for a time during a budget crunch. Think about it- if you've just been laid off, buying a car or new refrigerator is not your first priority. Also, as bankruptcies increase, the amount of "good credit" will decline, meaning that large purchases that are often financed will be delayed until the purchaser has enough cash. Be prepared if your job depends on the success of a GM, Ford, Sears, Home Depot, or Pottery Barn.
- **Retailers in general**- excluding the deep discount chains like Wal-mart who will be the first to squeeze suppliers and cut costs in a bad economy, most retailers will suffer tremendously. Malls in particular have a glut of capacity, as this premium retail space has expanded at 3 times the rate of population growth for over 10 years straight! This is a warning for those needing Dillard's, Macy's, Restoration Hardware, or any mid-to-high end retailer to stay in business for them to keep their job.
- **Construction Industry**- any company conducting business in, or providing supplies to, the construction industry and or supporting the continued growth of production capacity. If households delay buying a $20,000 car in a recession, what do you think they will do regarding a $300,000 mansion? Even more critically, what about companies considering a multi-million dollar new facility? Construction industries operate on the very margin of increased growth and capacity, and even the mildest recessions can send real estate and building material prices down the gutter. If commodity prices fail to fall as fast as demand for construction (all indications are that commodities will continue to fall, albeit at a slower pace since they have fallen so far already in the 90's), then suppliers of construction materials will be "squeezed" into bankruptcy within months. Beware of dependence on companies like Owens Corning, Lowe's, Centex, lumber companies, Square D, and firms with highly leveraged investments in real estate.

Stable and Predictable Industries in ANY Economy

The companies we're about to list are the best of both worlds: if the economy is good, you can take your paycheck and share in the wealth through the stock market; if the economy is bad, well at least you still have a paycheck!

- o **Food and Beverage**- Proctor and Gamble, Frito-Lay, Kraft, Nestle, Post General Mills, Kellogg, Coke, etc. Sure, there are generics on the market, but people tend to make their most irrational economic decisions on small purchases- like paying 70% more for Hershey's brand cocoa that was packaged with the same commodity cocoa as the generic stuff. Not only that, these companies have managed to achieve a markup so astronomically high relative to raw material costs (the packaging of Corn Flakes is more expensive than the product!) that they can easily absorb increased price elasticity- it might not be good for their profit growth or stock price, but they won't go bankrupt either.

- o **Beer and Cigarettes**- if you have an ethical problem with these companies, we completely respect that. Even so, these are probably the best industries for surviving a **depression**, not to speak of a recession. People buy alcohol and nicotine in any economy, and these companies show an unmatched record for consistent growth- meaning opportunities for not only continued employment but also genuine promotions and professional development. Companies like: Phillip Morris, RJ Reynolds, Anheuser-Busch, Coors, Miller, etc.

- o **Low Priced Consumable Essentials-** Ditto the same explanation as food and beverage- high margins, generics are not significant because of low price, and people have to buy them- stuff like toothpaste, razors, air filters, moisturizer, etc. Companies like Proctor and Gamble, Johnson and Johnson, Gillette, etc. The nice thing about working for a good "brand" is that the brand and products will likely survive a bankruptcy as long as the business model is still valid, of course under different ownership. An even better idea might be working for a manufacturer of generic rip-offs of brand name products- that's probably a growth industry, though not enough to bring the brands down entirely.

Growth Industries in a Recession or Depression

- o **Outgrowths of the Economic Environment**- in a bankruptcy, the lawyers get paid first, and then the creditors, then finally the shareholders- the employees, of course, get nothing. However, before there can be a bankruptcy, there has to be a collections agent and a team of bankruptcy attorneys. This could be a HUGE growth industry, as the supply of specialists in collections (especially collections from white-collar debtors, not just deadbeats who missed a weekly payment on their TV) and bankruptcy specialists is far less than the possible demand. If you have the resources, go to law school and become a bankruptcy lawyer. Or, go to work for a collections agency at minimum wage until you learn the ropes, and then start your own practice. This may be THE self-employment opportunity of the decade.
- o **Health Care**- the largest American generation in history, the Baby Boomers, ticks toward retirement every day. An older population means more medical care, more surgery, and more prescription drugs. Find a job in this field, and you will literally be set for life with job security. The possibilities are wide open- go to work for a manufacturer, work for a hospital, a nursing home, anything that will possibly increase in demand with an aging population. People will give their bottom dollar for their health, so this industry is as recession-proof as it gets.

We highly recommend that you give primary consideration to any job offer from the safe or growth industries. Such an offer is worth at LEAST 20% less salary than an offer in a risky business. The key to surviving an economic downturn is to maintain employment and keep developing yourself so you can fetch top dollar when things turn up- even during the Great Depression, 70% of the workforce was employed; **make sure you're in that 70%.**

Special Report: Are You Too Smart for Your Current Job?

Did you know that the best predictor of job performance is not a college diploma, not an interview, and not even grades or experience? Excluding past work performance, the best predictor of future work performance is a quality psychologists call "the g-factor:" general intelligence.

You may be wondering if you have "what it takes" for a certain profession: maybe a lawyer, doctor, engineer, or accountant. While intelligence doesn't explain everything (and certainly doesn't account for the vital necessities of a work ethic, motivation, and drive to succeed), all else being equal, it gives you the best measure of how you would stack up against others in a given field.

The number associated with intelligence is the Intelligence Quotient, or I.Q. The average for Americans is 100, and the standard deviation is 15. Standard deviation is a statistical term meaning, in plain language, "the typical distance from the average of the typical person." For example, though the average is 100, very few people have the exact IQ of 100. Because of the way it is computed, a person with a 115 IQ (the average plus one standard deviation) is in the 84th percentile of intelligence, smarter than 84% of the general population. Likewise, someone with an 85 IQ is in the 16th percentile.

How can you use this information? Simple- take an IQ test and determine your own IQ, and then compare your own IQ to that of the average person in your profession. If you are more than 15 points higher than the average person in your profession, you are probably too smart for your job, and would be better off in a higher IQ career! Your best bet is to research careers where you are above average but not by more than 15 points.

Here's a source for a free IQ test online:
http://www.emode.com/tests/uiq/

On the following table you will find the average IQ's of various professions:

Occupation	Average IQ
Professor/Researcher	133
Physician	128
Lawyer	128
Engineer	125
Teacher	122
General Managers	122
Nurses	119
Salesperson	114
Electrician	109
Foreman	109
Police	108
Mechanic	106
Machine Operators	105
Pipe Fitters	98

You can usually estimate the IQ of your own profession by comparing the complexity of the typical job at your pay rate (not necessarily YOUR job, since if you're smarter than average the company may be taking advantage of you by giving you harder work for the same pay) to the complexity of the above jobs. For example, accounting is more complicated than teaching or general management, but less complicated than engineering: reasonably, accountants probably have a mean IQ of about 123-124; of course, exact numbers aren't important in a statistical tool, since it only reflects a general trend, not the characteristics of every single accountant (in fact, nearly all will be significantly higher or lower than the average).

A practical example: If you're an administrative assistant with a 150 IQ, both you and society would see a greater benefit if you became a doctor or professor. Once you know your capabilities, make the most of them by considering jobs where you will be challenged to your fullest potential.

Special Report: Four Opportunities for Getting a Job NOW

Opportunity #1 – Nursing

Nursing is a wide-open field with great professional opportunities and high-income potential- here's the best part- they're BEGGING for people to become nurses. Nurses are much more than hospital maids or assistants, they are highly educated professionals whose practical functional knowledge of the human body and health compares to the theoretical knowledge possessed by a doctor. Here's what we like best about nursing- you get paid by the hour, including overtime and often double and triple time for holidays and call-ins! In a 40-hour week, a registered nurse will make about $40,000 a year- if they work 50 hours like the typical corporate salaried employee (who doesn't get paid anything for overtime), they rake in over $55,000 a year. Nurse practitioners working 50 hours make over $80,000 a year! To find out more about nursing, we recommend the following website:
http://www.discovernursing.com

Opportunity #2 – Military Officer

The military is always hiring. If you are under 27 and have a college degree (esp. if you are single), life as a military officer can be fun and rewarding. Military officers start at about $30,000 a year, and pay increases to over $50,000 very quickly- not only that, but the perks are unbelievable- paid food, housing, clothing, 30 days of paid vacation a year, tax-free shopping in non-profit stores, free travel, and full pension and retirement with lifetime health benefits after just 20 years of service. If you're 25 now, you could completely retire by age 45. We hear the Air Force treats their people best, followed by the Coast Guard, Navy, Marine Corps, and Army; one advantage of The Army is that they do not necessarily require a college degree for an officer commission, just a high enough test score on their recruiting test. All equivalent ranks get the same pay in all services. See the following sources for Armed Forces opportunities in the US:
http://www.af.mil
http://www.army.mil
http://www.navy.mil
http://www.uscg.mil
http://www.usmc.mil

Opportunity #3 – Teaching Under Alternative Certification

Most states now offer some sort of alternative certification for teachers. What this means is that anyone with a college degree can go to a two week "teaching boot camp" and be in a classroom immediately after (with full pay). States are hurting for new teachers, as most current teachers will retire in the near future. The pay is better than people realize (as you only work 10 out of 12 months), the hours can be reasonable, and the benefits and retirement packages of most states are quite generous. Not only that, but you'll make a real difference too. More information about teaching and alternative certification can be found here:
http://www.alt-teachercert.org

Opportunity #4 - Post 9/11 Federal Law Enforcement

The Feds are hiring, and don't think you have to sit behind a gray desk in Washington to get in on this opportunity. The most exciting opportunity in FedLand right now is with the US Border Patrol. You'll be protecting American jobs and security while earning a good paycheck in the CHEAPEST place to live in the country- along the US-Mexico border. We even hear they are offering signing bonuses for all comers, whether professional or operational (college degree and non-degreed positions). More information can be found here:

http://www.ins.usdoj.gov/graphics/workfor/careers/bpcareer/index.htm

Special Report: An Actual Top-Secret Corporate Interview File

The following pages reveal an actual behavioral interview guide used by interviewers and job recruiters at major US corporations. Read over the guide and you will see what the person sitting on the other side of the desk is using to "grade" your interview performance. By understanding the process, you will eliminate some of the unknown and be better prepared.

The interview form begins on the next page.

FOR INTERNAL USE ONLY – [COMPANY NAME DELETED] INC.
<u>Behavioral-Based Interview Questions</u>

When conducting job interviews, it is important to ask questions not only about an applicant's job knowledge and skills, but also of past work experiences. In particular, it is valuable to gather information in order to reveal how the applicant behaved in certain work situations. The applicant's past behavior often predicts how he/she will respond in similar future situations.

This information is important because how an employee behaves in completing responsibilities is as critical as what the responsibilities are in the actual job. Identifying and assessing required key behaviors should contribute to the overall success of an employee in their position.

Prior to asking the behavioral interview questions, it is recommended to begin the interview with general introductory questions. The following are offered as suggestions:

- Please highlight your past jobs telling me the employment dates when you worked for companies and what your job duties were (candidate should not have resume in hand, they should be able to recite from memory). If there are any gaps in employment, inquire about the situation(s).
- I have reviewed your resume but would like to ask you to begin by giving me an overview of your education and experience as they relate to this position and why you are interested in this position.
- Please elaborate on one of the work experiences listed on your resume.
- What were your major responsibilities?
- What were some of the most difficult duties of that job?
- Who did you report to and who reported to you (title)?
- What special skills and knowledge were needed to perform the duties in your previous jobs?
- Your resume/application lists many job changes. Tell me about that.
- How has your present/previous job changed while you've held it?
- What unique talent do you offer? Why do you feel it is unique?
- What else should I know about your qualifications for this job?

Organizational Success

Teamwork/Cooperation
- Gaining the cooperation of others can be difficult. Give a specific example of when you had to do that, and what challenges you faced. What was the outcome? What was the long-term impact on your ability to work with this person?
- Please give me your best example of working cooperatively as a team member to accomplish an important goal. What was the goal or objective? What was your role in achieving this objective? To what extent did you interact with others on this project?
- Tell me about a time when your coworkers gave you feedback about your actions. How did you respond? What changes did you make?
- Describe a project you were responsible for that required a lot of interaction with people over a long period of time.
- How have you recognized and rewarded a team player in the past? What was the situation?
- Tell me about a course, work experience, or extracurricular activity where you had to work closely with others. How did it go? How did you overcome any difficulties?
- Describe a problem you had in your life when someone else's help was very important to you.

Customer Orientation
- Give me a specific example of a time when you had to address an angry customer. What was the problem and what was the outcome? How would you assess your role in defusing the situation?
- Give me an example of when you initiated a change in process or operations in response to customer feedback.
- Tell me about a marketing promotion/initiative or information dissemination you developed. How did it meet the customer's need(s)?

Commitment to Continuous Quality/Process Improvement
- Tell me about a suggestion you made to improve the way job processes/operations worked. What was the result?
- Tell me about one of your workplace improvements that another department now uses.
- Give me an example when you initiated a change in process or operations.
- In your last job, what problems did you identify that had previously been overlooked? Were changes made? Who supported the changes as a result of your ideas?
- Describe something you have implemented at work. What were the steps you used to implement this?

Creativity/Innovation
- Describe the most significant or creative presentation/idea that you developed/implemented.
- Describe a time when you came up with a creative solution/idea/project/report to a problem in your past work.
- Tell me about a time when you created a new process or program that was considered risky. What was the situation and what did you do?
- Can you give me an example of how you have been creative in completing your responsibilities?
- Can you think of a situation where innovation was required at work? What did you do in this situation?

Flexibility/Adaptability to Change

- By providing examples, demonstrate that you can adapt to a wide variety of people, situations and/or environments.
- What do you do when priorities change quickly? Give me one example of when this happened.
- Tell me about a decision you made while under a lot of pressure.
- Tell me about a specific time when you were given new information that affected a decision that you had already made.
- Give me an example of a time when there was a decision to be made and procedures were not in place? What was the outcome?
- When was the last time you felt pressure on a job? How did the situation come about? How did you react? What made you decide to handle it that way? What effect, if any, did this have on your other responsibilities?
- What are some of the things your last employer could have done to keep you?

Continuous Learning/Development

- Describe a decision you made or a situation that you would have handle differently if you had to do it over again.
- When you have been made aware of, or have discovered for yourself, a problem in your work performance, what was your course of action? Can you give me an example?
- Tell me about a time when your supervisor/co-workers gave you feedback about your work/actions. What did you learn about yourself?
- What have you done to further your own professional development in the last 5 years?
- Tell me about a job that you had which required you to learn new things.
- Tell me about a recent job or experience that you would describe as a real learning experience. What did you learn from the job or the experience?
- Tell me about a time when you were asked to complete a difficult assignment even though the odds were against you. What did you learn from that experience?
- Discuss the highlights of your most recent educational experience. Did you accomplish any special achievements? What were your most difficult challenges?
- I noticed on your resume that you attended _____ training program. Please describe the training program. How have you applied what you learned to your current job?

Displays Vision

- Describe what steps/methods you have used to define/identify a vision for your unit/position.
- In your current or former position, what were your short and long-term goals? How long ago did you set them? Who else was involved in setting them? Which ones were achieved?
- How do you see your job relating to the overall goals of your present/previous organization?
- Tell me about a time when you anticipated the future and made changes to current responsibilities/operations to meet future needs.

Leadership/Initiative

- What are 3 effective leadership qualities you think are important. How have you demonstrated these qualities in your past/current position?
- Describe a situation in which you were able to use persuasion to successfully convince someone to approach things your way. What level was the person you had to persuade?
- What risks did you take in your present/previous job? Tell me about it.
- Tell me about your efforts to "sell" a new idea to your supervisor.

- 188 -

- Describe a leadership situation that you would handle differently if you had it to do over again.
- What one experience proved to you that you would be a capable manager?
- What have you done to develop the skills of your staff?
- Tell me about a time when you were able to provide a co-worker with recognition for the work they performed. What did you do?
- Tell me about a time when you reached out for additional responsibility.
- Tell me about a project/suggestion that you initiated. Explain how you communicated the project/suggestion.
- What have you done in your present/previous job that goes beyond what was required?

Making People Matter

Respect for Others
- Tell me about a time when you had to resolve a difference of opinion with a co-worker/customer/supervisor. How do you feel you showed respect?
- Tell me about a time when you needed to give feedback to an employee with emotional or sensitive problems. Was the outcome?
- Describe the way you handled a specific problem involving others with differing values, ideas and beliefs in your current/previous job.

Interpersonal Skills
- Give me a specific example of a time when you had to address an angry customer. What was the problem and what was the outcome?
- Tell me about the most difficult challenge you faced in trying to work cooperatively with someone who did not share the same ideas. What was your role in achieving the work objective? What was the long-term impact on your ability to get things done while working with this person?
- Describe a work situation that required you to really listen and display compassion to a co-worker/employee who was telling you about a personal/sensitive situation.
- Describe the way you handled a specific problem involving people in your last job.

Supports Diversity and Understands Related Issues

- Tell me about a time when you had to adapt to a wide variety of people by accepting/understanding their perspective.
- What have you done to further your knowledge/understanding about diversity? How have you demonstrated your learning?
- Can you recall a time when you gave feedback to a co-worker who was unaccepting of others?
- Can you recall a time when a person's cultural background affected your approach to a work situation?
- How have you handled situations in which you could not understand a customer's strong accent?
- Tell me about a time that you successfully adapted to a culturally different environment.
- Tell me about a situation in which you had to separate the person from the issue when working to resolve differences?
- How have you taken responsibility/accountability for an action that may have been offensive to the recipient?

- Tell me about a time that you had adapted your style in order to work effectively with those who were different from you.
- How have you reacted to conversations between co-workers that were clearly offensive to non-participants?
- Give examples of when your values and beliefs impacted your relationships with your co-workers.
- Tell me about a time that you evaluated your own beliefs or opinions around issues of difference.
- Tell me about a time when you avoided forming an opinion based upon a person's outward appearance.
- How have you made your voice heard in a predominantly male or female-dominated environment?
- What measures have you taken to make someone feel comfortable in an environment that was obviously uncomfortable with his or her presence?

Honesty/Fairness
- Tell me about a specific time when you had to handle a tough problem which challenged fairness or ethical issues.
- Tell me about a tough decision you made. What steps, thought processes, and considerations did you take to make an objective decision?

Builds Trust
- Think of a situation where you distrusted a co-worker/supervisor, resulting in tension between you. What steps did you take to improve the relationship?
- Keeping others informed of your progress/actions helps them feel comfortable. Tell me your methods for keeping your supervisor advised of the status on projects.
- If you can, tell me about a time when your trustworthiness was challenged. How did you react/respond?
- Give me examples of how your have acted with integrity (walked your talk) in your job/work relationship.
- Tell me about a time when you had to give feedback to an employee who displayed a lack of professionalism in their work relationships. What did you say? What standards did you set? What was the outcome?
- Setting high expectations implies you believe the employee can deliver. Give me an example of having done this.
- Trust requires personal accountability. Can you tell me about a time when you chose to trust someone? What was the outcome?
- Tell me about a time when you had to give the "benefit of the doubt" to a co-worker/supervisor. What was the outcome?
- Give me an example of when you 'went to the source' to address a conflict. Do you feel trust levels were improved as a result?

Recognizes Others' Achievements/Contributions
- Give me an example of how you and your staff have celebrated success in the past. What was the occasion?
- Tell me about a time when you were able to provide a co-worker/employee with recognition for the work they performed. What did you do?
- What consistent methods to you use to ensure that staff feel valued for their contributions?

Understands Others' Perspectives
- By providing examples, convince me that you can adapt to a wide variety of people.
- Gaining the cooperation of others can be difficult. Give a specific example when you had to do that.
- Tell me about the most difficult challenge you faced in trying to work cooperatively with someone who did not share the same ideas. What was the difference in ideas? What was the outcome? What was the long-term impact on your ability to get things done working with this person?
- Tell me about a time when you felt your staff was under too much pressure. What did you do about it?

Resolves Conflicts Constructively
- Give me an example of a time when you were able to successfully communicate with another person even when you felt the individual did not value your perspective.
- Tell me about a time when you and your previous supervisor disagreed but you still found a way to get your point across.
- Describe a time when you facilitated a creative solution to a problem between employees.
- Tell me about a recent success you had with an especially difficult employee/co-worker.
- Thinking of the most difficult person you have had to deal with, describe an interaction that illustrates that difficulty. Tell me about the last time you dealt with him/her? How did you handle the situation?
- Describe a time when you took personal accountability for a conflict and initiated contact with the individual(s) involved to explain your actions.

Positive Attitude
- What 3 specific things about your last job gave you the most satisfaction? Why?
- What have you done in your last job that makes you feel proud?
- Please think back to a time when setting a positive example had the most beneficial impact on people you worked with. How did you determine that a strong example was needed? What was the effect on the staff?
- Tell me about a time when you needed to address an employee's attitude. What did you say to that person? What was the outcome?
- Describe your best boss. Describe your worst boss.

Job Effectiveness

Planning/Organization
- Give me a specific example of a time when you did not meet a deadline. How did you handle it?
- Using a specific example of a project, tell me how you kept those involved informed of the progress.
- Are you better at working on many things at a time, or are you better at working on and getting results on a few specific things? Please give me two examples that illustrate this.
- Name one of your best accomplishments, including where the assignment came from, your plans in carrying it out, how you eventually did carry it out, and any obstacles you overcame.
- Of your current assignments, which do you consider to have required the greatest amount of effort with regard to planning/organization? How have you accomplished this assignment? Tell me how you handled it. How would you assess your effectiveness?

Problem Solving/Judgement

- Describe an instance when you had to think quickly to free yourself from a difficult situation.
- Tell me about a politically complex work situation in which you worked.
- Give me a specific example of a time when you used good judgement and logic in solving a problem.
- Give me an example of a time when there was a decision to be made and procedures were not in place? What was the outcome?
- How do you go about solving problems at work?
- Tell me about a specific time when you eliminated or avoided a potential problem before it happened.
- What types of problems do you most enjoy tackling? Give me some examples of such problems you faced. What did you enjoy about them?
- What types of problems do you least enjoy tackling? Give me some examples of such problems you faced. What was it about the problems that you least enjoyed?
- To whom did you turn for help the last time you had a major problem and why did you choose that person?
- In some aspects of work it is important to be free of error. Can you describe a situation where you have tried to prevent errors? What did you do? What was the outcome?

Makes Effective Decisions

- Tell me about a decision you made but wish you had done differently.
- Tell me about an experience in which you had a limited amount of time to make a difficult decision. What was the decision and the outcome/result of your decision?
- Give me an example of a time when there was a decision to be made and procedures were not in place? What was the outcome?
- Tell me about a time when you had to make an unpopular decision.
- Discuss an important decision you have made regarding work. What factors influenced your decision?
- In a current job task, what steps do you go through to ensure your decisions are correct/effective?

Takes Responsibility

- Give me an example of something you've done in previous jobs that demonstrate your willingness to work hard.
- What is the biggest error in judgement or failure you have made in a previous job? Why did you make it? How did you correct the problem?
- Tell me about a time when your supervisor criticized your work. How did you respond?
- Tell me about a time when you took responsibility for an error and were held personally accountable.

Achieves Results

- Describe a situation in which you were able to use persuasion to successfully convince someone to approach things your way.
- Give me an example of an important goal that you had set in the past, and tell me about your success in reaching it.
- What projects were accomplished during your previous job? How were these accomplished? What experiences did you have when meeting deadlines for project completion? Explain.

- Are you better at working on many things at a time, or are you better at working on and getting results on a few specific things? Please give me two examples that illustrate this.
- What do you consider your greatest accomplishments in your current/previous position?

Communicates Effectively
- Describe a situation in which you were able to use persuasion to successfully convince someone to see things your way.
- Tell me about a time in which you had to use your written communication skills in order to get an important point across.
- Give me an example of a time when you were able to successfully communicate with another person even when that individual may not have agreed with your perspective.
- Give me a specific example of a time when you had to handle an angry customer. What was the problem and what was the outcome?
- Tell me about a time when you and your current/previous supervisor disagreed but you still found a way to get your point across.
- Tell me about your efforts to "sell" a new idea to your supervisor.
- How do you make your feelings known when you disagree with the views of your staff?
- What have you done to improve your verbal communication skills?
- What have you done to improve your listening skills?
- Tell me how you kept your supervisor advised of the status on projects.
- How have you assessed your behavioral messages and what have you learned about yourself as a result?

Dependability/Attendance
- Give me a specific example of a time when you did not meet a deadline. How did you handle it?
- We all face times when personal issues pull us away from work responsibilities. If possible, tell me about a time when your dependability or attendance was challenged. How did you handle it and/or remain accountable or involved in work? How long did the situation last?

Job/Organizational Knowledge
- Describe how your position contributes to your organization's/unit's goals. What are the goal's/unit's mission?
- Tell me how you keep your job knowledge current with the ongoing changes in the industry.

Productivity
- Give me an example of an important goal that you had set in the past, and tell me about your success in reaching it.
- Tell me about a time when you had to complete multiple tasks/projects within a tight timeline.
- Tell me about a time when you had to go above and beyond the call of duty in order to get a job done.
- Give me a specific example of a time when you did not meet a deadline. How did you handle it?
- Give me two examples of things you've done in previous jobs that demonstrate your willingness to work hard.
- Describe a course, project, or work experience that was complex. What kind of follow-up did you undertake? How much time was spent on unexpected difficulties?

Additional Factors for Supervisors

Coaches/Counsels/Evaluates Staff
- Give me an example of a time when you helped a staff member accept change and make the necessary adjustments to move forward. What were the change/transition skills that you used?
- Tell me about a specific time when you had to handle a tough morale problem.
- Tell me about a time when you had to take disciplinary action with someone you supervised.
- Tell me about a time when you had to tell a staff member that you were dissatisfied with his or her work.
- Tell me about a time when you had to handle a highly emotional employee.
- Discuss a work situation in which you felt you successfully directed the work of others.
- Tell me about a time when your department was going through long-term changes or working on a long-term project. What did you do to keep your staff focused?

Identifies Areas for and Supports Employee Development Opportunities
- What have you done to develop the skills of your staff? How many of your employees have received training (any form) during the past year? What were the specific topic areas? Did they ask for the training or did your suggest it to them?
- Tell me about a specific development plan that you created and carried out with one or more of your employees. What was the specific situation? What were the components of the development plan? How long was the time frame from start to finish? What was the outcome?

Encourages Teamwork and Group Achievement
- Please tell me about your most successful attempt to encourage others to take action and get the job done. What led you to take these actions? Exactly how did you encourage others to take action or responsibility? What was the result of your efforts? Did anyone comment on your actions? Who? What was said? How often have you taken this type of action in the past six months?
- Tell me about a time when you needed to have co-workers working on a project who normally have different work styles/ideas. How did you pull them together?

Leads Change/Achieves Support of Objectives
- Tell me about a time when you were responsible for hiring and orientating a new employee. What did you do to help them adjust?
- Tell me about a time when your department was going through long-term changes or working on a long-term project. What did you do to keep your staff focused?
- Give me an example of a time when you helped a staff member accept change and make the necessary adjustments to move forward.

Enables and Empowers Staff

- Tell me about a time when you needed to delegate parts of a large assignment. How did you decide whom to distribute them to? What problems occurred? What was the outcome?
- What specific information do/did you share with your staff, how often do you share this information and why?
- Give me a specific example of how you have empowered your staff to make independent decisions.
- Tell me about the expectations you create for staff. What are they? What factors do you consider in setting/communicating expectations?

Strives to Achieve Diverse Staff at all Levels

- Give me a specific example of how you have helped create an environment where differences are valued, encouraged and supported.
- What have you done to support diversity in your unit?

Understands Diversity Issues and Creates Supportive Environment for Diverse Employees

- Tell me about the specific talents and contributions of your team/staff and how you have utilized these qualities to increase the effectiveness of the unit.
- What have you done to support diversity in your unit?
- Can you recall a time when you gave feedback to an employee who was unaccepting of others?

Appendix A: Government Job Listings

Federal Government (Highest Paying):
http://www.usajobs.opm.gov

State and Local Jobs (where websites are available):
http://statejobs.com/gov.html (if the links below do not work)

Alabama	Montana
Alaska	Nebraska
Arizona	New Hampshire
Arkansas	New Jersey
California	New Mexico
Colorado	New York
Connecticut	Nevada
Delaware	North Carolina
Florida	North Dakota
Georgia	Ohio
Hawaii	Oklahoma
Idaho	Oregon
Illinois	Pennsylvania
Indiana	Rhode Island
Iowa	South Carolina
Kansas	South Dakota
Kentucky	Tennessee
Louisiana	Texas
Maine	Utah
Maryland	Vermont
Massachusetts	Virginia
Michigan	Washington
Minnesota	West Virginia
Mississippi	Wisconsin
Missouri	Wyoming

Appendix B: Cover Letter Template

```
Your Address
Your Address
```
Date

```
Contact Name
Contact Title
Company Name
Company Address 1
Company Address 2
Company Address 3
```

Dear Mr./Ms. Contact Last Name:

First Paragraph: Indicate your interest in the organization, its products or services. State your source of information about the employer (Internet, news media, career center, employer directory, i.e., Peterson's Job Opportunities in Engineering and Technology, or employment service). If you were referred, indicate your contact's name, title, and employer where applicable.

Second Paragraph: Outline your strongest qualifications, focusing on the broader occupational and/or organizational dimensions. Include academic background, work experience, internships, participation in cooperative education, or any extracurricular involvement/leadership positions. Highlight strengths, skills, and accomplishments, describing how your qualifications match the work environment.

Third Paragraph: Refer the reader to the enclosed resume or employment application which summarizes your qualifications, training, experiences, and education. Be careful not to repeat your resume entirely in your letter. Provide details and explanations that are not found on your resume. Do some personal marketing here. Convince the employer you have the personal qualities and motivation to make a contribution to the organization. Do not inquire about what the organization can offer.

Concluding Paragraph: Suggest an action plan. Indicate that you will call during a specific time period to discuss interview possibilities. Indicate your flexibility. Repeat an e-mail address or a phone number (or add a different address or number where you can be reached, if appropriate). You may even want to ask if the company will be recruiting in your area, or if any additional information or references from you would be helpful. Finally, thank the reader for his/her time and consideration.

Respectfully,

Your Name

Enclosure

Appendix C: Model Resume

JOHN SMITH
123 Any Street
Any City, Any State 12345
123-456-7890
e-mail: jsmith@anywhere.com

OBJECTIVE

To obtain a position as a Distribution Manager that utilizes my 7 years of distribution and logistics management experience, my experience founding and managing a small business, and my bachelor's degree in business administration.

PROFESSIONAL SUMMARY

Experience with successfully managing all aspects of a large distribution center including implementing automated distribution systems; selecting, managing and training staff; developing and managing the departmental budget; establishing and monitoring productivity goals; and leading cross-functional teams on key projects. Have designed the layout, organization, processes, and procedures for a distribution facility. Proven leadership skills gained from managing a large distribution center as well as founding and managing a multi-million dollar business.

EXPERIENCE

General Manager, Distribution
ABC Companies, Any City, Any State, 1989 – 1999.

- Reporting to the Executive Vice President of Operations, responsible for managing all aspects of operations for a 270,000 SF distribution center with a 94-person staff and a $3.4 million budget.
- Processed 8 million units annually while managing 5,700 SKUs to supply appropriate product to over 500 different locations during off-peak times and 750 locations during peak times.
- Developed operating budget for Distribution Center based on detailed forecasts and managed Distribution Center to operate effectively within the operating budget.
- Reduced Distribution Center expenses by more than $1.5 million, a 30% reduction, over a 2-year period while maintaining productivity levels, service quality, and inventory accuracy.
- Designed an employee productivity improvement incentive program that resulted in a 28% increase in productivity.
- Developed a seasonal staffing program that eliminated the need for temporary labor resulting in a $500,000 savings.
- Directed the successful start-up of a new distribution facility achieving within the first quarter of operation a distribution volume that exceeded plan by over 200%.
- Selected and implemented a warehouse management software system, trained users, and developed procedures to integrate the computerized system.
- Led cross-functional team integrating the distribution system with a new database merchandising system.
- Redesigned receiving and picking operations to incorporate an automated system completing the project on time and under budget.

Founder and President
XYZ, Inc., Any City, Any State, 1982 – 1989.

- Founded and led a 14-employee company generating a peak of $4.7 million in annual sales.
- Responsible for residential construction projects for over 150 new single-family homes.
- Managed the complete project including bidding, design, scheduling, purchasing, subcontracting, and customer service.
- Scheduled subcontractor activities and oversaw multiple subcontractors to ensure construction projects were completed on time and within budget.
- Developed, marketed and sold residential real estate by establishing affiliations with CDE Group, A-1Bank, Top Realty, and Best Realty.

EDUCATION

Any University, Any City, Any State
Bachelor of Arts, Business Administration

SKILLS

DMS, MS Office, Spreadsheet Software, ORACLE

PROFESSIONAL DEVELOPMENT

World Class Logistics, CLM Annual Conference
Supply Chain Management, CLM Annual Conference

PROFESSIONAL AFFILIATIONS
Member, Council of Logistics Management

Secret Key #1 - Guessing is not Guesswork

You probably know that guessing is a good idea - unlike other standardized tests, there is no penalty for getting a wrong answer. Even if you have no idea about a question, you still have a 20-25% chance of getting it right.

Most test takers do not understand the impact that proper guessing can have on their score. Unless you score extremely high, guessing will significantly contribute to your final score.

Monkeys Take the Test

What most test takers don't realize is that to insure that 20-25% chance, you have to guess randomly. If you put 20 monkeys in a room to take this test, assuming they answered once per question and behaved themselves, on average they would get 20-25% of the questions correct. Put 20 test takers in the room, and the average will be much lower among guessed questions. Why?
1. The test writers intentionally writes deceptive answer choices that "look" right. A test taker has no idea about a question, so picks the "best looking" answer, which is often wrong. The monkey has no idea what looks good and what doesn't, so will consistently be lucky about 20-25% of the time.
2. Test takers will eliminate answer choices from the guessing pool based on a hunch or intuition. Simple but correct answers often get excluded, leaving a 0% chance of being correct. The monkey has no clue, and often gets lucky with the best choice.

This is why the process of elimination endorsed by most test courses is flawed and detrimental to your performance- test takers don't guess, they make an ignorant stab in the dark that is usually worse than random.

$5 Challenge

Let me introduce one of the most valuable ideas of this course- the $5 challenge:

You only mark your "best guess" if you are willing to bet $5 on it.
You only eliminate choices from guessing if you are willing to bet $5 on it.

Why $5? Five dollars is an amount of money that is small yet not insignificant, and can really add up fast (20 questions could cost you $100). Likewise, each answer choice on one question of the test will have a small impact on your overall score, but it can really add up to a lot of points in the end.

The process of elimination IS valuable. The following shows your chance of guessing it right:

If you eliminate wrong answer choices until only this many answer choices remain:	1	2	3
Chance of getting it correct:	100%	50%	33%

However, if you accidentally eliminate the right answer or go on a hunch for an incorrect answer, your chances drop dramatically: to 0%. By guessing among all the answer choices, you are GUARANTEED to have a shot at the right answer.

That's why the $5 test is so valuable- if you give up the advantage and safety of a pure guess, it had better be worth the risk.

What we still haven't covered is how to be sure that whatever guess you make is truly random. Here's the easiest way:

Always pick the first answer choice among those remaining.

Such a technique means that you have decided, **before you see a single test question**, exactly how you are going to guess- and since the order of choices tells you nothing about which one is correct, this guessing technique is perfectly random.

This section is not meant to scare you away from making educated guesses or eliminating choices- you just need to define when a choice is worth eliminating. The $5 test, along with a pre-defined random guessing strategy, is the best way to make sure you reap all of the benefits of guessing.

Secret Key #2 - Prepare, Don't Procrastinate

Let me state an obvious fact: if you take the test three times, you will get three different scores. This is due to the way you feel on test day, the level of preparedness you have, and, despite the test writers' claims to the contrary, some tests WILL be easier for you than others.

Since your future depends so much on your score, you should maximize your chances of success. In order to maximize the likelihood of success, you've got to prepare in advance. This means taking practice tests and spending time learning the information and test taking strategies you will need to succeed.

Never take the test as a "practice" test, expecting that you can just take it again if you need to. Feel free to take sample tests on your own, but when you go to take the official test, be prepared, be focused, and do your best the first time!

Secret Key #3 - Test Yourself

Everyone knows that time is money. There is no need to spend too much of your time or too little of your time preparing for the test. You should only spend as much of your precious time preparing as is necessary for you to get the score you need.

Once you have taken a practice test under real conditions of time constraints, then you will know if you are ready for the test or not.

If you have scored extremely high the first time that you take the practice test, then there is not much point in spending countless hours studying. You are already there.

Benchmark your abilities by retaking practice tests and seeing how much you have improved. Once you score high enough to guarantee success, then you are ready.

If you have scored well below where you need, then knuckle down and begin studying in earnest. Check your improvement regularly through the use of practice tests under real conditions. Above all, don't worry, panic, or give up. The key is perseverance!

Then, when you go to take the test, remain confident and remember how well you did on the practice tests. If you can score high enough on a practice test, then you can do the same on the real thing.

General Strategies

The most important thing you can do is to ignore your fears and jump into the test immediately- do not be overwhelmed by any strange-sounding terms. You have to jump into the test like jumping into a pool- all at once is the easiest way.

Make Predictions
As you read and understand the question, try to guess what the answer will be. Remember that several of the answer choices are wrong, and once you begin reading them, your mind will immediately become cluttered with answer choices designed to throw you off. Your mind is typically the most focused immediately after you have read the question and digested its contents. If you can, try to predict what the correct answer will be. You may be surprised at what you can predict.

Quickly scan the choices and see if your prediction is in the listed answer choices. If it is, then you can be quite confident that you have the right answer. It still won't hurt to check the other answer choices, but most of the time, you've got it!

Answer the Question
It may seem obvious to only pick answer choices that answer the question, but the test writers can create some excellent answer choices that are wrong. Don't pick an answer just because it sounds right, or you believe it to be true. It MUST answer the question. Once you've made your selection, always go back and check it against the question and make sure that you didn't misread the question, and the answer choice does answer the question posed.

Benchmark
After you read the first answer choice, decide if you think it sounds correct or not. If it doesn't, move on to the next answer choice. If it does, mentally mark that answer choice. This doesn't mean that you've definitely selected it as your answer choice, it just means that it's the best you've seen thus far. Go ahead and read the next choice. If the next choice is worse than the one you've already selected, keep going to the next answer choice. If the next choice is better than the choice you've already selected, mentally mark the new answer choice as your best guess.

The first answer choice that you select becomes your standard. Every other answer choice must be benchmarked against that standard. That choice is correct until proven otherwise by another answer choice beating it out. Once you've decided that no other answer choice seems as good, do one final check to ensure that your answer choice answers the question posed.

Valid Information
Don't discount any of the information provided in the question. Every piece of information may be necessary to determine the correct answer. None of the information in the question is there to throw you off (while the answer choices will certainly have information to throw you off). If two seemingly unrelated topics are discussed, don't ignore either. You can be confident there is a relationship, or it wouldn't be included in the question, and you are probably going to have to determine what is that relationship to find the answer.

Avoid "Fact Traps"
Don't get distracted by a choice that is factually true. Your search is for the answer that answers the question. Stay focused and don't fall for an answer that is true but incorrect. Always go back to the

question and make sure you're choosing an answer that actually answers the question and is not just a true statement. An answer can be factually correct, but it MUST answer the question asked. Additionally, two answers can both be seemingly correct, so be sure to read all of the answer choices, and make sure that you get the one that BEST answers the question.

Milk the Question

Some of the questions may throw you completely off. They might deal with a subject you have not been exposed to, or one that you haven't reviewed in years. While your lack of knowledge about the subject will be a hindrance, the question itself can give you many clues that will help you find the correct answer. Read the question carefully and look for clues. Watch particularly for adjectives and nouns describing difficult terms or words that you don't recognize. Regardless of if you completely understand a word or not, replacing it with a synonym either provided or one you more familiar with may help you to understand what the questions are asking. Rather than wracking your mind about specific detailed information concerning a difficult term or word, try to use mental substitutes that are easier to understand.

The Trap of Familiarity

Don't just choose a word because you recognize it. On difficult questions, you may not recognize a number of words in the answer choices. The test writers don't put "make-believe" words on the test; so don't think that just because you only recognize all the words in one answer choice means that answer choice must be correct. If you only recognize words in one answer choice, then focus on that one. Is it correct? Try your best to determine if it is correct. If it is, that is great, but if it doesn't, eliminate it. Each word and answer choice you eliminate increases your chances of getting the question correct, even if you then have to guess among the unfamiliar choices.

Eliminate Answers

Eliminate choices as soon as you realize they are wrong. But be careful! Make sure you consider all of the possible answer choices. Just because one appears right, doesn't mean that the next one won't be even better! The test writers will usually put more than one good answer choice for every question, so read all of them. Don't worry if you are stuck between two that seem right. By getting down to just two remaining possible choices, your odds are now 50/50. Rather than wasting too much time, play the odds. You are guessing, but guessing wisely, because you've been able to knock out some of the answer choices that you know are wrong. If you are eliminating choices and realize that the last answer choice you are left with is also obviously wrong, don't panic. Start over and consider each choice again. There may easily be something that you missed the first time and will realize on the second pass.

Tough Questions

If you are stumped on a problem or it appears too hard or too difficult, don't waste time. Move on! Remember though, if you can quickly check for obviously incorrect answer choices, your chances of guessing correctly are greatly improved. Before you completely give up, at least try to knock out a couple of possible answers. Eliminate what you can and then guess at the remaining answer choices before moving on.

Brainstorm

If you get stuck on a difficult question, spend a few seconds quickly brainstorming. Run through the complete list of possible answer choices. Look at each choice and ask yourself, "Could this answer the question satisfactorily?" Go through each answer choice and consider it independently of the other. By systematically going through all possibilities, you may find something that you would otherwise overlook. Remember that when you get stuck, it's important to try to keep moving.

Read Carefully

Understand the problem. Read the question and answer choices carefully. Don't miss the question because you misread the terms. You have plenty of time to read each question thoroughly and make sure you understand what is being asked. Yet a happy medium must be attained, so don't waste too much time. You must read carefully, but efficiently.

Face Value

When in doubt, use common sense. Always accept the situation in the problem at face value. Don't read too much into it. These problems will not require you to make huge leaps of logic. The test writers aren't trying to throw you off with a cheap trick. If you have to go beyond creativity and make a leap of logic in order to have an answer choice answer the question, then you should look at the other answer choices. Don't overcomplicate the problem by creating theoretical relationships or explanations that will warp time or space. These are normal problems rooted in reality. It's just that the applicable relationship or explanation may not be readily apparent and you have to figure things out. Use your common sense to interpret anything that isn't clear.

Prefixes

If you're having trouble with a word in the question or answer choices, try dissecting it. Take advantage of every clue that the word might include. Prefixes and suffixes can be a huge help. Usually they allow you to determine a basic meaning. Pre- means before, post- means after, pro - is positive, de- is negative. From these prefixes and suffixes, you can get an idea of the general meaning of the word and try to put it into context. Beware though of any traps. Just because con is the opposite of pro, doesn't necessarily mean congress is the opposite of progress!

Hedge Phrases

Watch out for critical "hedge" phrases, such as likely, may, can, will often, sometimes, often, almost, mostly, usually, generally, rarely, sometimes. Question writers insert these hedge phrases to cover every possibility. Often an answer choice will be wrong simply because it leaves no room for exception. Avoid answer choices that have definitive words like "exactly," and "always".

Switchback Words

Stay alert for "switchbacks". These are the words and phrases frequently used to alert you to shifts in thought. The most common switchback word is "but". Others include although, however, nevertheless, on the other hand, even though, while, in spite of, despite, regardless of.

New Information

Correct answer choices will rarely have completely new information included. Answer choices typically are straightforward reflections of the material asked about and will directly relate to the question. If a new piece of information is included in an answer choice that doesn't even seem to relate to the topic being asked about, then that answer choice is likely incorrect. All of the information needed to answer the question is usually provided for you, and so you should not have to make guesses that are unsupported or choose answer choices that require unknown information that cannot be reasoned on its own.

Time Management

On technical questions, don't get lost on the technical terms. Don't spend too much time on any one question. If you don't know what a term means, then since you don't have a dictionary, odds are you aren't going to get much further. You should immediately recognize terms as whether or not you know them. If you don't, work with the other clues that you have, the other answer choices and terms provided, but don't waste too much time trying to figure out a difficult term.

Contextual Clues

Look for contextual clues. An answer can be right but not correct. The contextual clues will help you find the answer that is most right and is correct. Understand the context in which a phrase or statement is made. This will help you make important distinctions.

Don't Panic

Panicking will not answer any questions for you. Therefore, it isn't helpful. When you first see the question, if your mind goes blank, take a deep breath. Force yourself to mechanically go through the steps of solving the problem and using the strategies you've learned.

Answer Selection

The best way to pick an answer choice is to eliminate all of those that are wrong, until only one is left and confirm that is the correct answer. Sometimes though, an answer choice may immediately look right. Be careful! Take a second to make sure that the other choices are not equally obvious. Don't make a hasty mistake.

Check Your Work

Since you will probably not know every term listed and the answer to every question, it is important that you get credit for the ones that you do know. Don't miss any questions through careless mistakes. If at all possible, try to take a second to look back over your answer selection and make sure you've selected the correct answer choice and haven't made a costly careless mistake (such as marking an answer choice that you didn't mean to mark). This quick double check should more than pay for itself in caught mistakes for the time it costs.

Beware of Directly Quoted Answers

Sometimes an answer choice will repeat word for word a portion of the question or reference section. However, beware of such exact duplication – it may be a trap! More than likely, the correct choice will paraphrase or summarize a point, rather than being exactly the same wording.

Slang

Scientific sounding answers are better than slang ones. An answer choice that begins "To compare the outcomes…" is much more likely to be correct than one that begins "Because some people insisted…"

Extreme Statements

Avoid wild answers that throw out highly controversial ideas that are proclaimed as established fact. An answer choice that states the "process should be used in certain situations, if…" is much more likely to be correct than one that states the "process should be discontinued completely." The first is a calm rational statement and doesn't even make a definitive, uncompromising stance, using a hedge word "if" to provide wiggle room, whereas the second choice is a radical idea and far more extreme.

Answer Choice Families

When you have two or more answer choices that are direct opposites or parallels, one of them is usually the correct answer. For instance, if one answer choice states "x increases" and another answer choice states "x decreases" or "y increases," then those two or three answer choices are very similar in construction and fall into the same family of answer choices. A family of answer choices is when two or three answer choices are very similar in construction, and yet often have a directly opposite meaning. Usually the correct answer choice will be in that family of answer choices. The "odd man out" or answer choice that doesn't seem to fit the parallel construction of the other answer choices is more likely to be incorrect.

Additional Bonus Material

Due to our efforts to try to keep this book to a manageable length, we've created a link that will give you access to all of your additional bonus material.

Please visit http://www.mometrix.com/bonus948/tabe to access the information.

A information can be obtained
ww.ICGtesting.com
ed in the USA
IW102232191218
0757LV00015BB/459/P

9 781516 705300